FROM NOWHERE TO Somewhere
MY POLITICAL JOURNEY

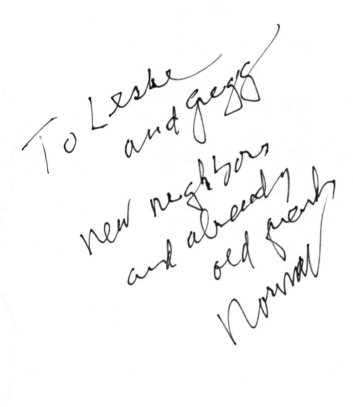

To Leslie
and Gregg
new neighbors
and already
old friends
Norm

FROM Nowhere TO Somewhere

MY POLITICAL JOURNEY

A MEMOIR
OF SORTS

Norman Sherman

天 First Avenue Editions
Minneapolis

First Avenue Editions
An imprint of Lerner Publishing Group, Inc.
241 First Avenue North
Minneapolis, MN 55401 USA

Website address: www.lernerbooks.com.

Cover photo: At work in flight aboard Air Force Two, 1965
Back cover photo by Emily McDermott
Design by Zach Marell

Main body text set in Janson Text LT Std 12/17.
Typeface provided by Linotype AG.

Library of Congress Cataloging-in-Publication Data

Sherman, Norman, 1927–
    From nowhere to somewhere : my political journey : a memoir of sorts / by Norman Sherman.
        pages cm
    ISBN 978-1-5124-0404-3 (pb : alk. paper)
    1. Sherman, Norman, 1927– 2. Political consultants—United States—Biography.
3. Humphrey, Hubert H. (Hubert Horatio), 1911–1978—Friends and associates. 4. United States—Politics and government—1963–1969. 5. Democratic Party (U.S.)—Biography.
6. Political activists—Minnesota—Biography. 7. Democratic Farmer Labor Party—Biography. 8. Minnesota—Politics and government—1951– 9. Minnesota—Biography.
I. Title.
E840.8.S5325A3 2016
977.6'053092—dc23
[B]   2015020757

Manufactured in the United States of America
1 – BP – 12/31/15

Table of Contents

To Ginny with love and appreciation
and
To the memory of Hubert H. Humphrey
who changed my life as well as the nation's

1. Who Am I?

Writing accurately and honestly about your own life is hard. Memories fade. The urge to make things neat and positive takes over. Leaving out overwhelms putting in at the slightest doubt of how what you say may appear next year or 10 years from now if anyone reads your story.

William James, the American philosopher, wrote over 100 years ago, "The most frequent source of false memory is the accounts we give to others of our experiences. Such acts we almost always make more simple and more interesting than the truth. . . . Our wishes, hopes, and sometime fears are the controlling factors."

I have tried to avoid the dangers James describes as I recount my life of 87 years, most of them pleasant and fulfilling. I think I have done reasonably well in my life both personally and professionally, and I have tried to tell my story accurately in the pages that follow.

I have also written here about others, some of whom I admired, some of whom invited mixed feelings, and some I just didn't like. I have tried for accuracy and fairness as I describe each of them. Most of those I write about are people I met in my work in liberal politics since I was in my early twenties.

One person, Hubert H. Humphrey, mayor of Minneapolis, U.S. senator from Minnesota, vice president of the United States, influenced much of my life. In some ways, he is more important in my story than I am myself, as odd as that sounds. That is not humility, but history.

What he did, and what I watched close-by for unforgettable years, made the lives of millions of people here and abroad better, safer, and healthier. I don't pretend he was perfect, but he stood alone as a man of intellect, heart, and decency among all the powerful and famous folks I have known.

Now, as one of my kids said in a family discussion, "Let's get back to me." In the interest of honesty, and keeping William James in mind, here's part of a *New York Times* article that described our Humphrey staff as the presidential election of 1968 was about to begin with Humphrey as the Democratic candidate: "Mr. Sherman, 40, a self-described 'political hack' who made good, threatens occasionally to break out of anonymity through wit and irrepressibility. He comes as close to an eccentric as anyone of the Humphrey staff." Modesty prevents me from denying it all. Or any of it.

Making good as a political creature was not inevitable, or even likely. It was not so much a chosen career as happenstance. Politics became a consuming interest of mine before I was old enough to vote. I don't know quite why. My parents were poor immigrants who had come to the United States from the same area of Romania. The hostile and threatening acts against Jews in the last decades of the 19th century and the atmosphere leading up to the Kishinev pogrom in 1903 drove them and their families out.

If my folks had political views about government, elections, or candidates when I was growing up, or even when

I was an adult, I don't remember any conversations or pronouncements of the sort. There may have been some, but my mother and father were focused on family and getting by, their condition most of the time after they got off their boats, and certainly in the years after their children were born. I also don't know precisely when my focus on the political and social world began, but a neighbor friend tried to get me to read *Das Kapital* when I was about 14. I must have, in my pre-adolescent way, expressed interest in making life better for all mankind. My introduction to Karl Marx was a flop. I read a page or two and gave it up as boring and beyond me. Yet, looking back, whatever brought me to it must also have nurtured my growing interest in political matters and activity in my later years. No one else in the family got the bug.

I think my near-fixation was, in fact, latent in the atmosphere of poverty. Being poor, having parents uncertain about food for tomorrow or rent for the next month may be beyond a child's total understanding, but the feeling, at least in my case, got through in an unsettling and lasting way. You may be too young to fully comprehend, but I think you are never too young to feel the anxiety that surrounds you. I can't be sure, but my urge to remake the nation, and maybe the world, likely grew out of that fertile soil.

Politics, for whatever reason, has been a chronic condition for a long time. It has been my drug of choice. It is a condition for which there is no political penicillin. There was no escape, and I'm glad. In a bizarre pattern of starts and stops, it has made my life fun and interesting and satisfying for about 65 years. It was short of an obsession, but a good deal more than a hobby. None of what took place was likely considering my early work life.

As a teenager, I worked as a soda jerk in our neighborhood

drug store. I dug ditches for the Minneapolis Gas Company to run pipes from the main to new houses being built after World War II. My foreman, a Pole from northeast Minneapolis who had never met someone like me, used to repeat, with a headshake, "I'm working with a Jewisher." It seemed less prejudice than novelty, but I had to restrain myself from repeating a bit of learned wisdom available for use with a number of folks: "My people already had diabetes when your people were still painting themselves blue."

I never stayed long at anything. I taught briefly as a graduate student at the University of Minnesota. Over the years since, I ran a bookstore and a small publishing company. I worked for a major farm co-op and a municipal bond company. I wrote the narration for a film on safely refueling nuclear submarines.

I have worked for public officials at all levels, often writing their speeches or running a campaign or just stuffing envelopes. At various times, I wrote for congressmen—Don Fraser of Minnesota, Jim Wright of Texas, Bill Gray of Pennsylvania, among others. Several senators hired me for speech writing, including John Kerry when he first came to Washington, although after my second and final speech, my style, not my writing style, bugged him. Senator and Majority Leader George Mitchell was another one. I wrote for cabinet secretaries and their underlings. I worked in federal departments and agencies.

I published, and partially owned, a newsletter devoted to women in sports about the time I also worked for the International Monetary Fund. I helped create a company in 1969 that used computers to get out the vote. I wrote for the Embassy of Greece and the Treasurer of the United States, the head of Avis car rental, and a paper box manufacturing company.

I was central in setting up a liberal think tank and I worked for National Public Radio. I ran a foundation concerned with communications and one devoted to hospice care. I helped several people write their memoirs.

But, for all of that, it is easy to identify the best, most fulfilling part of my peripatetic career: my work in liberal politics. I first volunteered in 1954 in campaigns of Orville Freeman for governor of Minnesota and of Hubert H. Humphrey for re-election to the United States Senate. Both men were founders and leaders of the Minnesota Democratic Farmer Labor (DFL) party.

Humphrey had been mayor of Minneapolis from 1945 to 1949, and then U.S. senator beginning in 1949. He was vice president of the United States from 1965 to 1969. I served as his press secretary for most of his vice presidency and during his unsuccessful campaign for president in 1968, and I edited his autobiography.

Along the way, I have known two more men—Walter Mondale and George McGovern—who were the nominees of the Democratic party for president of the United States and three—Eugene McCarthy of Minnesota, Paul Simon of Illinois, and Morris Udall of Arizona—who tried but didn't get the nomination. (I don't count Kerry and Al Gore, both of whom I met or talked to several times, but didn't really know.)

I ended my working life as a professor at Louisiana State University where I held a chair in political communications, an unexpected end considering my earlier academic life, but flowing easily from my later political work. A captive audience of youthful faces and eager minds made the trip to the South, a place I feared I would hate, worthwhile. Gumbo was an added reward.

Through it all, I kept in mind my father's encouraging

words: "Norman, go somewheres." Fame and fortune were never my goals. I never became rich. I never found lasting glory. But I had a fulfilling life for a long time. It has been one of upward mobility. Looking back, it was a journey of some errors, some disappointments, but I wouldn't do much differently even if I could redo it all. It was an unexpected trip. It was often a delight, more laughs than tears, more successes than failures.

2. A Poor Start

Here is how it started.

My mother, Lena, was born in 1884 to Abraham and Anne Drucker in a small village, Faleshty, in the easternmost part of Romania (now Moldova), next to Russia. In my parents' day, about 4,000 people, three-quarters of whom were Jewish, lived there. Then and later the Jews survived in a hostile, murderous environment of anti-Semitism.

Maternal Drucker grandparents and relatives from Faleshty, Romania, circa 1910, New York

Soon after the turn of the century, the Drucker family sailed for the United States, arriving at Ellis Island in New York. Their departure had been dramatic. My mother and her two sisters were hidden under hay in the back of a wagon (like "Fiddler on the Roof"), running from hostility that had threatened and taken the lives of Jews for years.

Pogroms by Russian soldiers had ravaged the area since the 1880s and were a continuing, violent ordeal for Jews, certainly through the devastating Kishinev pogrom in 1903. Even later, during World War II, Germans and their allies enslaved or murdered many Jews, including, in one instance, forcing a rabbi and his flock to chop through the winter ice on a nearby frozen river, jump through the holes, and thus all drown by their own hands, strong enough to swing a pick, but too weak to resist. The alternative was a bullet.

The unknown in the New World was a step up from the known. The family, parents and five children, were, like other immigrants, ready to face the hardships they would find in the United States. The two male children learned some English and were ultimately successful businessmen. They were bright and competent and recognized the opportunities in their new surroundings. The three girls were married young and to less successful men.

My mother spoke Yiddish all her life, but improved her rudimentary English after a decade here when my brother Fred brought home books from elementary school. She read with him, learned as he did, and ultimately became fluent and then read newspapers and magazines that were easily at hand. By the time I was born in 1927, she spoke only English with her children.

My father, Louis, was born in 1886 near Faleshty on what passed for a farm, but which provided only a meager existence.

He was one of three brothers who came to this country about the same time as my mother and her family. Harry and he went to Richmond, Virginia, which apparently needed tailors. Another brother, Morris, soon found work in one of New York City's garment trade sweatshops. The family of Natan, the brother who remained, ended up in Israel many years later. One of his kids, apparently having somehow evoked the wrath of God, died while in the synagogue praying. A second was in the Russian army in World War II and was killed when a fellow soldier found he was Jewish.

My dad and his brother were not the first Jews to arrive in Richmond. Jewish immigrants had arrived around 1760, first from England and then Germany, and enough followed so that the first synagogue was organized in 1789. A hundred years later, their well-established community welcomed the Eastern Europeans.

Harry opened a grocery store and later, during Prohibition, took up bootlegging before becoming a grocer again. My father became a tailor and began his lasting profession as a CPA — Cleaning, Pressing, and Alterations. But he felt isolated in Richmond from his *landsmen*—the people who had come from the same area where he had grown up.

At that time, many immigrants with common roots in the Old Country and now living in New York got together periodically for a social evening, which let them lament their common past and share their New World

Parents Louie and Lena Sherman, circa 1910, New York

beginnings and their hopes, however meager. More important, gathering provided an opportunity for young people to meet, court, and marry. My father-to-be took the train from Richmond to New York, where he was introduced to Lena at a gathering of folks from Faleshty. The courtship was brief. They married and set up a home in Richmond around 1910.

Long before I was born my dad went from impecunious immigrant to fairly successful businessman, earning enough to make an adequate life for his family. Then, about the time I was born, he was talked out of his business by a slick faker in a swap for a failing grocery store. The store went down the tubes quickly while the CPA shop continued to thrive under new management.

Duped, my dad went to court with someone's guidance and won back his shop. Then he proceeded to sell it to the same man, but this time legally. Beaten down, overwhelmed, he left my mother in Richmond while he worked to recover his balance on a farm near Mantorville, Minnesota. I am not sure how my mother survived with her brood while he was on the mend and out-to-pasture, but she did. She was a quietly strong woman and must have attracted help from other Jewish families. By then, there were five children: Fred born in 1911, and then Rose, Marvin, and David before I was born in 1927, seven years after Dave.

After six months or so, my dad had gotten himself together enough for us to be a family again in Minneapolis through the beneficence of my mother's cousins who had gone there directly on arrival in the United States. They apparently had been urged to go to Minnesota since they were harness makers in Bessarabia, and Minnesota had horses. My folks became part of a small, but growing Jewish community. When they arrived in 1929, there were about 14,000 Jews in a city of several hundred thousand. By 1943, Jewish residents had almost doubled, still a small minority, but with a larger place in a usually friendly, but sometime hostile, community.

For my parents, however, even in a new and growing area, only dreary days soon followed their move. The Great Depression prevented it from becoming a move up. Rare work, little income, new surroundings, and a large family made things tough. They were not alone, of course. About a third of Minneapolis residents, Jews and gentiles, lived in a household where the expected breadwinner was unemployed. Much later I was told that my parents vowed that I, still a small child, would not miss a meal, even if the others did. I was fed, but somehow soon sensed, almost preternaturally, the tension of poverty. I think in a child's way, I shared their discomforts even as I ate.

I also think we consumed and were sustained by about three tons of *mamaliga* over those years. All you needed was water, corn meal, and, when extravagant, a bit of salt. It was not particularly tasty or nutritious. Filling was enough. *Haute cuisine* was for others. I still eat corn meal mush out of the need to keep those memories alive. I, in my comparative affluence, also add a bit of butter or cottage cheese as well as the salt to my discomfort food.

(Much later, the cuisine of Romania, and its gypsies, captivated my daughter, Anne, a teenager filled with a romantic search for her heritage. We were browsing in a bookstore one day when she found a Romanian cookbook and asked if she could buy it. I said, "Only if it is authentic." She then asked how she could determine that, and I said, "Check the section on omelets. If it says steal two eggs, it's real." She frowned at what she thought was an insensitive ethnic slur and stalked away. In a moment, there was a squeal. She had opened it as I suggested and found an author's note: "We decided to collect a dozen eggs from barns, attics, or any dark corner where hens were setting. . . . To our young minds it didn't seem to be a crime." I still have the book.)

Beyond food, our surroundings were meager and seemed always uncomfortable. At one point, we rented a second floor flat in an area filled with people like us—immigrant Jewish parents, young families, little money, and burdensome language problems. On the corner was an empty lot where someone kept goats whose bleating frightened me. Bearded orthodox Jews walked the streets dressed in black, and they were frightening, too. It was not quite an enforced ghetto, but close to a *de facto* one without easy escape.

Those beards also appeared at our orthodox synagogue, Tifereth B'nai Jacob, but by then I was older, and they were not so scary. As part of our orthodoxy, the women sat together isolated from the men, who were closer to the rabbi and symbolically, I suppose, closer to God. My mother, a premature feminist and not so religious, hated it. She lit the Sabbath candles on Friday night, chanted a prayer, but it was soon clear, even to me, that her heart was not really in it.

Young as I was, I didn't completely know what poor meant, but I did feel its consequences even then if my memory of a single night is real. I was awakened, carried in the dark by my mother down the stairs and told not to cry or make any noise. I much later learned we couldn't pay the rent, and we disappeared in the darkness before we could be thrown out in the light. We must have had little to carry, few clothes, not much food, and I don't know how we made it to our next destination.

We moved later to Logan and Sixth Avenues North. The neighborhood was a haven for poor Jews and equally poor Italians, though some of them, the lucky ones, worked regularly in the wholesale fruit and vegetable market downtown. The Jews were often peddlers, using a horse-drawn wagon on a route through neighborhoods without grocery stores close-at-hand and on to nearby country roads to isolated farms. My father apparently tried peddling for a short time when he wasn't able to find work as a tailor. He was a flop. He didn't like horses and didn't do math too well.

He also tried to be an insurance salesman. Many years later, already married and in graduate school, I had to deal with a Metropolitan Life Insurance agent who suddenly stopped in mid-sentence and asked, "Are you the son of Louis Sherman?" When I said I was, he couldn't resist telling me that, decades after the fact, other agents still talked and laughed about my dad as "the worst agent in our history." He had made his mark as a fecal Midas, a talent he developed in Richmond, if not before. (I was no insurance-smarter than he. When I was in college I was riding in a friend's car involved in an accident resulting from his careless driving. When an insurance agent came to interview me and ask what compensation I wanted, I asked for $13 to replace my broken glasses, not understanding liability. I probably could have paid for my entire college tuition if I had been smarter.)

On Logan, we lived a few houses from the corner. Streetcars clattered to and fro on the metal rails on Sixth Avenue. When it rained heavily, a few tar-saturated blocks holding the rails apart absorbed the water, expanded, and popped up. As soon as the rain ended, my brothers and I would be sent out to gather the loose blocks, certainly not what the streetcar company wanted. It was a bit of understandable, if not excusable, thievery. Maybe excusable. Our choice was stealing or freezing. In the winter, those free blocks, gifts from the rain of God, took the place of some costly coal in our furnace, and our chimney belched forth a heavy, dark cloud of smoke. My mother would look out our window at neighboring chimneys and note which other houses looked like ours. Lighter smoke generally meant someone was working, and they could buy coal. Ours told another story. My mother involuntarily transmitted her humiliation. She should not have been ashamed. The conditions we endured were widespread among Eastern European Jews in Minnesota.

As the depression wore on for the country, it lifted some for us. My brother Fred found work at Sears, Roebuck and my father resurrected his career in front of the pressing and sewing machines. That was enough to make upward mobility real. We moved to slightly better neighborhoods, renting one place and then another. The streets weren't suddenly paved with gold, but we didn't have to sneak out at night. We paid the rent. We moved in the light of day and I went to my second school.

At Grant School, my second grade teacher took me to the principal's office and had me read to her. I moved along until I was stumped by the word "grandfather." I noticed a picture on the opposite page of an old man. When I blurted "grandfather" as though I had read it, they moved me up a grade. Quick was as important as smart.

The black ghetto began nearby and black students came to Grant. One day, students were lined up in the gymnasium where a nurse (I remember her as a giant) checked us for head lice. I was lice-free, but wanted to cry. Her barked orders frightened me. It was worse for others whether they had head lice or not.

When I got home, I told my mother what had gone on and asked her in my child's way why Negro (the term of the time) kids were treated differently, why they were pushed around as we were not, why they were singled out. She had no blacks as friends, although she had known a few in Richmond and referred to them in Yiddish as "Schwartzes." I think she used it as a descriptive word, not a pejorative one. In any case, she did not hesitate a minute in condemning what I had described. She said strongly that the nurse's behavior wasn't right.

That may have been my first lesson on civil rights and democracy and one I did not forget. (I thought of that scene when I met Martin Luther King during the battle for civil rights legislation in 1964. Things had changed and things had not changed. Here we are 50 years later and that is in many ways still true.)

My school in third grade, Willard, was almost entirely Jewish, filled with the children of families on the rise economically, many still poor, but assimilating as much as possible. I did well, except for my effort to blow the bugle. In the fifth grade, I proudly became a member of our drum and bugle corps and tooted my way through weeks of learning. When spring came and a recital was announced, my teacher called me in and said that she wanted me in the recital, but when I lifted the bugle to my lips, she hoped that I would not blow. My tone-deaf condition was not a public humiliation, but a private (and lifelong) burden to carry. It was taps for my musical career, or even serious listening. (My wife, a wise and compassionate person, laments that they didn't switch me to the drums where a sense of rhythm might have sufficed.)

To pay for his tuition and to help us at home, Fred worked at Sears as a clerk in their pharmacy section while he also was a student in the pharmacy school at the University of Minnesota. After classes and work, he would walk home, miles away, to save the streetcar fare—about a dime, maybe less—and arrive home, late, tired, and with blistered, bloody toes after his endless day on his feet.

When he got his pharmacy degree, he moved up at Sears and, about that time, my father found a better mediocre hotel for his tailor shop. My sister worked at W.T. Grant, a downscale department store. Their combined wages meant we could cut down on the corn meal mush, and, when I was about 12 years old, we moved to the more affluent south side of Minneapolis. There were a few very elegant houses and many substantial ones not far away. In some sections, neighbors were likely to be doctors and lawyers and up-scale businessmen. Even where we lived, there were no peddlers or market workers. Lower middle class was better than before.

With mother Lena on a Brooklyn rooftop, 1939

It was a delicious step up, but we still lived in an apartment in a fourplex, a distance from the fancier folks. My dad had begun to earn a regular, if not large, income and the pride of leaving where we had been, of moving up, was palpable. In retrospect, it is odd. The move was only a little more than a geographic one, but it meant an immense amount to my folks. It was living their American dream.

I soon went to Hebrew school at the nearby Conservative synagogue, Adath Jeshurun, in a weekly after-school ritual. That led to my bar mitzvah preparation, the coming-of-age rite in which 13-year-old boys chant a verse from the Torah. The chanting was inevitably taught by an old man in the congregation who looked like he had been at the Wailing Wall when it had been built. They must be cloned.

The ceremony takes place on a Saturday morning around your birthday before the congregation, or at least those who had nothing better to do than pray. The bar mitzvah boy is decked out in the uniform of passage—a new prayer shawl, a *talis*, and a *yarmulke*, the little black cap that sits on the back of your head.

In an un-Christian moment during my final days of preparation, my tutor shook his ancient head and said, "Norman, that is the worst *haftorah* I have heard in all my years." I knew I had a hard time carrying a tune or chanting a chant. I just didn't expect it to be confirmed publicly in my synagogue. It's like saying your circumcision was cut on the bias.

With parents Louie and Lena in Minneapolis, early 1940s

But it got worse. You also gave a little speech on becoming a man. (Among the presents that came with the event was almost always a Parker pen and pencil set, leading to the mocking joke, "Today I am a pen and pencil.") Word came to my class one day that the rabbi wanted to see me. When I got to his office, Rabbi Gordon said, "Here is your speech." I said, "Rabbi, I have written my own speech." He responded without a smile or any warmth, "If you want to have a bar mitzvah, you will give this speech." (About 25 years later, when I traveled with Vice President Humphrey to Boston, the rabbi, now at a fancier synagogue, came to a gathering of Humphrey contributors and friends. I reminded him of the event and my story. Once again, he did not smile.)

I did not spend all my time in school. Bryant Square, a park across the street from our apartment, brought other pleasures. We hung around a clubhouse sort of building with pingpong tables inside, and swings and slides and tennis courts and ball fields outside the door. In summer, we played softball against other parks, and in winter ice-skated on the flooded courts. That public park was my country club.

One year, our softball team played for the city championship in a field with bleachers around it and with some guy in a booth manning a loudspeaker system. Ted Williams could not have felt more excited in his first all-star game than I was at the little field. When I got to the plate as our leadoff batter, the voice boomed out to the near-empty stands, "Sherman, second base, Sherman." I led off the game with a single, scored the first run, and made no errors. It was the highpoint of my athletic career, but not because I didn't aspire to more.

In the midst of this good fortune, World War II had begun. Fred went off to Italy and France as a medical administrative officer because of his pharmacy degree. In his distinctive way, he left guidelines for me to follow. They were mounted, in my absence, on my bedroom wall on green cardboard about four inches high and about a foot and a half long. One read, "4/7ths work; 3/7ths play." (How he decided to divide by seven was never explained.) Marvin, with a gentile wife not yet embraced by the family, went to the Pacific as a civilian working on installing and repairing refrigeration equipment, having studied at Dunwoody, a local trade school. When Marvin and Marie married, my mother, despite her lack of deep religious commitment, sat *shiva*, the Jewish lament for the dead. The ritual—hair let down, breast-beating, weeping—was frightening.

Before Marvin and Marie left, I was invited, as the only member of the family then talking to them, to lunch in their tiny basement apartment. I looked over the counter at a plate of green jello in which there were slivers of carrot. Jello was not kosher. I had never seen it at home, and I thought Marie had inadvertently dropped garbage in it. I ate it, but thought it was odd that they served it.

David became a navy pilot, training in Pensacola, Florida before being assigned to submarine patrol out of Trinidad looking for any German effort to damage or destroy the Panama Canal or impede shipping to countries in South America. It seemed routine and not dangerous since it was so far out of a real war zone. We had nothing to fear.

One Sunday morning my dad, on an errand, had gone down the stairs to the front door of our building where he met a Western Union deliveryman who asked where the Shermans lived. My dad identified himself, and the messenger handed him a telegram. It read "The Navy Department regrets to inform you that your son, Ensign David Sherman, is missing following a plane crash on 15 July 1944 in the performance of his duty and in the service of his country. The Department appreciates your great anxiety, but details are not now available and delay in receipt thereof must necessarily be expected. To prevent possible aid to our enemies, please do not divulge the name of his ship or station."

Upstairs, we knew nothing of the meeting until my sister, now married and whose apartment was about 10 blocks away, called. She was weeping, and my mother heard not only her words, but my dad sobbing in the background as well. Dave was my father's favorite child. He was always at ease and witty. He got an art scholarship when he was in high school and he was on the freshman wrestling team at the university before he enlisted. It took my dad decades to recover from his death. Soon after the telegram, my brother was declared dead, and a bit later a box of his belongings arrived. It was four or five feet long and a couple of feet high. My mother called my dad to tell him, and he forbade us from opening the box until he got home. He was certain that Dave's body was inside, despite my mother assuring him it was not.

He oddly did not come immediately home, but stayed in shock and tears until his normal closing hour. When he got home, he stood behind me, breathing heavily, sobbing, while I pried the box apart. Inside were books, personal belongings, but, of course, no body. I got over it, but my father seemed burdened by it all for years.

We later learned that Dave had written Fred saying the engines on the planes they were flying chronically broke down. On Dave's fateful flight, his two-engine plane was on patrol when the first engine stopped. He was gliding to a landing when the second also stopped. The plane flipped and crashed into the sea, killing him and one other. (When I read Arthur Miller's play, *All My Sons*, shortly after it came out in 1946, I was struck by its central fact: defective equipment had been sold to the military for profit when the seller knew it was bad. Greed easily overcame patriotic goodness. In the play, 21 planes had crashed and people like Dave had died as he had. Needlessly.)

His memorial service at our synagogue was delayed several times. My mother believed it was because we were relatively poor and the few other grieving families were well off. I think she was right. In any case, she rarely went back after the service was finally held, and she never forgot what she thought was a slight to her son.

By the time I was a teenager, my dad had pursued his same work in different places. He went from one to another second-rate hotel, transient or permanent home for traveling salesmen, underpaid schoolteachers, professional athletes of one sort or another, rural folk who had come to see a doctor or a relative or to shop. I only recently learned that the last two of his shops were in hotels frequented by the underworld, including John Dillinger, FBI designated public enemy number one.

For my dad, things did get more interesting. Many of the Minneapolis Millers, our minor league baseball team, stayed at the King Cole Hotel, his best location. Among the guests was Ted Williams before he went quickly to the Boston Red Sox and a major league Hall of Fame career. (He once took my dad and me to a wrestling match, my one night out with an All-Star.) Williams was young and shy. In the off-season when he came back to Minneapolis, he would not eat his meals in the public dining room. He ate with the staff and my dad at a table behind the kitchen.

Not all of Louie's clients were as illustrious. His best client for tailoring was the well-dressed proprietor of a bordello at 242 Hennepin, until a new mayor, Hubert Humphrey, closed it. Betty, our favorite madam, was unable to make ends meet and had no cash for tailoring services. Her new situation left my dad sad for her professional loss and for his diminished income as well.

My father had another vague connection to the Kosher Nostra underworld. He knew an immigrant Jewish family nearby. Their son, later disowned, brought unwanted notoriety to them. In 1945, just before Humphrey became mayor, the underworld thrived in Minneapolis. The previous mayor was on the take, the police chief as bad. For years, muckraking journalists had flourished, publishing erratically, skipping an edition when they were bought off to keep something quiet. Two had been murdered in the mid-thirties. Another quasi-journalist and their heir, Arthur Kasherman, had worked with both of them and produced a periodic little newsletter in their tradition.

The circulation of his newsletter was not high, but it produced a fair income. Kasherman, like the others, would find some scandalous or illegal behavior and threaten to publish it. If the perpetrator would pay him off, he would kill the story. It was a form of first amendment blackmail, and he had served several years in the state prison for a shakedown the victim made public.

One night, he had a dinner date. His companion suggested they eat at Hannah's Cafe, a restaurant that attracted the underworld types and was probably owned by one. After dinner when they returned to his car, they found its tires slashed, but got into it. His lady friend slipped hurriedly out the passenger side door and ducked. At that moment, a bullet smashed the driver-side window and killed Kasherman. It was a set-up, and she was a cooperating lady.

About a dozen years later, my father and I were talking about my work, and I explained with some pride that I worked for important political people, often writing speeches and press releases. He didn't quite understand my explanation and asked, "Norman, do you remember Art Kasherman? You don't write like Art, do you?" I assured him I did not, but wasn't sure he was convinced.

My dad's work also provided me with a job. I was barely as tall as the pressing machine, but to help him I struggled to press pants and jackets and keep smiling. One summer, when I was not quite 15 and really underage, he also got me hired as a dishwasher. I was about 5 feet tall, maybe 100 pounds. It was hot, heavy work for a runt.

The waitresses would haul in trays loaded with dirty plates and silverware and dump them on a huge metal table. I stacked it all in wooden racks, lifted the door on one end of the huge dishwasher, shoved in a rack and started the steamy hot machine. I couldn't keep up with the accumulating dishes, which would often be used again as soon as they were clean and dry. The waitresses growled at my lack of skill and speed. I ached and cursed my benevolent dad. On my first day, the diners and the staff were long gone while my bedtime passed and I still sweated.

My job was usually held by a drunk, bum, or floater who stayed a short time and was replaced by a similar, temporarily sober, soul. I understood their longevity. I lasted that one shift, leaving unwashed dishes for the next day and a new dishwasher. I also left a short note explaining that I would not be back. The hotel, I hoped, had seen the last of me. That turned out not to be quite so.

I was hired as a bellhop a couple of years later, hauling luggage up to plain if not tacky rooms, helping drunks off the floor into their beds, watching gentlemen my family knew check in with a bottle of whiskey and a woman, putting a priest from Duluth to bed when he would visit and consume more spirits than was healthy, wise, or holy.

The job was not what a teen-aged idealist needed to experience, but did no lasting harm, as best I can tell. And it was a little more money and made me proud to be contributing even a bit to our family's tiny income. Years later the hotel was purchased by a Christian group, which turned it into the Evangeline Residence for Women. I have always hoped they had an exorcism ceremony.

3. Growing up Jewish

At West High School I tried out for the basketball team and, despite my height, I made it. It was no small accomplishment for a little squirt. For two years during practice, I ran, sweated, and leapt about, sometimes getting great laughs with a "broken-leg" dribble I invented. It amused my teammates and me, but apparently not the coach. When Friday came, the day real games were played, he never selected me to suit up. I sat behind the bench in my street clothes.

The coach was like the rabbi. He would have you do things his way or not at all, and my broken-leg charade was not his way. When I realized that I was only on the team so that there were enough players for two teams to practice during the week and would never share the Friday glory, I turned in my jockstrap.

I had to find another outlet. I had read, although I am not sure it is authentic, that Jews in ghettoes had said, "Humor is the ghetto's only form of defense." I wasn't in a real ghetto, but I discovered I could make people laugh, and, looking back, it may have been my personal defense. To some extent every Jew in Minneapolis then needed it.

I don't recall feeling deeply that I was part of a

discriminated-against minority, even though I would from time to time hear the words "kike" or "sheeny," pejoratives used by some of my classmates, not necessarily for my ears, but possibly so. Certainly there was no escaping totally from the atmosphere of separation. A well known and honored journalist and author, Carey McWilliams, writing about anti-Semitism in the United States in the forties called Minneapolis its capital and for good reason. Under the guise of Christianity, there were several noisy evangelical pastors preaching hate to huge congregations who carried the message from on high to many people below.

Two brothers, Luke and Paul Rader, had a popular tabernacle with a movie-house sign in front advertising their sermon of the week with a misleading title, often speaking of Christian love when they truly spoke pagan hate. Another evangelist, William Bell Riley, was an almost equally bigoted voice of anti-Semitism in the guise of Holy Scripture.

No matter what the cover, there was really no ambiguity in their preachments: the Jews were the anti-Christ and to be shunned, at the least. If the voices and words of those men of the cloth were not heard in every corner of Minneapolis, the spirit of their religious rage and biblical distemper seeped out from their pious cesspool to the ears and hearts of many.

Their audience may have been mostly the unwashed, but even the more up-scale secular places and people were not welcoming to Jews. The Minneapolis Athletic Club and the Minneapolis Club, gathering places for the well-to-do, did not admit Jews of whatever means as members until 1960. One can only assume that all of this didn't happen without discussion and deliberate action by those who did belong: the establishment of retail giants, businessmen, manufacturers and millers, bankers and financiers, doctors and lawyers.

Oddly, even the American Automobile Association, hardly an exclusive haven for the elite and ordinarily eager elsewhere for members of any sort, would not accept identified Jews as members. Nor would the Lions, Kiwanis, and Rotary clubs. That only began to change in 1946 after the election of a new mayor, although the venom didn't disappear quickly or totally.

In 1970, a rotund, prematurely-balding young man, Mike Berman, worked long hours in a DFL campaign, arriving early each day wearing a tie, leaving late with the tie long off and hanging on a door knob near his desk. Often after midnight he would stop at the Minneapolis Club to buy the early edition of the next morning's paper. One night, taking home a week of ties, he was in the lobby about to pay for his paper when a drunken member came off the elevator, saw him, and gasped loudly, "Oh, my god, what's a fat Jew doing selling ties in our lobby at two o'clock in the morning?"

As late as the mid-seventies, women could not be members, and female guests of members, including wives, could not enter through the front door. When Muriel Humphrey was appointed to the U.S. Senate in 1978, after her husband's death, she was automatically made a member as both U.S. senators were. She refused to be a back door member and with a grin of satisfaction came in out of the cold the front way. She didn't eat there often.

Worse than all the social exclusions was the world of medicine where lives, not just status and acceptance, were at stake. Except for the University of Minnesota Hospital and the city's General Hospital, Jewish doctors were not permitted to affiliate formally. Only Jews who were patients of non-Jewish doctors had a chance to sneak in to the other hospitals. The private hospitals, most of which began with religious sponsors, declared in effect that Jewish interns as well as doctors were toxic and sent them away. As a result of all that, Jewish people in need of care or surgery in a hospital, or just to deliver a baby, were not able to get help easily. It was not until 1951, when a Jewish hospital available to everyone including gentiles opened its doors, that the other hospitals began to change. Non-sectarian death was available.

Ultimately, Hubert Humphrey as mayor inspired, wrangled, forced a more benevolent spirit on the city. He enlisted many church leaders not burdened with prejudices like the Raders and Riley to speak out. He used government agencies to foster a more caring community for all. Some change also came home with the veterans who had seen places where prejudice reigned and had seen its destructive effects. They fought it overseas and at least some were ready to fight it at home.

Humphrey had begun to make a mark nationally, too. Though young and relatively new on the national scene, in 1947 he joined other progressive Democrats and liberal leaders of the labor movement in organizing the Americans for Democratic Action. The founders included theologian Reinhold Niebuhr, United Auto Workers president Walter Reuther, and Eleanor Roosevelt. ADA became a significant presence in advocating social programs and justice in Washington.

Even as he became a national leader, however, he kept his focus at home, and what Humphrey did in those years bore fruit for a long time after. The positive changes that had begun under him in fighting anti-Semitism slowly blossomed in the 1960s with the election of Jews to major public office. Arthur Naftalin, a Humphrey political colleague from the beginning, had been among a small group who helped create the DFL. Naftalin worked in the mayor's office for Humphrey, became a professor at the University, and was

Freeman's Commissioner of Administration, but had never run for office. Then, in 1961, he ran for mayor and won. He was re-elected three times, ending his service in 1969.

The first Jewish U.S. senator from Minnesota, Rudy Boschwitz, a Republican, was elected for two terms beginning in 1978. He lost to another Jew, Paul Wellstone, in 1990. Wellstone died in a plane crash in 2002 and was soon succeeded by Norm Coleman, a Republican, who was also Jewish. Then in 2008 both major parties nominated Jews, and Democrat Al Franken won. Beginning not long after the American Automobile Association in Minneapolis ceased preserving its Aryan purity-on-wheels, one Minnesota U.S. Senate seat has been filled by a Jew.

The change even showed up in a minor way in my high school where I first heard Humphrey speak in 1944. There were social clubs, sort of spring training for college fraternities, sponsored by the Young Men's Christian Association (YMCA). Each " Hi-Y" had an identifying three-letter acronym always including an X, which stood for Christianity.

With the war ending and slogans if not always the spirit of democracy everywhere, the only "Negro" in the school, Don Brown; the only Japanese, Johnny Oshima, whose parents had been in a federal internment camp; and I were invited to join the Hi-Y. Up until then it had been made up entirely of boys from a suburb, Edina, whose real estate covenants permitted no Jews to live there, and certainly no blacks. My club had a three-letter identification that stood for Loyalty, Obedience, Christianity or LOX, the Jewish word for smoked salmon, an ethnic delicacy often served with bagels.

Like the other members, I wore the little black club pin, LOX, proudly on my shirt and joined in the laughter that my closer friends who lived nearby, and not in Edina, could not contain. I was of both Jewish and gentile worlds and thought life was good and prejudice on its way out. I was a bit premature. Certainly, at that moment, I should have found whoever suggested the expanded membership. I suspect his parents were among those still living, maybe cherishing, their minority-free lives in their clubs and in their community. (I don't think I ever asked myself why I was the chosen one.)

A jarring moment, soon after my induction, brought me up short. The school counselor, Malvina Lockwood, who was also the faculty adviser to our student council, one day put her arm around my shoulders as we were on the way to a meeting and said, "Norman, you should try to act less Jewish." I shrugged, a little bewildered. I thought she should have acted less like a bigoted fool. I couldn't be oblivious all the time.

Years later, at a class reunion, a girl I had taken out on several occasions during those years asked me if I ever wondered why I picked her up at another classmate's house and not at her own. When I said I had not ever thought about it, she explained that her father would not let her date Jews. He was a top executive at General Mills, part of the upper crust, and, apparently, an anti-Semite whose bad genes didn't get to his daughter.

On balance, those teen years were good ones and left me excited in anticipation of a bright, if not easily defined, future. With my bugle long gone and my jockstrap hung up, I left high school with a satisfying sense that I was a reasonably good student, had a talent for making people laugh, and that was enough; certainly more important than being the valedictorian or gentile.

4. Political Beginnings

My passage from high school to college was not a smooth one. My brother Fred, always rigid, determined, and interfering, had gotten hooked on the idea of my going to the University of Chicago. Under a legendary educator and innovative president, Robert Hutchins, it attracted bright students from all over the country to a program of accelerated study, which put them in advanced classes as they qualified on entrance exams or demonstrated in basic classes. Fred thought the system was made for me.

I reluctantly complied and applied. I had never been away from home. In fact, until the previous year, I had not even been to St. Paul, our adjacent twin city. My college-bound friends were going to the University of Minnesota. I wasn't a genius and early graduation meant nothing to me. I wanted to be where I was comfortable among people I knew.

The weeks of summer passed, and we heard nothing from Chicago. As fall approached, I, relieved, prepared to register at Minnesota. Fred insisted that we contact Chicago again. Surprisingly, I had been accepted, and the letter telling me had apparently gone astray. I reluctantly gave in and took the train to Chicago, registered, and found a place to live. That turned out to be the high point. My room was on the top floor of a fraternity house that had more empty rooms than resident members and the fraternity had to rent out space to the unwashed. When asked to become a member, I declined the opportunity.

I should have stayed home. A private college drained more than we could possibly afford (although it was nothing compared to today), and I was lonely from the moment I stepped off the train. Then I met other students. Their self-approval overwhelmed me. I would introduce myself, give my name, smile, and too often hear my new classmate humbly say, "Hi, Norman, I have a 180 I.Q. What's yours?"

Each time I heard that question, and some version came regularly in the early weeks, my inclination was to say 90 and vanish. Instead, I mumbled some inane response first and only then moved on to the next resident genius. There was no escaping the overwhelming atmosphere of self-esteem.

Since I had heard from the university late, I did not have the chance to take the exams that might have given me advanced placement on entrance. I started at the entry level and only then took the tests. With the results, I was placed in several advanced courses. It surprised me, gratified Fred, and left me behind since it was the third week of the semester. I moved ahead and fell behind.

When I got home at Christmas break, I announced that we couldn't afford the tuition, room, and board, that I hated being away from home, that I couldn't stand most of the people I met, and that I was not going back. I didn't stamp my foot; I didn't cry, but my obvious discomfort brought the embrace, or at least understanding, of most of my family.

Even then there were hurdles. It was 1946, and veterans of World War II had been coming home in large numbers.

Because of their G.I. Bill of Rights, they had overwhelmed the university. As a transfer, I had to plead to get in. Finally I was admitted and registered where no one asked my IQ or told me his. I suddenly could enjoy the excitement of interesting subjects and inspiring professors in a comfortable environment.

I thrived as an English major. Before I was done, I took courses from two novelists of acclaim: Robert Penn Warren and Saul Bellow. In the openness of Minnesota, I got to know both a bit in social and informal ways. Other faculty members were just as welcoming and I aimed at a degree in English literature with a new passion.

While I was still an undergraduate, my mother fell ill in 1949. She went to her Jewish doctor who looked after a good share of our community. People lined up beyond the waiting room to see him. My mom, self-diagnosed, told him she had colon cancer. He checked and said she did not. She came home and stoically went on for another six months before returning even more convinced. This time the doctor said she was right, but, of course, her cancer was much further along. She was a diabetic (as I have been for 40 years) and didn't heal easily or well after the belated surgery.

Her operation was at the University hospital and I became the designated visitor. I was nearby. My father cried too easily to visit very often. Brother Fred worked long hours seven days a week and was too parsimonious to hire a relief pharmacist. My sister, Rose, had begun her family and had two young sons. Marvin lived far away. So it was left to me to comfort, to hold hands, to cry a bit, trying to be encouraging to a dying mother.

No day was easy, but one day was memorable. When I arrived, I could see my mother was upset in a different way. Before I could inquire why, she cursed my father for sending a rabbi to see her and in explicit, impassioned words said I was to tell him never to do that again. She didn't need prayer and she didn't want solace from a stranger, however holy or anointed. She was a feisty lady even as she accepted that she had not long to live. And by then she was still Jewish, but not religious, unable to forget her sense that in our synagogue rich and poor were treated differently, maybe by God, certainly by the rabbi. (I am fortunate, I think, that I inherited more from her than my father, although I do show a bit of his more fatuous ways.) After she came home and soon died, I turned my full attention to school and work. Because she had been the glue that held the family together, I was on my own.

What I learned outside of class during those years remains with me while much else has been forgotten. The man who ran the campus bookstore where I worked bought a small fishing resort in northern Minnesota. It had eight cabins, a little store, and boats for rowing or for a small outboard motor. For several springs I would join him to clean the cabins and in the fall to close them. One day he asked me to take his two dogs for a run in the woods. As they ran and I walked, I spotted a huge bird on a tree trunk. It had a dazzling red crest extending back into a point, and white stripes on a body of black feathers and a long tail. I was certain I had found a prehistoric creature and took off running faster than the dogs back to the house to share my discovery. Lyman, my friend and an accomplished bird watcher, said, "Oh, it's a pileated woodpecker," as though it were a sparrow. Though deflated then, I have continued bird watching, now following my wife who has become far better than I ever was at identification. It has been my only hobby beyond politics.

As an undergraduate, I was a creative, if not a great or consistently successful English major. But I was attracted to a young woman who was. In a large English class, one student often answered the professor's questions. Jane Klingel wore attractive clothes, including a lovely white blouse that seemed unlike any other I saw. Romantic that I was, I assumed she must have sewn it herself when she wasn't studying. It turned out that she bought her outfits at the campus branch of our fanciest department store, Dayton's. Overcoming my disillusion, I soon convinced her to marry me. The wedding was a casual affair. We met two friends at the courthouse in downtown Minneapolis and were married in a moment by a judge in his chambers.

Despite my intellectual flaws and irreverent nature, and my new marital burdens, I began my graduate work in the fall of 1951, able to do so because I became a teaching assistant and then an instructor in the humanities program. I was proudly the only one of my fellow teaching assistants promoted that year. It may not have been my excellence entirely. A faculty member got a late fellowship and took off for a year, leaving a vacancy to be filled at the last minute.

Then a preeminent professor, William Van O'Connor, asked me to be the managing editor of a national literary quarterly devoted to the study of William Faulkner. *Faulkner Studies* had been produced in mimeographed form by graduate students at the University of Montana. These students, with a Ph.D. in hand, were now teaching in various universities and their publication needed a new home. I again saw a glorious career in my future as a college professor and scholar.

I soon made the "journal" into an 18-page quarterly. Since I had read so little Faulkner, I recruited several others who had. In addition to me, there were two editors and a staff of six, including my wife and her next husband. One of my recruits, Jules Chametsky, went on to an illustrious career as an English professor at the University of Massachusetts and editor of scholarly journals. Another was an eccentric bookstore owner and college dropout, Melvin McCosh, who was a good friend and who had read every word Faulkner had published. Melvin was a scrawny guy with a beard before they were common, and generally spoke in a whisper. We quickly built up the paid subscription base to dozens before giving it up.

McCosh and I later started a publishing company appropriately named: McCosh and Sherman. We published a book of cartoons on motherhood, *Premier Fruit*, by a French artist, and a book of sketches by Faulkner, *Mirrors of Chartres Street*, that had never been published in book form before and had languished in the files of the New Orleans *Times Picayune* for years. O'Connor had somehow found them. We got a fellow student to illustrate the book and hit the big time. The *New Yorker* reviewed it. "Eleven sketches disinterred from the dusty files of the *Times Picayune*. Better left undisinterred. Tortured illustrations by. . . ." That didn't stop us. Money did.

Isaac Rosenfeld, a fiction writer and professor, was acclaimed for his short stories. He gathered them, we printed them, but had no money to bind them. They were ultimately tossed away. Melvin and I ended our publishing career quickly.

Melvin was a mythic creature whose store became a second home for a motley crew, including me. We hung around, had deep intellectual conversations, and occasionally bought a book. (He also rented out rooms in his Dinkytown house next to the campus. One of the later renters was my future wife, Ginny, who lived there briefly around the time I first met her.)

Some of the books that filled his dusty shelves came from the Salvation Army store, which sold donated books as well as used kitchen appliances, tools, and old shirts, pants, and dresses. Melvin worked there for a pittance when his own meager sales were slower than usual. It was an economic step up. Despite his slow sales, if he found a customer somehow irritating, he wouldn't sell to him.

Melvin was not exactly mainstream. When Marlboro brought out a "crushproof" cigarette box, he drove over one with his ancient Cadillac and displayed it in his window alongside the ad touting it. He featured a sign once a year that said, "Homecomers Go Home." He once called Northern States Power Company, our electric company, and asked a bewildered telephone operator to speak to Reddy Kilowatt, the company's cute symbol, and when the bewildered operator said he wasn't really real, Melvin said, "But he signs my bills."

Later, when he bought a surplus firehouse from the city, he had the only bookstore in America with poles. Unfortunately, there were no fire trucks remaining on the first floor and no books on the second floor. The poles stood glistening, but unused. The university literary magazine, *Ivory Tower*, did a profile of Melvin repeating stories, some mythic, some real, that he had told to the reporter who wrote the article. Melvin responded with a letter asking, "Why did you make up those lies about me?" The conscientious reporter was bewildered.

The real significance of *Faulkner Studies* was meeting my printer. When I decided that the baby journal should grow up from mimeograph to print, I found a person who changed my life forever. Fortunately, my brief whirl as a scholar had that singular, lasting result.

I went to the University of Minnesota Press and asked them to recommend an inexpensive printer. They directed me to Gerry Dillon, the partner of two men he had met while he was a reporter at a daily paper in Indiana. The three of them bought a print shop in Minneapolis. It was in a small, unimposing brick building that shouted "inexpensive." I liked what I saw and was further delighted when Gerry's secretary turned out to be someone from my high school class. Out back, there were a couple letterpresses, racks of type, shelves of paper, and not much else. The two Hoosiers ran the printing presses, and Gerry worked the streets. The business was so limited that he also drove a taxi at night to earn enough to feed his growing family.

He was a literate printer. He said he had written a paper on Faulkner when he was in college and wondered if I would like to publish it. I didn't ask to read it. It remained unpublished, but our laughter and my comments became a bonding moment.

His shop was perfect for us, but it was his political activity that influenced my life beyond the friendship that began then and lasted until his death in 1993. When we finished talking Faulkner (it took minutes), we talked politics (that lasted years). I later told people who asked how I got infected by DFL politics that I caught it off a toilet seat at Meyers Printing Company.

Our meeting just then was premature. I was still trying to be a radical. I was uncomfortable in the mainstream and outraged, still, by Senator Joe McCarthy riding high in his red-baiting vilification of those he sneeringly identified as Communists, and thus enemies and traitors. Many of those vilified were, of course, not "Reds," but liberals of one sort or another. I attended a McCarthy rally at the University wanting to see evil up close. If he wasn't drunk, he must have had a mild seizure that made his tongue thick, his brain thin, and his stance unsteady.

The first political rally I attended was for Henry Wallace at the Minneapolis Armory in 1948. He was running for president as the candidate of the Progressive Party, the far-to-the-left alternative to the Democratic Party and Harry Truman. The sense of mission, the goal of creating a more perfect world that seemed to flow from the movement attracted me.

That night the Armory was packed with a full house of exuberant people (among them Walter Mondale, although I didn't discover that coincidence until years later). We were often out of our seats and on our feet for every speaker, cheering and applauding, and especially so when Wallace was introduced. It was my first experience with palpable political ecstasy.

After the early rousing oratory, the house went dark, a spotlight playing on the black curtain at the back of the stage behind which Wallace waited out-of-sight as the anticipation grew. Then, the spotlight shown on the left and Wallace stumbled in from stage right, bumping into a chair and almost falling on his way to the podium and microphone. It was not Karl, but Groucho and Harpo; a Marx brothers entrance, comic, silly, clumsy; all irrelevant, but somehow immediately diminishing my enthusiasm. It seems absurd now to think something so petty would have had that effect, but it did. I recovered a bit as Wallace regained his balance and began to speak words I wanted to hear.

The Communist Party was active and relatively strong in Minnesota, though still small, and it dominated our local Progressive Party. Those who identified themselves proudly as Stalinists were not easy to like. I didn't see them as revolutionaries ready to overthrow the government, but as bores, self-righteous, and humorless.

After Wallace spoke, leaving many of us, but certainly not everyone, a little disappointed, the head of a major Minneapolis labor union worked the crowd into a kind of frenzy. Then he called for a "sea of green." People, including me despite my doubts, led by shills among us, raised and waved a dollar or a five or maybe more, over their heads. Party workers raced up the aisles and through the audience grabbing the money, stuffing it into buckets they carried. It was effective fundraising by gimmick. I was a conflicted innocent of good heart and simple mind, a bad combination. But this was off-putting, a gross bit of manipulation, the work of ideologues.

I was participant, observer, and victim. Later, the more I thought about the evening, the less appealing Wallace and his party became to me and, I thought, inevitably to other voters. It got worse. An ardent Communist Party member named Les came out from New York City to run us rubes. He didn't ask; he ordered. He didn't appreciate; he expected. He offensively exuded, like body odor, the attitude that each of us lackeys "would be free my way."

I can see his arrogant, unsmiling face even yet. He was not a Communist as I understood them to be in my more generous moments, but a thorough little fascist. He had the warmth of an igloo and the affect of a stump. My growing disaffection diminished my commitment. The more I read and understood about Joe Stalin and the Soviet Union, the less I liked what I learned. My disillusion, set aside for a while, now grew quickly. I didn't parrot Joe McCarthy, but I did silently question my new leaders.

Soon after the rally a fellow student at the University, listening to my doubts, sneering in disgust, delivered the ultimate insult: "vacillating bourgeois." I was furious, but he was right. A couple of months later on a clear November day, two weeks after I turned 21, I voted for Harry Truman. (I actually owed President Truman a lot. When I turned 18, I had a pre-induction physical at Fort Snelling and was given 1A status. Days later, he decreed that 18-year-olds would not be drafted.

A year later, I went through the same ritual and so did he. He announced that 19-year-olds would not be drafted. The war ended without me in uniform.)

That 1948 election night, I went with a good friend, David Seham, and his doctor father to my first listening party. It took place at the elegant home of a prominent lawyer and local Democratic leader. It was a new world of affluence and power I hadn't known, seen up close, or even fully imagined. There was style in dress, food, and even furniture. We listened, standing around several radios. The evening wore on with the Republican candidate, Thomas E. Dewey, seemingly destined for victory. (The little joke at the time, originating with Harold Ickes, Franklin Roosevelt's Secretary of the Interior, was that the "E" in his name stood for "Elusive," a quality I have since found in other Republican presidential candidates. Later as a columnist for the *New Republic* magazine, Ickes took on Senator Joe McCarthy when few others did.)

David and I left the party, depressed, convinced our candidate would lose and the world would come to an end, but as we drove, the results and our mood changed. The numbers grew closer and closer. In our excitement, hanging on every broadcast word, and actually cheering aloud the newest results, we ended up driving from south Minneapolis to St. Cloud and back, about 120 miles, to savor a couple of hours of rising hopes and then victory.

I was really hooked after that, although for a few years I was unnaturally serious while I got my B.A. and unsuccessfully pursued a Ph.D., first in English literature and then in American Studies. Politics was not a constant part of my life over the following half-century, but it was close. Virtually everything I have done in a work or professional way has revolved around it or at least permitted me to stay close and active in some fashion, sometimes as a volunteer, more often paid. I would do virtually anything that let me participate, organize, persuade.

It seemed my ordained lot. At the university in 1952, I became the head of an *ad hoc* Student Action Committee set up to raise hell about the firing of a black faculty member, Forrest Wiggins, from his position in the philosophy department. There were only a handful of African Americans on state university faculties in the country, and he was the first of two then at Minnesota.

The fervor of anti-Communism during those McCarthy years was high. Ultimately, two DFL state legislators from St. Paul led a campaign to get Wiggins fired because they whispered that he was probably a member of the Communist Party or at least, in a regurgitated phrase of the time, a "fellow traveler." Actually, I think he was singled out for no other reason than teaching while black.

Forrest had been vice president of the Minnesota Progressive Party and supported Henry Wallace in 1948, as many faculty did, and he had made a speech the next year, not in class, but in a public meeting in Duluth, where he said, "business was destructive of the public good." No one took to the barricades, but the two legislators, conservative folks disguised as liberals, took to the microphone and their bullying pulpits.

An absurd, near-hysterical campaign was begun to get him fired, and it was successful. That he was some form of a socialist was undisputed; that he was a member of the Communist Party much less certain, unlikely, and quite irrelevant to the subject matter of his teaching. There was never any allegation that he was distorting philosophical truth in some secret Communist way. The philosophy department unanimously opposed his firing and urged instead his promotion, but in the craziness of the time, that didn't matter.

We didn't save his job, but I liked my role and, particularly, moving an audience. I spoke once to a hall overflowing with cheering students. I was quoted in the campus newspaper, which said there were 800 students there, although it seemed like thousands. I appeared less successfully before the Board of Regents to make our case. It was a memorable occasion anyway. I had no shirt that was clean and adequate for the occasion so I went to Dinky Dayton's and bought a shirt and tie. I took them home, put on the shirt, and discovered the sleeves were way too long. Under time pressure, I raced back angry and berated the clerk for selling me a defective shirt. He explained to my bewilderment that what I had were "French cuffs" and needed cuff links. I may still have them.

We put out a kind of manifesto that I had largely written calling for Wiggins's reinstatement. A professor, Franz Montgomery, who taught some writing courses, stopped me one day to say that he was a staunch (his word) conservative, but had used our document in several of his classes as an example of superb (also his word) writing. That was not faint praise.

I remained an ideologue in search of radical company. I had found the Socialist Workers' Party (SWP) through a fellow graduate student who had come to Minneapolis from Detroit ostensibly to study for a Ph.D. in American Studies. But what really drew him was the SWP office in Minneapolis run by icons of the national Trotskyist movement. My erstwhile friend once appeared at my door after some controversy and dramatically announced in a grand cliché, "You have nothing to lose but your chains." He delivered the wisdom as if he were Moses with a brand-new commandment. I couldn't find my chains in any case.

Vincent Ray Dunne, one of three Communist brothers,

who had led an historic strike by teamsters of Local 574 (later 544) in 1934 in Minneapolis, was our local guru and leader. He had been convicted of violating the Smith Act of 1940 for "advocating the overthrow of the U.S. government." The Supreme Court overturned the law in 1957, but long before that Ray and 11 others served time in the federal penitentiary at Sandstone, Minnesota. Ray was in 16 months. Most of the others spent a year there. To stop the revolution, to clear the barricades, to end subversion, a total of 213 people were charged, not nearly enough for even a half-assed insurrection.

They opposed our entry into World War II, something I would not have agreed with. But if the Smith Act had still been on the books during Vietnam days, it would have sent not a couple hundred, but hundreds of thousands to jail. To be anti-war seems a right, not an offense worthy of incarceration. That Ray and Grace Carlson, his political associate, came out of jail without discernible rage surprises me even now.

Ray sat on a secular throne of our making; we worshipped him, and I think he deserved it. I didn't know then that he had started working in a lumber camp when he was 14 years old. He was an extraordinary man, with a first-rate formally untutored mind, a student of American history beyond the labor movement. He was a social philosopher with the strong hands and body of a working stiff and the stronger brain of a professor. If he was a rabble-rouser, as some had charged, he was a quiet, dignified one. He never puffed himself up, never bragged about what he and his brothers and allies had done to improve the lives of others.

He was a fervent follower of Leon Trotsky, the flip side of the Communist coin from Joe Stalin. (The Stalinists called them Trotskyites as a kind of putdown instead of the preferred Trotskyists. I never understood the difference in my most Trotskyist or Trotskyite days.)

I didn't know of the effort to organize workers in the wholesale fruit and vegetable markets when it was happening since I was not yet 10 years old. But many of our neighbors who worked in the market had children I played with every day and with whom I remained friends for years. I heard talk of the battle later after we moved away. Our neighbors weren't radicals, certainly belonged to no union when the strike began, but knew their lives had been made better by what the Dunne brothers and a few others organized and ran. I somehow absorbed some of their positive recollections before I met Dunne. (One Dunne sibling, Bill, was a Stalinist and still a union organizer. I was told, not by Ray, that they had not spoken for several years when they found themselves, by accident, in a bar in New York City. Standing about six feet apart, their eyes met for a moment of recognition and then they turned their backs on one another and did not speak. Ideology took precedence over family.)

When I met Ray, he talked revolution as though it might come soon and be led by his compatriots, maybe including me. It was heady stuff. Along with his incendiary talk, however, from time to time he wore *pince-nez* glasses, imitating Trotsky himself. It was an odd bit of affectation, though slight, and easily ignored. Glasses or not, he was my leader. He remains today one of the more exceptional people of integrity, coherence, and compassion I have ever known. That I ultimately did not share his vision of how we would create a more perfect world has in no way diminished my feelings about him.

The sense of the impending revolution he described was brought home at a social gathering (in other circles called a Christmas party) in our headquarters at Fourth and Hennepin in downtown Minneapolis. It was on the second floor and had a couple of offices, a library, a meeting room, and a kitchen. It was a church basement upstairs.

I sat with a couple who owned a small grocery store in a suburb of St. Paul. Before supermarkets and easy transportation, small grocery stores seemed to be a step up on the economic scale for many people, including truck drivers. Everyone bought groceries. Every family knew its neighborhood grocer. Pork chops and broccoli, and everything else, created a continuing opportunity for this couple to sneak in a bit of revolutionary talk.

My tablemate had been in that historic strike almost 20 years earlier. Though now a mini-mini-capitalist, he was devoted to Dunne and the movement. Between bites, his face suddenly grew serious, and he asked, "What will we do with Christmas when the revolution comes?" When I said, "We'll make it a workers' holiday," a smile wiped out the troubled look and an aura of a combined Trotskyist and Christian joy enveloped him.

I also went to the headquarters for lunch from time to time. Our repast was prepared and served by Grace Carlson, a quiet presence and former University of Minnesota professor, and clearly a better cook than Ray. She had run for the U.S. Senate in 1940 and the U.S. House in 1950. After serving her 16-month Smith Act incarceration, she had been the SWP vice presidential candidate in 1948, the first time the party had run a national ticket. She and Farrell Dobbs, the presidential candidate, (who was occasionally around and had been a major leader of the strike) got 13,614 votes out of almost 50 million cast. She was the first person I knew to run for vice president of the United States.

If Grace was a revolutionary worthy of jail and capable of inspiring others to the barricades for the overthrow of the government, it was not apparent in her voice or style. She spoke softly, never moved frenetically, gave no orders, made no demands. She was a gentle soul. Resident cook she may have been, but she was always an active and equal participant in our discussions and never deferential to the male leaders. A few years after I met her, she went back to the Catholic Church, a true believer still, but of a different sort.

In 1952 when I voted for the SWP national ticket, with Dobbs once again at the top, but with a new running mate, the total vote had dropped back to 10,312, a small force for our mission. In fact, my SWP ran last among the candidates of six protest parties, including Douglas MacArthur as the Constitutional Party candidate and Darlington Hoopes, the Socialist Party candidate with an exquisite name. That wasn't its lowest point, but it wasn't the highest either. In 1976, the SWP got about 90,000 votes. But in 2012, it was back down to just over 4,000.

I ultimately did not see the world quite as they did, but my brief dalliance with them reinforced my sense that life could be made better for lots of people if we worked at it. Better was possible; perfect might not be. I had to move on.

Soon after the 1952 election, I decided that Yom Kippur could not be a workers' holiday and that my visionary excursions led nowhere, that my lust for political action and a better society was misplaced on the far left. It was a time when I saw my wonderful dreams for what they were in the context of an America of Joe McCarthy, Congressman Howard Smith and his contemptible Smith Act, segregation, unchanging economic disparities. What I indulged myself in was, I decided, endless talk, a kind of decent delusion of Nirvana on the horizon, a verbal massage that felt good, but was not the real thing and cured nothing. I reluctantly gave it up.

5. Into the Political World

I had already accepted that my graduate school efforts were not going well and would not get better. I had accumulated more incompletes than "A" grades. A Ph.D. was clearly beyond me. So, I found work in bookstores and briefly ran a small one, earning little. Then, by luck, I became a technical writer at Minneapolis Honeywell, and soon a speech writer, titling my first speech, "Air Conditioning: A Hot Subject."

If I have had a profession, it grew out of that. I have been a ghostwriter, an odd career not chosen, but begun almost by accident. A couple of years earlier, still an undergraduate and single, I was at a bus stop on Olson Highway (the renamed and repaved street where I lifted those tarred wooden blocks) near our new home bought with the insurance money from Dave's death. A car pulled up and the driver asked if I was on my way to the University. When I said yes, he offered a ride. He pointed at the empty ashtray on the dashboard and said the first ride was free, but if I rode with him again, I needed to put a dime in. That seemed fair. We picked up several other students with their dimes ready.

The driver was a Ph.D. candidate in psychology. He and his wife and their two kids lived a couple of miles up the road.

I became a regular passenger, and we became friends. Later, when I was married, we saw them regularly.

One day, in a rather formal fashion, he called and asked to see me. We set an appointment hour at his insistence. When we met, he said he had been asked to leave the University after he had solicited a campus cop staking out the men's room in Northrop Auditorium, home of the Minneapolis Symphony Orchestra. My immediate reaction was to ask, "Would you like an affidavit that you have never made a pass at me?" He broke up at my disingenuous response. He went from the men's room to work at Honeywell, and it was through him that I was hired when I finally gave up my illustrious academic career.

I went on from my first speech to what might have been a successful career, writing mostly about thermostats, heating, and cooling. My colleagues and I also developed a list of "zircons": phony jewels of wisdom that some salesmen, literal and simple, might use. My first, "A carpenter without confidence drives a crooked nail," was delivered seriously. Others should have been, but were not. "You can't scrape bottom in an empty barrel." "When the man above you on the ladder of success is backing down, that's the time to nose ahead."

My work drew praise until a fateful moment. My boss, who oversaw about 50 of us, sat in a glass-walled office at the head of the floor, fully visible to all. What was not so clear was that he was an alcoholic. Despite being a friend of the founding family and major officers of the company, he was demoted, in fact, if not in title, but not fired. He kept the office and was grandly anointed "Director of Creative Services," although he no longer had anyone working for him. He sat in solitary splendor.

At the time, a thought-process dubbed "brain storming" was a silly fad. It was the main theme of a book by a New York advertising executive. It was nonsense disguised as pseudo-psychology. John, our deflated boss, asked five of us deemed the most creative of our lot to a meeting where we could practice thinking creatively. It was my downfall. I should have thought more and been less creative. Or I could have just shut up.

At the end of a tedious hour of psychobabble, we were handed little pieces of paper and told we were going to do some exercises in brainstorming. And so he began. "There is a bomb on the fourth floor (two floors below us), and it's going to go off in one minute. Write down what you would do." He counted down the minute: "50 seconds, 40 seconds.... Okay, the minute is up." He then started around the table, calling on one of us after another. Each muttered, shrugged, and said nothing. He called on me, and I said, astounding even myself, "I'd piss out the window and float downstream." I thought that was creative thinking as soon as I heard it.

Muffled laughter was followed by quick dismissal of the session and, shortly thereafter, me. I looked for another job, and with the help of a neighbor I got one as a night janitor at our local daily paper. Soon after I began, I noticed that all the janitors near me disappeared at midnight for about 20 minutes. It was mysterious. A couple weeks went by before I was inducted into the fraternity and invited into the nightly excursion.

On the roof of our building, there was a huge neon sign advertising our circulation. I knew the numbers. What I didn't know was that many nurses working at the Minneapolis General Hospital lived in a dorm across the street. When midnight came and their shifts ended, the nurses readied for bed, stripping down to panties and bra while my fellow workers climbed the sign or danced on the roof, shouting various gentle obscenities. The night one nurse pulled down the shade on which she had written, "Good Night," I gave up my week-old career as a voyeur.

I did not give up ghost writing entirely. The *Tribune*'s humor columnist, Will Jones, often ended with a short paragraph of several lines, dubbing them "Day Brightener" or "Day Spoiler." I would leave notes in his typewriter with a few sentences that fit one or the other category. When he used them, he identified the source: "The Night Janitor says . . ." I combined a large audience and anonymity.

I did reach beyond that on one occasion. Once a week, editors would issue a memo, TRIButes and TRIBulations, of good and bad things that had happened. Other janitors shared my pride when we read, "Norm Sherman of maintenance spotted the wrong cut in Bob Short story and called the error to cityside's attention."

I also had a moment of real stupidity, doing something that embarrasses me to this day—sort of. Once a week, I worked in the basement of the building at a waste compressor that turned out huge, heavy bales of detritus brought down from offices, the newsroom, and lavatories above. On a slow night, I began to read discarded carbon copies of letters, often torn in half down the middle. One caught my attention and I searched through the trash until I found the other half. It was a response to a letter from Ed Thye, Minnesota's other, and Republican, senator. He had written to Gideon Seymour, the executive editor, to complain about the greater amount of publicity Humphrey got and the outrageous fact that headlines often read "Humphrey, Thye" when he was the senior senator and should be named first.

Seymour responded, emphasizing his greater friendship for Thye. "Humphrey is busy making news all over the place, he is ingenious, wily and boundlessly energetic. What is more, he has a staff trained and geared to get every last crumb of publicity and to work effectively with the avenues of publicity.

"Those, including yourself, who criticize the Minneapolis papers for giving Humphrey so much publicity have this much justification: he is banging at us with printable acts and statements so constantly and from so many different angles that no matter how much we throw away, he still winds up with more than his fair share."

With it in hand, I made my first trip to a senatorial office. I took the copy of the letter gleefully to the Humphrey office in downtown Minneapolis and gave it to Herb Waters, Humphrey's top aide. I was a stranger, and he glanced at the letter quickly, asked me where I got it, and, as I answered, led me to the door and returned "my" letter. He shut what had been an open door.

Despite that excursion into spying, I was a good janitor and probably could have remained there until retirement, but politics called. With Gerry Dillon's counsel, I had become active in the DFL Second Ward Club, filled mostly with University faculty, students, and a few outsiders. He introduced me to several men who remained part of my life for a long time: Karl Rolvaag, then DFL state chairman, later lieutenant governor of Minnesota, governor (winning by 91 votes out of 1.3 million cast), and the U.S. ambassador to Iceland; Orville Freeman, soon to be Minnesota's governor and later appointed by John Kennedy as the U.S. secretary of agriculture; and Walter Mondale, Minnesota attorney general, U.S. senator, vice president, and Democratic candidate for president.

The DFL has been an essential and satisfying part of my adult life. It brought me friends, purpose, and focus. I was still in high school when it came into being, but most of the people who put it together were themselves then only in their thirties. Hubert Humphrey, with major help from Orville Freeman and a few others, was the prime mover in combining the Democratic Party and the Farmer Labor Party into one. The two parties had divided the liberal vote, thus providing the conservatives a relatively unchallenged acquisition of power. Neither seemed likely to win a statewide election. Without their people ever in the highest offices, hope for the progressive legislation they both wanted was slim at best.

Despite that, the fusion was accomplished as an uneasy alliance. The Democrats were largely urban (and Irish Catholic in their stronghold in St. Paul) and often, if not always, interested largely in patronage jobs when there was a Democratic administration in Washington. The Farmer Laborites were more rural, Protestant, Scandinavian, German, Finnish, and more driven by ideology, with roots stretching back to the Non-Partisan League, the farmers' strong voice in the 1920s. There was also a small coterie of urban union members, a handful of Jews, and a few liberal lawyers, college professors, and small businessmen.

With Humphrey and the folks around him leading the way, leadership in both parties finally found common ground. The Farmer Labor group was dominated by the left wing, including some Communist Party members who jumped when they thought the Soviet Union called, sometimes switching major positions overnight without embarrassment. At the moment of merger, they were in a conciliatory posture, talking of a "United Front." It was an uncomfortable, but fortuitous, alliance for the moment, vital in establishing a new party.

Humphrey, in any case, was soon able to make the left-bloc peripheral and bring in representatives of the growing labor movement and progressives from the Farmers Union. Without the money and manpower of both national and local unions, DFL growth and success would have been difficult, if not impossible.

I think it is ironic that a strong labor movement had only become possible in Minneapolis because of the 1934 strike. If it had not broken the domination of business interests who had kept Minneapolis an open, non-union town, unions of any sort would never have had breathing space to grow and would never have become the strong base of the DFL that they did. No one praised the Dunnes for what they had done, of course, and I suppose it may never have occurred to them. The labor movement was moving ahead nationally, but the defeat of the Citizens' Alliance, the bosses' militant and well-financed tool, was a vital part of liberal emancipation in Minnesota.

Humphrey was the inspiration for the success of the new party; Freeman was the perspiration. Freeman traveled the state endlessly as party leader, driving 100 miles and more to meetings of half-a-dozen people gathered around a farmer's dining room table, finding a couple of union leaders on the Iron Range and in Duluth, hoping to reach their membership. Seeking publicity for the party, he called on weekly newspaper editors in small towns and found most indifferent or conservative.

As the DFL amalgamation began, old animosities and suspicions did not go away. Two years in, the 1946 convention was acrimonious. The old hands were derisive of "Humphrey and his diaper brigade," a label that opponents (including the underworld) had begun to use. They were almost right. The leaders were young. Freeman was 30, Arthur Naftalin was a year older, Gene McCarthy 34, and Humphrey only 37. The Humphrey-Freeman side was dismissive of left-ideologues who would never win an election in their purity and doctrinal rigidity.

One useful thing coming out of the convention was the formation of the Young Democratic Farmer Labor Party, or YDFL. It was created and run primarily by Bill Kubicek, a professor of physical medicine at the University of Minnesota medical school, and its purpose was simple: start early in order to get young people to the caucuses in 1948 so that the Humphrey-Freeman bloc would be victorious in platform disagreements and in endorsements.

Bill, earlier on, had gotten off a plow at the family farm in southeastern Minnesota and announced that he would not get back on. He came up to Minneapolis and worked his way through the University, possibly the first in his family to go to college. He also met Freeman during that time and became both an adviser and acolyte. He was a wise and unassuming man, with great political instincts and no need to be in the spotlight. Unsung hero understates his role. He was secretary of the state party for years and a magnet of political wisdom for younger, eager activists, including Walter Mondale. He was an extraordinary combination of ward heeler and scientist.

Though Freeman was elected state chairman of the senior party in 1948 with significant help from the YDFLers, the next convention was more contentious, filled with the undiminished rancor of contending blocs. In the end, however, Karl Rolvaag was elected state chairman in 1950 to succeed Freeman and all the other state party offices were allies as well. Freeman had his eye on the governorship, but didn't have the endorsement votes and reluctantly ran for attorney general.

In 1952, the DFL was still a bare-bones operation. The tiny office almost closed for lack of funds. It took several years before it had a functioning organization, however small, in every county in the state. But each year it grew stronger, becoming a seriously contending party. And that is when I arrived on the scene. By then Orv had run for both attorney general and governor unsuccessfully, but defeat doesn't always deter another run for something, and certainly did not for Orv. He was still merely a "hopeful" when we met by chance, and he asked me to play a role in his campaign and, thus, the DFL.

At Christmas in 1953, Gerry Dillon and his wife, Uva, invited me to a party at their home. Among the other guests were Freeman and his wife, Jane. Her father, James Shields, had been the Progressive Party candidate for the U.S. Senate in 1946. He was a left-wing candidate, and his opponents whispered that he was a Communist. Jane's mother went her separate way as a stalwart DFLer, chairwoman of a working class ward in Minneapolis.

At one point during the evening I found Orv sitting at my feet, looking up with a smile made crooked by a rifle bullet injury to his jaw during a Marine landing at Bougainville in the southwest Pacific. He asked, "Norm, do you really like to write?" I thought the question a bit odd, but I answered, "Yes."

He then asked if I would be a volunteer in his campaign. I eagerly said that I would. His invitation was an unexpected Christmas present. There was my future wrapped in a ribbon. I was in the inner circle, on the ground floor, on my way up.

As the 1954 state convention time approached, I was elected a delegate. The convention was held in Albert Lea, a small town about 100 miles south of Minneapolis. It was exciting. Speeches and caucuses and votes and serious folks added up to an exhilarating time. It didn't have quite the intensity of a Ray Dunne lecture. It wasn't revolution, but I comforted myself with purpose: it was the road to a better world, step by step. And I had a role, if only a tiny one.

I sat on one committee with a couple of members of the state legislature and other old hands. I was last among equals, but spoke out with great certainty on several issues, ending up on the losing side, almost alone, each time. (Almost 60 years later, I still think I was right. I just don't remember the issues.)

The purpose of the convention was to endorse our candidates, as well as to write our manifesto and elect officers to run the party. When the election of the state chairwoman took place, I learned a lesson, in those pre-feminist days, of how women were judged. The two candidates were quite different. One, Geri Joseph, had been a journalist and was beautiful, smart, and elegant. She was married to a well-to-do businessman, maybe the only Jew in the top-tier grain business. The other, Marge Maki, came from the Iron Range, was smart, but unpolished.

They had been nominated by several effusive speeches, but had not appeared on the stage. A farmer from northwestern Minnesota whom I had just met was near the back of the hall. He rose and, ignoring a nearby microphone, shouted from where he stood, "We heard about 'em. Let's see 'em." In a couple of minutes, Geri glided on stage, well-coifed and wearing an elegant tweed suit. Marge, a tall woman, lumbered on stage in a skirt and blouse and klutzy shoes. The farmer, still standing, immediately shouted, "Let's vote." Geri won.

Hubert Humphrey had, of course, been nominated for re-election to the U.S. Senate, and Freeman had been nominated for governor, a position the DFL had not held during its brief existence. The Humphrey acceptance speech, my first real opportunity to hear him speak politically, was extraordinary. He had a lot to say and he said it at length, moving his audience to cheers and tears and a sense of mutual mission. What I saw that day would be recognized by millions over his entire career.

Harry Truman once said, "Hubert is a Rembrandt with words." Less generously, still in the Senate, Lyndon Johnson said, "Hubert has the greatest coordination of mind and tongue of anyone I know." Senator Barry Goldwater, the Republican candidate for president in 1964, said, in a kindly, not sneering way, "Hubert speaks at 275 words a minute with bursts to 340." Years later a photographer got laughs when he said he took a picture of Humphrey with a hummingbird hovering just over his shoulder and "the wings were in focus, but the lips blurry." And even Mrs. Humphrey had an opinion. She said to her husband, "You don't have to be eternal to be immortal."

Humphrey once told me of a speech he had given during his first run for the Senate. He was addressing an audience, mainly of Finnish farmers, in New York Mills, a small town in central Minnesota. Stereotypically, the Finns did not express public emotion easily. Humphrey said, "I gave them the goddamnedest speech I could. No claps during the speech and an unenthusiastic few claps at the end. You know how I am. I gave them another speech without stopping. I sweated. My shirt stuck to my skin. I got the same result. So I gave them a third speech and finished exhausted and deflated. When I shook hands at the door as they were leaving, one after another said, "Best speech I ever heard."

In Albert Lea, there were not a lot of Finns among the delegates. As the convention drew to a close, Humphrey, Freeman, and the rest of the ticket stood together on the stage before an excited and demonstrative crowd. Freeman approached the podium, grabbed its sides, exhibiting the kind of rigidity and determination he often displayed in walk, talk, work—really in everything he did. Ambiguity or nuance rarely intruded.

He began his acceptance speech with a roar, "Folks, we

have to get the meat from Senator Humphrey's speech here yesterday, get it digested, and get it out into some of your hands." I was sitting next to Mary Ann Jones, a fellow delegate and the wife of the journalist who used my end-of-the column bits and around whose desk I swept. She turned to me and said, "It sounds like shit to me." From a lady I barely knew, it was surprisingly vulgar, hilarious, and unforgettable.

A couple of weeks after the convention Jane and Orv came to our ward club meeting, and I told the story to Jane, who laughed and muttered through her glee, "You've got to tell that to Orv." "No!" I barked, aware that he had no visible sense of humor, particularly about himself. But she called him over and goaded me into telling the story. It was one time when I knew I should shut up, not try to be funny, but she insisted. I repeated my story, doom hanging over me, and Orv, indeed, did not laugh. I think I was on his digested meat list from then on.

At other times, I irritated him more with proposed bumper stickers. One for the Duluth docks was "Save Your Seamen With Orville Freeman." Another later was for Eugenie Anderson, a grand and dignified lady, when she sought the nomination to run against Senator Thye. "Two Thighs Are Better Than One" seemed apt. It didn't seem so to Orv. Once again, I was a slow learner with an unfortunately quick tongue and no censor. And little sense.

By the time I became active in 1954, old divisions and battles had diminished. Remnants of hostility and competition remained, but the party belonged to my new friends, and I got to work on projects in the evenings and on weekends that fed my sense of involvement and let me learn things about organizing, persuading, including the use of radio and television, and getting out the vote.

Radio was still the dominant mass media outlet, and much

of our campaign communication consisted of our few one-minute spots running over and over again. That was handled by the advertising agency I later joined, but I had nothing to do with it. Television was slightly different. I was peripherally involved, doing some writing for candidates.

Bill Kubicek came up with the idea of buying the same half-hour on all the television stations that had an audience in Minnesota. On five occasions, we were simultaneously on 11 stations—three in the Twin Cities; two in Duluth; one in Rochester; and the single stations in Valley City, North Dakota; Fargo, North Dakota; Sioux Falls, South Dakota; Mason City, Iowa; and LaCrosse, Wisconsin, whose signals crossed the border into Minnesota. Anyone watching television had to be watching our program. There were an estimated 750,000 viewers each time.

There were two other innovations where I was again only peripherally involved, but close enough to learn a lot about getting out the vote. Candidates, good ones and bad ones, almost always believe that their charisma, charm, and gift of oratory make them unique. That may be true in some cases, but the mechanics of a campaign make a real, and maybe the ultimate, difference in a campaign. Without the ability to get out the vote, except in rare cases, all is inevitably lost.

In 1954, two events were special in inspiring enthusiasm in party workers and then attracting voters' support and getting them to vote. The first, suggested and defined by Bill Kubicek, was the use of a sample ballot. With limited funds, the DFL contacted about half the voters in the state, concentrating on heavy Democratic precincts since we couldn't isolate DFLers, there being no party registration. Each household received a 5½" x 8½" card listing all the statewide candidates, the incumbent congressman or candidate, and the appropriate state legislative candidates. The card was perforated down the middle into "His" and "Hers" sides, something that would probably not be acceptable today, but was not controversial then.

It was an immense undertaking, covering new ground with absolutely no precedent in Minnesota, and possibly anywhere in the country. A young law student, a friend of Walter Mondale, was hired to oversee the project. Mondale stole Bill Canby, then just 23 years old, from his summer job in the shipping department of a battery factory. I didn't learn until much later that Bill had graduated from Yale *summa cum laude* and as a Phi Beta Kappa member. (He later became a federal circuit court judge.)

For the first time, the DFL endorsed candidates before the primary in the hope that people loyal to the party would win, thus making the general election an affirmation rather than the election of someone with no strong party allegiance. Early endorsement was new and crucial.

Mailing a uniform piece of campaign literature would have been easy, but this one required the overlay of postal routes and legislative district boundaries before the age of computers. The ballots had to be mailed to arrive as close to election day as possible to diminish the chances that they would be lost or forgotten, but early enough to guarantee delivery before votes were cast. They had to be dropped at different postal stations all around the state. Some postal districts involved more than one legislative district requiring further separation. Bill oversaw it all.

Printing was complicated, as well. Varying quantities for each district had to be printed and then packaged carefully. Fortunately Gerry Dillon, with enthusiasm, turned his printing presses and his political mind to the job. I sealed boxes at his shop as my contribution. It was a massive undertaking that cost $18,000, a comparatively large amount considering that the entire Freeman-Rolvaag campaign cost only $49,000 beyond that. One measure of the sample ballot success was the election of Frank Larkin to be clerk of the Supreme Court. Frank had driven a milk truck for his living, and his election so aggravated the conservatives in the state legislature that, as soon as they could in a subsequent session, they abolished the job as an elected one, making it an appointed position. No milk truck drivers need apply and certainly ought not to be elected.

Several months earlier in the campaign, Jerry Heaney, a Duluth lawyer and our national committeeman, later a federal judge, came up with the idea of an event with a large crowd, cheap food, and lots of speeches. Its only purpose was to provide take-home enthusiasm. We filled the Minneapolis Auditorium with 15,000 people (more than the national vote for my SWP presidential ticket in 1952) for a bean feed, a dollar to get in and gorge on a plate of beans and wieners, mostly served by members of the Restaurant Workers' Union.

It was an explosive event sending people back home across the entire state with an excitement of message, a sense of political power, and a stronger hope of victory. They worked their towns and villages as no political party in Minnesota had before. It was neighbor-to-neighbor where persuasion was less needed than friendship and presence. And victory came—certainly from the quality of our candidates, but certainly also as a result of our grassroots organizing, our new techniques, and the enthusiasm of a growing party.

During that 1954 election, I suddenly became a television writer, although I did not own a set. With television so new, anyone who could hold a pencil or type qualified to be a TV ghostwriter. With the slightest of credentials, I was asked to do a script for a half-hour show that featured congressmen from the Twin Cities area. One, Roy Weir, had never missed a vote from the time he arrived in the House of Representatives in 1949. When I gave him what I had written, he read it quickly, took a cigar out of his mouth and said, "Look, Sonny, you may talk like this, but I don't." He put the cigar back, handed me the script, and ad libbed his part of the show. He wasn't as eloquent as he might have been, but he was himself and he was re-elected without my help. Beyond that, he taught me, inadvertently, a good lesson for a working ghost. "Know the speaker, hear the voice, forget who you are."

At the same time, I met Eugene McCarthy, who was also part of the program. We talked the same language, but he for the most part depended on his natural eloquence. I was a twice-deflated ghost, but McCarthy after that at least made a point of talking to me whenever we were at the same event or meeting.

Not solely because of my volunteer efforts, Humphrey was re-elected with 56 percent of the vote and Freeman and Karl Rolvaag were elected governor and lieutenant governor with 53 percent. We had done old political things. We had done new ones. It somehow all seemed to work. Orv had come a long way from sitting at my feet.

The next year at a Midwest Democratic Conference held in Chicago, I met another person, Max Kampelman, who later became a good friend. Our friendship, however, did not begin smoothly. Minutes after we met, I started a monologue blasting the Communist Control Act of 1954. It made membership in the Communist Party a crime punishable by a $10,000 fine and five years in jail. It labeled the party "an agency of a foreign power" that was "conspiring to overthrow the republic." Hyperbole and nonsense were the most generous and polite words I could find. The "conspirators" amounted to far less than one percent of our population, were barely visible in most of the country, and militant in word, but clearly not in action. If they made no dent during the Depression of the 1930s with unemployment and misery widespread, it seemed unlikely to me that they would suddenly threaten the country in the 1950s.

Max was the main drafter of the bill, the inspiration for it, and a vehement anti-Communist. Humphrey had been its main sponsor. As I listened to Max defend it on democratic principle and the safety of the country, I divined a secondary purpose: give the conservatives no opportunity to attack Democrats as weak on Communism in the next election. The Red Scare hysteria that had been fed and led by Senator Joe McCarthy was strong and politically threatening, but I thought then, as I still do, that the bill was an egregious political pander. As it turned out, no administration, right or left or in the middle, ever used it. And by then U.S. Communist Party membership was down. At its peak in the forties, it was 70,000. Add in "fellow travelers," sympathizers, and dupes and it still did not merit what it elicited.

In 1991, long forgiven for my angry words, I helped Max when he wrote his autobiography. (He later gave me full credit for getting him to write it. If I did, I don't remember any resistance.) He had served with great distinction as U.S. ambassador to several international conferences, one on nuclear and space arms reduction and a second one on human rights. He was a foreign policy star for Ronald Reagan who said of him, "Your success will benefit millions for generations to come." Reagan also said that what Max had reached, "was one of the high watermarks in the history of my administration."

That Max could serve Reagan after his close association

with Humphrey for so many years disturbed some of us, but he focused on the issues and seemed always true to how he felt. (Reagan had made a political commercial endorsing Humphrey in 1948. He was a public liberal in those days, although it may have only been a script he memorized.) Max and I remained close friends until his death in 2013.

In 1956, the Democratic National Convention was in Chicago, and I wanted to go to it. I was working again as a janitor at the *Star Tribune*. As always, I was short of money and went to the employee credit union to borrow what I needed. My loan officer asked what I intended to use the money for. I gulped and hesitantly explained why. There was silence, a raised eyebrow, a quizzical smile and, I thought, impending rejection.

Her eyes said what her voice did not. "A janitor going to a national political convention?" My mind responded to her silence. "Should I have lied? Pay bills. Take a vacation. Buy new blue jeans." But after a pause she approved my loan of a couple hundred dollars, and I soon joyously took off. With the loan, I would be where I wanted to be. Without it, it was only television on someone else's set.

With my newly found, if borrowed, wealth, I registered for my own hotel room, a luxury I had not previously had at any political gathering. Generally, I roomed with someone equally broke. I had hardly settled in my room when Jack Puterbaugh, my buddy from Honeywell and now executive secretary of the DFL, one of four employees, came to my door to say a room was needed for a fat cat who had decided at the last minute to attend and found no room available. Mr. Money Bags went to our state chairman, Ray Hemenway, with his problem, and Jack and Ray, my political benefactors and most powerful close friends at the moment, asked in desperation for my room. I ended up sleeping in Jack's bathtub on some cushions and pillows. If Jack had taken a night shower, I would have drowned.

For one of the sessions, I, with a borrowed badge, joined friends in the Minnesota alternate delegate section. We were seated in the rows that sloped up from the main floor. Just behind us were folks from Georgia. A Minnesotan, Bob Short, a major contributor with political aspirations, was fairly conservative, but had been given a liberal speech with six or eight questions and delivered it with the passion of a true-believer. He talked jobs and housing and retirement. "Don't you think every child should have the opportunity for a good education?" "Shouldn't every one of us have good health care available?" After each question, the Georgians roared, "No."

When the session adjourned, I was standing in the aisle taking in the scene when one of the Georgians came down the stairs and ran his hand over my brush-cut hair. I wheeled and said to the grinning fool, "I don't even let my mother do that." He looked shocked and gasped, "Why ... why ... don't ya love your mutha?" I said, irritated, "Well, not particularly." He reared back in shock, a miserable bigot with family values, "I don't know how to talk to a man what don't love his mutha."

The period was not without some personal failure. My marriage was about to end, something I learned while I was away for a long weekend of political work for pay in northwestern Minnesota, about five hours away. On Thursday when I left, I kissed Jane goodbye. On Sunday when I called to say I was on my way home, she said she wanted a divorce. So much for the kiss that turned into a kiss-off. It made the trip home terrible, as the next months were. Maybe years. (You will have to compare the end of this marriage to the next one. My early wives had a talent for saying goodbye.) It was not just that I had somehow failed in what I thought was an okay marriage, but I doted on my two kids, loved that they gave me a kind of family life different from what I had known. I dreamed about their futures with me there. But, with no choice, I moved out.

After the 1954 election, I had hoped to be hired by Freeman in or around the governor's office, but my past verbal sins made that impossible. Instead, Orv arranged for me to work, at a distance, for the advertising agency that handled the State of Minnesota tourist trade account. I went from janitor to account executive. I wore a tie, clean shirt, and pressed pants. I had a desk and a secretary. Some might have considered it a promotion. I hated it. My supplicant callers were advertising space salesmen. "An ad in our magazine will bring thousands of people to Minnesota." I was always a bit catatonic as they spoke so they, desperate for some connection, invariably asked what I did before I came to the agency. When I told them I had been a night janitor for the local paper, they were silent and bewildered.

Profit, not politics, surrounded me. Slick was more important than substance or truth. One day, the head of the agency, the son of the cousin who took my family in when we arrived in Minneapolis, called all of us account executives together. I should have taken the day off. We were part of a national company that had been hired by the American Medical Association to organize and publicize a campaign against health care legislation before Congress. I had read the bill because health care was something of interest. When my boss misstated its content, I rose and said he had it wrong. I then started to explain to him and the others in the meeting what the truth was. Cousin Sam ambiguously said, "Sit down and shut up." Once again I was on my way back to my interrupted career as a janitor. It was a promotion, but only a temporary one.

I was soon taken from my second tour of duty when Gene McCarthy hired me for his 1956 reelection campaign. He had been a congressman since 1949 and had a safe seat. When he hired me, he said he wanted me to join his staff in Washington after the election. He won handily, and I was excited at my impending new world. I had given up my apartment and packed my bags, figuring the call would come. I sat by the phone among my few belongings, but heard nothing from him for a couple of days.

When he did call, he told me that his payroll budget was used up on his current staff and he couldn't take me along. It was immensely disappointing and a bit embarrassing, but I had no reason to doubt his explanation. Many years later, Dick Stout, a journalist and McCarthy admirer, wrote a book about the 1968 presidential campaign, focusing on McCarthy. At lunch one day after its publication, he asked me if I had ever wondered why I didn't get the job I expected in 1956, a dozen years before. I was surprised that he knew about it, and even more surprised by his explanation. He said, "Abigail (Gene's wife) said she would not have someone who was divorced on their staff." They later separated after Gene got messing around with a female reporter, but they did not divorce. Strangely, Abigail and I became better friends after their parting.

But there were moments in those years that made up for any periodic discomfort. It was out of the tub, off the floor, up from the basement and into the stratosphere where I had already begun to fly. I met three people who were idols of mine: Eleanor Roosevelt, Harry Truman, and Adlai Stevenson.

Stevenson came to Minnesota in 1955 in anticipation of his next run for president. Before Stevenson arrived, I had been talking to Governor Freeman about some ideas I had for the speech Stevenson would give. I figured if Orv liked the ideas he might repeat them to Stevenson, probably as his own. The afternoon Stevenson hit town I was in the basement of the hotel where the temporary DFL office was. Someone came to me and said, "Orv wants to see you upstairs."

I went to his room, knocked on the door, which he opened. There sat Stevenson, his glasses soon in his hand gesturing toward me as he said, "I understand you have some ideas for my speech." I about wet my pants. My candidate for president, an eloquent orator, a national figure considered an intellectual, was asking for my words and thoughts. I repeated whatever I had told Orv, and when I heard Stevenson that night, I thought I heard echoes, maybe the exact words, of my advice.

Stevenson's visit was highlighted in a negative way by attendance at a University of Minnesota football game. Freeman had been a second-string player during his time in college, possibly more dedicated than talented, and loved the game. He was a jock. He insisted that it was a great common touch for Stevenson to be in the stands and be introduced. Humphrey disagreed. He said whenever a politician played that card, he was booed by half, cheered by the other half, and accomplished nothing. Stevenson, in a thin coat, froze in the early-season cold and listened to the boo-birds. It took him a couple of hours to recover from the cold. The booing probably lasted in his soul for a longer time.

Harry Truman was less inclined to listen to me. He had come to town for our annual Jefferson-Jackson fundraising dinner in 1956. Television was still relatively new and black-and-white, of course, and when you bought a half-hour as we had done that was what you got. No wiggle room. Start when the cameraman signals. Stop when the half hour was up. They went to commercial and you were history. (I suppose it may still be the same, if you can get the time.) I was directed by Bill Kubicek to sit at the press table below the podium and give Truman signals as the end of *our* time approached.

I had to explain it all to him so I went up to the head table, broke in and explained where I would be sitting, and that I would raise four fingers when that was the time left, then three, then two, then one, a bent-over index finger for thirty seconds, and a neck-slashing gesture with seconds left. The president than repeated my gestures, nodded, and thanked me. A symbiotic relationship was established with me in charge.

I took my place, and as the president neared the end of our time, I gave him my signals, ending with a final one I had not expected to use: that finger cutting my throat. Truman smiled down at me and went right on for about ten minutes, maybe more. Television and Sherman be damned.

Serving Eleanor Roosevelt was my transcendent moment. To meet her would have been magnificent, but there was more. In 1956, I was assigned to drive her around for parts of two days and look after her. When she first got into the car, she said, "Mr. Sherman, (we were on a last-name basis), a woman my age needs rest, so please excuse me if I doze off and don't speak between meetings." It was a burden to be quiet, but I managed.

One of my other duties was to hire a plain-clothes cop to stand guard at her hotel room door. After a glorious day, I was relaxing, indeed glowing, when word came that Mrs. Roosevelt wanted to see me. I raced to her room, urging the elevator to go faster.

I knocked. She opened the door and invited me in. With door closed and speaking softly, she said, "I don't have this kind of protection in New York. I cannot imagine that I need it in Minneapolis. Please send that nice man home." I sent the nice man home, quite overwhelmed that this special lady cared about others as she did. But there was even more.

The next day, we ended up in Hibbing, a town on Minnesota's Iron Range, about 200 miles from Minneapolis. After the meeting that night, she was going on to Duluth for her flight home. Someone else would drive her. We were in the high school gym for a large gathering and I, toward the end of the evening, was across the basketball floor from where she stood talking to people. Suddenly, she left the group and started across the floor. I couldn't imagine where she was going, but she seemed to be heading toward me. And, by god, she was. She said as she shook my hand, "I want to thank you for all your help." I was barely able to respond. Eleanor Roosevelt thanking me. That was certainly the high point of the year, maybe of the decade.

But, soon, after the 1956 campaign, after a bit of embarrassment and overcoming my disappointment with McCarthy, I decided to leave Minnesota and maybe politics.

6. In the Trenches

A friend and coworker from my Honeywell days had moved to Connecticut and was working at Electric Boat, the submarine factory in Groton. I went to stay with him and his family. During my visit, he urged me to apply for a job there. I was hired, and added submarines to thermostats about which I knew little and wrote much.

One unexpected task was writing the narration for a film on the refueling of the Nautilus, our first nuclear submarine. The boat had been built and refueled there. Messing with nuclear reactors was dangerous work, and the entire process had been filmed before I showed up. I edited the film and wrote the narration, calling it, "No Second Chance." And there wasn't any. Every worker was tethered so he couldn't fall into the radioactive area and die; even each tool was, too. Dropped, it could have resulted in horrific consequences. It was eerie to even screen what had been filmed.

The film was to be used to train future crews doing similar work. I hoped it would win the Naval Academy Award, but top-secret documents don't qualify. There was recognition enough, since it was, in fact, shown for many years afterward and no one fell in.

Eager to experience a submarine ride, I had arranged with great excitement to do so when two things intervened. After about a year, my security clearance was still being held up. I assumed it was my lunches and meetings with Ray Dunne and Grace Carlson, but I wasn't able to check before I left. I thought I might have been fired had I tried to stay and wanted to spare others my embarrassment, and maybe theirs.

Luckily, before my crisis at Electric Boat, I had written a letter to Chester Bowles, a former titan of the advertising world who had founded with future Senator Bill Benton the giant firm of Benton and Bowles. (Benton introduced a resolution to expel Joe McCarthy from the Senate.) When Bowles gave up advertising, he ran for governor of Connecticut and was elected. He later served as ambassador to India and then undersecretary of State, appointed by John Kennedy. He was a man of some distinction. I volunteered to help him by writing speeches and press releases in his 1958 effort to get the U.S. Senate nomination, and my offer led me to his home office in Essex, an upscale community close by. I drove my little Renault 4CV out to his home, turned off the public road into a mini-forest with a mansion at its center. It was an extraordinary sight of establishment and affluence that I had not seen up-close before.

I did a bit of volunteer work, and he soon asked me to join his staff full-time as a paid assistant. I was back from the depths of the submarine factory. Unfortunately, he lost the nomination to Abe Ribicoff at the state convention. Governor Ribicoff won with the ardent help of State Chairman John Bailey who was later chairman of the national Democratic Party when John Kennedy was president. Bailey had pledged to Bowles that he would stay neutral, but he was obviously duplicitous, supported Ribicoff, and got his way. I, an anonymous face, followed him as he walked around the convention floor, quietly barking at delegates, "Vote for Abe or you're dead." When I heard it, I suddenly knew what a party boss was and how different politics there was from the openness of Minnesota. That kind of threat would have brought only laughter and an obscene gesture on the prairie.

The day after defeat, Doug Bennet, the college-age son of a good friend of Bowles who had unsuccessfully been the Democratic candidate for Congress two years before, took two Bowles daughters, his sister, and me for a relaxing, therapeutic sail on the Connecticut River. As we sailed, I spoke in vulgar, descriptive words about Bailey. Doug, the straightest of arrows, told his parents immediately after we docked of my offensive monologue, and they carried the message quickly to Bowles.

When I got to work the next morning, I was told Chet and his wife, Steb, (nicknames everyone used) wanted to see me. In the office, Chet sat at his desk; Steb stood next to him, hand on the back of the chair (modern American Gothic), as they chastised me and explained that I had behaved in an unacceptable way. They had considered firing me, but had decided to give me a second chance. Much later, after he overcame his Boy Scout posture, I worked with Doug, the tattletale, in several places before he ended up as president of Wesleyan University for 12 years. He did that without me, and, I think, never swore.

Chet and Steb, in sadness and disappointment, soon went to their second home on an island off the coast of Maine. They were barely gone when Ken Wynn, the other half of our two-man staff, and I decided to try to persuade Chet to run for the House of Representatives. We drove along the coast through areas I had never seen. When we got to the port close to their island, Chet had sailed in to pick us up. The harbor was loaded with elegant, expensive boats.

I was carrying my change of underwear and toothbrush in a brown paper bag and in land-locked words said I would take my stuff "downstairs." I didn't know it was the "hold." When I dashed back up, Bowles had swung the boom over in preparation for leaving, and I ran into it at full speed, damn near knocking myself out, driving my head down to about my waist or so it seemed in my confusion. Land lubberhood was confirmed, but I did not again speak vulgarly. I only thought the forbidden words.

We did succeed in getting Bowles to run for Congress, and he won. I wanted to go to Washington with him, but I was once again carrying the burden of loose lips. I was not asked to be on his congressional staff. I returned to Minnesota. With no money and no job, I slept on a couch at Gerry and Uva Dillon's house and looked for more political work.

When Humphrey decided to seek the 1960 Democratic nomination for president, an office was set up the year before in St. Paul as a home base. Karl Rolvaag, still lieutenant governor, a part-time job without much responsibility when the legislature was out of session, ran it. He hired a secretary and me. I held a job of little consequence, and the office was ultimately closed when John Kennedy bumped Humphrey out with an unexpected, shocking primary victory in West Virginia. It was a state of strong unions and a weak economy, with a lot of people living in near poverty. Catholics were few and considered virtually an alien culture.

It was a state seemingly perfect for Humphrey both economically and religiously. But, merit ran second to money. Joe Kennedy, John's father (and a flagrant anti-Semite), dumped a small fortune in the state, paying off anyone who could be bought. At the time no one talked much about what went on. Only recent historians have catalogued the abuse.

It wasn't only money. John Kennedy turned people on in a way other candidates did not. He had a presence and charm that no one could match. And he had a family that exuded glamour. Though fewer than a dozen altogether, they moved like an army of thousands through primary states. Humphrey was often quoted as describing his situation as an "independent merchant running against a chain."

When Humphrey lost, he withdrew, without rancor or visible disappointment, and gracefully endorsed Kennedy the day after his defeat. Some of the rest of us were not so quick to forgive or to forget. We worked for Kennedy's election, we voted for him, but it was hard to get over that a daddy's fortune essentially bought the election.

In that brief primary campaign I learned something more about Humphrey. Our tiny St. Paul office was understaffed and the campaign underfinanced. What funds we had were allocated mostly to radio and television, to rallies and press releases. Among my other menial duties, I watched over a teletype machine that carried speeches, schedules, and other essential data to the campaign in the field. It also brought back messages from the traveling party.

At least once a week, sometimes once a day, the machine would ring and then bang out an urgent message from Humphrey himself: "Where are the campaign buttons? We have run out of buttons." The first time I thought he was very strange to care about buttons. Few people, after all, wore them throughout the campaign. Most buttons disappeared into a desk drawer or wastebasket in about two hours. When I joined the campaign entourage, I realized why they were so important.

For Humphrey, the campaign was not just the message, not just the mass media and large meetings. It was also those buttons he could pin on people. He liked the one-on-one contact, the passing intimacy, the smiles of appreciation. I have never met anyone else who truly cared about that kind of campaigning. Indeed, it would be hard to imagine John Kennedy doing the pinning, much less enjoying it. Adlai Stevenson once said to Humphrey, incredulity dripping from his patrician voice, "Hubert, you really enjoy all of this." Humphrey did.

Humphrey was not at his best at the 1960 national convention held in mid-July in Los Angeles and his behavior left Orville Freeman furious. It wasn't pretty. The day after his primary loss in West Virginia, Humphrey had declared his support for John Kennedy, as I have noted. But the presidential bug remained despite having fewer than 50 delegates pledged to vote for him. He couldn't quite shake the desire. And if that didn't work out, he dreamed that Adlai Stevenson, if nominated instead of Kennedy, would make him the vice presidential nominee.

Yet, at the same time, he urged Freeman to try to get selected to give the nominating speech for Kennedy. Humphrey saw it as a step toward Orv becoming the vice presidential nominee if Kennedy won. A Midwestern governor with a liberal record, Protestant, and close to Humphrey made political sense. Orv understandably expected that Humphrey would unequivocally and publicly support Kennedy. He didn't. He went mute. Freeman was for Kennedy, Gene McCarthy was for Stevenson, and Humphrey appeared to be for both.

As a result, the day before the voting would take place, the Minnesota delegation caucused for hours after the convention session ended, rancor replacing Minnesota nice. At Arvonne Fraser's creative and wise suggestion, the delegates sat in a circle, leaders and followers on the same level. There was an intensity of difference without hope for consensus. Everyone wanted to be heard, and speeches were endless, repetitious, and unpersuasive. It was one time I yearned for a political boss.

Orv later wrote, "Gene McCarthy then spoke and ripped into Kennedy very strongly, relating his legislative record and indicating he had no confidence in him in no uncertain terms." McCarthy's animosity certainly derived from policy differences, but I think it also grew out of his feeling that he was a far better Catholic than Kennedy and if a Catholic were to be the nominee, it should be he.

The caucus stayed in session until well after midnight. Then a handful of leaders adjourned to Humphrey's suite. When they left at dawn they were no closer to agreement on candidate or tactics, each left to go his angry way. At noon, Freeman was informed that he was the Kennedy choice for the nomination speech if he could assure them that Humphrey would not be speaking for Stevenson. They talked and Humphrey told Orv that he was not giving the speech, but had announced that he was for Stevenson, not Kennedy. He also said that Gene McCarthy would nominate Stevenson. Orv spent not only that day filled with a sense of betrayal, but many after. When the teleprompter failed during his presentation that night, he labored on. It was an appropriate end to his chaotic week. (When the role was called, Humphrey and Stevenson combined got 8 percent of the vote; Kennedy won overwhelmingly and took Lyndon Johnson, not Orv, as his vice presidential running mate.)

Humphrey later wrote honestly about his ambiguous behavior, acknowledging that Orv, with good reason, was outraged. They made up, they remained friends and allies on liberal issues, but I think their friendship suffered at least for a short time, maybe longer. It was not improved when Humphrey, at Kennedy's request, asked Orv to be secretary of Agriculture. Orv rejected the offer. He apparently thought it was Humphrey making up for their convention strife. He also thought if Kennedy wanted him, Kennedy should ask. He got over his pique in time to reconsider and take the job.

Memories of the year were hard to shake. In 1968, Humphrey visited Cardinal Richard Cushing in Boston with two men who had been important Kennedy aides, Larry O'Brien and Ken O'Donnell. The Cardinal, who knew and liked Humphrey, said he thought the country was ready for a Cushing-Humphrey ticket, but knew certainly that a Humphrey-Cushing ticket, if it must be that way, would work.

After the laughter and some serious talk, the Cardinal said, "Hubert, it was in this very room that Joe Kennedy and I decided how much to offer ministers in West Virginia. I'm embarrassed to say we gave less to the Negro ministers than to the whites." He was both Cardinal and ward-heeler, and, for all his political sins, immensely appealing and delightful. When he met someone new and Catholic, he would extend his hand with his blessed ring for kissing and say, "Hi, I'm Dick Cushing."

We had not been entirely innocent in West Virginia. A local custom was to give cash to the person in each county, often sheriffs, who could deliver votes on election day. In local parlance, it was called WAM, or walking around money, and sometimes FAM. We couldn't cover the state, but we did the best we could. One day our man in Charleston got two calls. We had been substantially outbid by the Kennedy campaign. These two "honest" guys felt they shouldn't double dip, and wanted to return our gift. The silent majority apparently weren't troubled and kept ours and theirs.

With Humphrey out after West Virginia, I began a couple more years of floating about, doing political jobs of various sorts, living hand to mouth, earning enough for child support payments, food, and rent and not much more. I did serve my country in a special way, involving a chair and a president. In October 1962 President Kennedy came to Minneapolis to speak to the DFL bean feed. On Saturday morning I was given an important assignment: find a rocking chair for the waiting room at Ryan Field, the airport in St. Paul from which the president would leave. On a weekend and at the last minute, that was tough, but I found one to borrow from a DFLer who sold furniture.

The president's trip was around the time of the Cuban Missile Crisis. The previous year at the Bay of Pigs, 1,500 Cuban exiles who had been trained by the CIA beginning under Eisenhower got their chance to launch a counter-revolution. The plan was simple. Once on shore, they would lead the natives in an effort, bound to be successful, to overthrow Castro. It didn't work out that way. A third of them ended up dead on arrival and the rest were captured. There was hardly a battle, much less an uprising.

With that past disaster still fresh and faced with a nuclear face-off, a president could not be seen doing a political thing in the boonies. Kennedy went quickly to mass at St. Olaf Church and then to the airport. As the plane was readied, he sat in a dingy room in a rocking chair to relieve his ailing back. Without me, God knows what he would have suffered.

The years that followed were, of course, awful. The decade of the 1960s was an extraordinary one on several levels. Calm eluded us. An assassination of a first-term, immensely attractive young president left a mourning nation with Lyndon

Johnson as president. That he was vice president at all is a political sin for which I do hold the Kennedys responsible. I have read that Bobby Kennedy opposed his selection, and I wish he had been successful. I assume Johnson was selected primarily, if not exclusively, because of electoral votes.

Some southern states, ordinarily Democratic, were viciously anti-Catholic, suspicious of Kennedy on civil rights, and just not comfortable with him. Though the election was very close, less than one percentage point separating the candidates in the popular vote, the electoral vote was not. Nixon got 219 while Kennedy got 303, carrying Texas, Louisiana, Arkansas, Georgia, South Carolina, West Virginia, states for which Johnson is often given credit. The Democratic ticket would have had to lose all of them and one other state to have changed the electoral results and, thus, given the presidency to Nixon.

Johnson's presence may have provided the margin in some of those states, but I think he gets more credit than he deserved. The ticket carried Georgia 62 percent to 37 percent and Louisiana 50 percent to 28 percent, margins that cannot be attributed entirely to Johnson's presence on the ticket. Kennedy, I think, would have carried them with L'il Abner as his running mate and would have won the election.

The country was fortunate that Kennedy, not Nixon, began to deal with a rancorous period in our history. The civil rights protests and advocacy brought chaos, anger, and some success. The war in Vietnam would soon divide the nation. The intensity of protest on both issues grew explosively everywhere, and I should have been out marching and waving a sign. But, I was largely a spectator, not active in any of the protests or events. My own life continued with highs and lows, with little planning or clear purpose. It was a stumble-forward process once again to places I had not anticipated even in my fantasies. It started slowly enough.

In 1960, after Humphrey pulled out of the presidential race, I worked at the state capitol for Rolvaag. I had first met Karl in 1954 when he was the state chairman of the DFL, and I had traveled some around the state with him during his campaigns for lieutenant governor.

Karl was not charismatic or a facile orator, but he had a clear and extraordinary commitment to liberal government and a better society that I liked. It took us about an hour to bond and we grew closer, our relationship stronger the more we worked together.

His campaign had little money as always, and we stayed in cheap motels around the state in a single room with two old beds. I never had a clue that he was an alcoholic, as he had been since he was a teenager, or even that he drank much. Booze-in-excess was a 50-year career for him, begun when he was 15 and only over in his sixties.

When I first went to work for him, I lived in downtown St. Paul in a shoddy walk-up, third-floor apartment over a dusty picture-framing store and with a clear view out back

of a couple of loading

Campaign literature for my losing legislative race, 1960, the "great Kennedy-Sherman year"

docks and garbage cans. I decided to run for the state legislature. My adopted district had two more years of life before disappearing for lack of people, and I looked forward to that long-term service. Once hired by the voters, I couldn't be easily fired no matter what I said.

I was one of about a dozen people in the primary, but I had both DFL and labor endorsement and thought I was a cinch for getting through the primary and into the general election as one of the top two vote-getters. Then public office: State Representative Norman Sherman.

I asked Gene McCarthy to arrange a meeting for me with the mother superior (I privately referred to her as the Mother Shapiro) at a convent of nurses working at Saint Joseph's Hospital. I went at the appointed hour to see Sister Marie DePaul. She sat in her white nursing habit with the cowl round her face behind a desk in a tiny office on the main floor of the hospital.

She asked, "Mr. Sherman, what can I do for you?" I said, "Sister, I'm a divorced Jew and I need your help." It was not a line I had practiced. She fortunately burst out laughing, excused herself for her reaction, then told me, after a bit, that she didn't dictate to the other sisters how to vote, but asked me to leave 42 pieces of my campaign literature.

On primary election night, my hopes for a legislative career were dashed. I ended in sixth place. I got a total of 87 votes with 42 of them coming from one holy precinct, and a maximum of eight in each of the others. The nuns, obviously, were in the habit of voting for quality. As least I thought so as solace, but in the eyes of my would-be constituents, the winners were better qualified than I. One was a desk clerk in a flophouse hotel; the other a bartender in a cheap joint. In the general election, the desk clerk won. Once again, I was ready to move on.

In the spring of 1962, a state legislator, Ben Wichterman, whom I had gotten to know and like, told me he intended to run for the U.S. Congress from the huge Ninth District in northern and western Minnesota. He asked me to run his campaign, although he had little money. I agreed to be his entire staff, demanding he cover my monthly obligation to my ex-wife. Beyond that I said I would, in my repeatable style, work essentially for room and board.

Ben, who hadn't gone beyond high school in his formal education, lived on a large farm which I later described as harvesting alternate crops—one year, dust; the next year, mud. It was a hard life, made more difficult by the size of his Catholic family of nine kids.

Devout, he went to mass every Sunday, family in tow. One Sunday, he came home from church and repeated what the priest had said in his sermon. It was out-of-date and out-of-step with the modern church. I told Ben that I had copies of an encyclical, *Mater and Magistra*, in the trunk of my car and that he ought to take one to the priest who obviously had not read what Pope John XXIII had decreed the previous year. He had written on Christianity and social progress, and I was determined to spread the doctrine.

I am not sure now why I had purchased a few copies, except the message had clearly moved me. Ben took the copy, delivered it, and, I thought, immediately became a better Catholic, as the priest may also have. I savored my unlikely role and wished I could talk to "my" nuns at St. Joseph's to brag about proselytizing a priest in partial payment for their support.

Some weeks later, we were many counties and miles away from home when we ran into the local priest on the street. The good father said he had heard that Ben campaigned with an encyclical in his hand, praised him, blessed him, and asked how he happened to do that. Ben said, "I have a Jewish campaign manager," and introduced me. It was a good moment, but being Jewish on the prairie was not always so great.

Ben and I visited Chippewa (now Ojibwe) Indian reservation and met with their three top leaders, one of whom, Roger

Jourdain, I had known from his lobbying in the state legislature. Roger was joined by two sub-chiefs, Otto Thunder and Danny Needham. They told us horror stories of life on the reservation: few teachers in run-down schools; inadequate health care facilities or professional aid for the sick; few jobs and, thus, little income. The misery was endless and real.

When they paused, Ben said that an Area Redevelopment Act had passed, part of the social legislation pushed by President Kennedy's New Frontier administration. Because of that, there was support now for industry to move to places like the reservation. Roger said he knew the legislation because they had had a serious inquiry from a California furniture company. It proposed a manufacturing plant on the reservation, employing about 75 people. "But," he said, his face showing some unease, " they're Jews."

After Ben lost in the primary, there was a gathering of some of his closest supporters. One of them, a pharmacist in a nearby town, embraced me as I got ready to leave the district and said that he hoped I would stay with him and his wife if I ever came up to the area again, "You will be as welcome as a Jew in Hell."

With that sendoff, I went back to the Twin Cities and quickly was hired by Don Fraser, who was also running for Congress. Don and his wife, Arvonne, were very close friends of Gerry Dillon. I had known them for almost a decade because of that and Don's service as a state senator while I was around the capitol with Rolvaag. Don was quiet and unassuming, but a superb legislator, a guy of great integrity, and I admired his extraordinary abilities to push liberal programs that seemed part of his political soul. He was able to steer a Fair Housing bill through the state legislature in 1960, a remarkable feat considering how many conservatives were there and how few

African-Americans in the state. One, a leader still a leader in the black community came from the gallery in tears; we embraced and she whispered in my ear, "My mascara is going to run."

I was more ambiguous about Arvonne, who had testified for my first wife in an uncontested divorce proceeding, apparently working out her feelings about her own divorce in a marriage before Don. Even with a non-contested divorce, the instigator of the proceedings has to find several grounds to justify the decree. Jane noted that I did not bathe often enough. Arvonne was not able to testify on that particular matter, but found something negative to say. Later, she became a respected public servant. She held important jobs in government and was our ambassador to the United Nations Commission on the Status of Woman in 1993 and 1994. She wrote a very good book, and remains a friend today. Together, I think the Frasers may be the best political couple I have known. They had a dedication to public service, and combined that feeling with political skills leading to significant accomplishments.

Our campaign, benefiting from some redistricting, was successful against a long-time Republican incumbent, Dr. Walter Judd, and I was announced as Don's chief of staff. I went off to Washington to begin hiring other staff. When I got back, Don told me that he and Arvonne had changed "his" mind and that I would be second in the office. That was the fastest demotion in my career (although not the first, and possibly just part of a previously described pattern) and a publicly embarrassing one, so I told Don in rather vulgar terms where to put his job and walked out.

The unstated reason, I was later told and am inclined to believe, was because Arvonne's sister had a boyfriend of sorts who would be the top aide. Apparently, the Frasers hoped they might marry. (They didn't.) While I pouted, Gerry Dillon urged me to reconsider my decision and to take the job since I had no other and at the same time save Don any embarrassment before he even left for Washington. Gerry persuaded me. It turned out to be good counsel and, my accepting it, a wise decision.

I had already called Bill Connell, Hubert Humphrey's administrative assistant and chief aide, and asked if he had a job for me. He did not, but he, too, advised me to take the Fraser job since it was easier to find another one in Washington if you were already there and employed. I swallowed my pride, took back my ugly words, and packed my bags. I told Don that I would leave as quickly as possible. I didn't want to work for the guy who replaced me before I even got started, but I soldiered on.

7. My Nation's Capital

After only a few weeks, Bill Connell called and said he had a perfect job for me since the person who handled constituent service was leaving. The rest of Humphrey's staff was mostly involved with legislation and national programs. But, Bill said, the home base was not only essential and vital to Humphrey's re-election, but reflected his deep affection for our state and its people.

He also said that, while I had the job, Humphrey liked to interview prospective employees "at my level" and that he had set up a *pro forma* meeting the following day. It was scheduled for 10:00 a.m. in Humphrey's Senate whip office, a narrow two-room suite in the capitol where a secretary-receptionist and another staff person sat in the front room and a single door led to Humphrey's inner office.

I arrived early, giddy with dreams of a brighter tomorrow. The appointed time came and went. I waited for another 45 minutes, got up, approached the receptionist, and said, "Please tell the senator I am no longer interested in the job. I don't wait 45 minutes for anyone." It was clear that Humphrey did not want to hire me, probably, I thought, because of my reputation as a left-wing flake. There seemed no other explanation for his solitary confinement and my public isolation.

Almost 50 years later, I am still shocked by my stupid, arrogant, self-important behavior. Fortunately, Bill saved me. Soon after I got back to the Fraser office, there was a call from him assuring me that Humphrey wanted me, was very busy at my appointment hour, and would I please come to a meeting set up for the next day.

I reluctantly agreed. At precisely ten, I was ushered into the inner sanctum where Humphrey stood behind his desk, dusting it. I later learned that, as a carryover from South Dakota dust storms of the 1930s, he dusted when nervous. He didn't look up, but said, "Hi, Norman." I returned the greeting and stood waiting.

After a bit, maybe only a few seconds that seemed like 45 minutes, he looked up, broke the awful silence to ask, "Do you know I have work coming out of my ass?" I said, "Yes, sir, I do." He said, "Okay, you're hired." Silence followed so I backed toward the door. He looked up again and said, "Norman, do you type?" I said, "Yes, sir, I do." He then explained that every time he hired a male, the new employee expected a secretary. He said there just wasn't staff money enough for that. I was both amused and confused to hear that coming from a senator endlessly attacked then and later as a big spender of taxpayers' dollars. It was a strange, ambiguous beginning; a pithy interview with typing skills paramount in addition to understanding the physical base of the work load.

My quizzical mood did not last long. I was soon inspired. The most pedestrian job seemed important, somehow contributing to Humphrey's sense of service as a senator and being of some value to the constituents. Humphrey had begun his stay in the Senate with a simple demand of his then small staff: every letter should be answered the same day it was received unless it required contact with a federal agency for information. Even if it did, it ought to quickly get an acknowledgement. He said that many people got little or no mail and that they ought to hear from him without delay. I should have understood that. In 1954, when I was working as a volunteer at the DFL booth at the Minnesota State Fair, an old man came in and asked if "Hubert" was around. He took out a folded letter, a little smudged, a little crinkled at the corners, a response to a letter he had written about some farm issue. It was a couple of years old and had clearly been reread many times, and he wanted to continue the discussion with "Hubert," someone he had never met, but who was a first-name friend.

Humphrey's staff from the beginning worked long hours, but Humphrey himself often arrived at the office earlier than some and stayed later than most. The staff got used to his late night scouring the office to look for unanswered mail. (Some staff took mail home and brought it back the next morning.) It was a near compulsion that was not lost on his constituents. They spoke. They asked. He responded. It might be about a lost Social Security check. It might be about a multi-million dollar contract that meant jobs and profit. It might be the death of someone he knew well, or it might just as easily be in response to a high school assignment to write to a public official.

(Years later working on his autobiography, I found a classic Humphrey response to a letter from the Georgia Peanut Princess. He wrote, "I agree with you that peanut butter is as much or more of a household treat as mom's apple pie . . .. Also I like peanut butter and cheese on crackers. Give me the crunchy or the smooth, I'm not fussy. In other words, I just love peanut butter." There were a couple of other unappetizing variations. Had I read the letter before election day in

1968, I would still have voted for him, but with some pause as I considered what his culinary taste might do to the White House kitchen.)

Shortly after I went to work, he summoned me. Virtually every other office in America with two or more rooms had a telephone intercom. You dialed a single number or two and a phone rang in a nearby office. Not so in our office. Humphrey wouldn't spend the federal dollars to replace a buzzer system. He had a panel of buttons on his desk with a staff name next to each one. He pushed, and a beckoning sound was heard and heeded.

When that happened one day, I raced from my desk in the farthest office in the suite to his. He handed me a handwritten letter on paper torn from a lined pad bought at the drug store. It recounted that he had twice helped the family before. The first time, the woman had written to say her husband was serving time for a felony at the federal prison in Leavenworth, Kansas, too far for the family to visit often. At her request, Humphrey got the man transferred to Sandstone, the federal prison in Minnesota, so they could meet with less difficulty. When the husband had served his time and was released, he couldn't find a job, and she had written again asking for Humphrey's help. He got the man a job in a small town near his Waverly home. It was in a family-run slaughterhouse with, until then, no outside employee, and not covered by unemployment insurance. Now, the guy had been laid off when the plant closed. He once again needed work.

Humphrey said, "Get him a job. You know everyone in Minnesota." That was a bit of an exaggeration, and I put the letter in a tray for future fulfillment. A week went by and my desk buzzed again. I did my steeplechase race, got to his desk, and he asked, "Have you found (using the guy's name) a job?"

I said, in my brilliance, "Who?" The letter was still in my to-do tray. I had forgotten the name and I had done nothing. I whimpered how busy I was, and he said firmly again, "Get him a job."

I finally did. I got the governor's office involved and they found him a job driving a truck for the Highway Department. I reported my success to Humphrey. Then I got word that his old friend, and my new one, had flunked whatever test they gave a beginning truck driver. I informed Humphrey and thought I was done with it. Humphrey said, "Get him another test." I did, he passed, he worked.

I go on here at length about a minor and not earth-shaking event because it is a clear picture of who Humphrey was. The felon couldn't vote, his family probably didn't, and they wouldn't tell their neighbors about it. I learned then, if I had not known it before, that public service in an elected official's office meant caring for people you didn't know and wouldn't meet or hear from except in difficult moments. At least that was so in Humphrey's office.

Some offices, I learned, almost ignored their mail. Others responded slowly and cursorily. In the Humphrey office, the mail was my salvation. I went from a borderline hire to an embraced employee. I wrote a lot of letters, maybe more than anyone else, and the senator thought they sounded quite precisely like him. Once, later when he was vice president, I went into his office for something, and he asked, "Do you want to see a great letter I wrote?" I read the letter and agreed that it was a great one, but said, "I wrote it." He said he did, I said I did, and we repeated the dialogue until he buzzed his secretary to get the carbon copy from the files since each letter had the initials of the writer half-hidden in the letterhead. I was smugly right, and he just shook his head and smiled.

I also learned quickly that Humphrey was the fastest study I had ever met. One afternoon there was a meeting with several executives from Honeywell, a major employer in Minnesota, about a problem the company had with the Department of Defense. Humphrey had had a busy day on the Senate floor, and I had no chance to brief him beyond a few words and handing him a background paper of two or three sheets. He absorbed it all as we raced down the hall to the meeting room, spoke as though he had been thinking about nothing else for hours, if not days, and left the supplicants of whatever political leanings with the sense that they had a friend as well as a senator. They did, at least for the moment and until the problem, if it had any merit at all, was resolved.

Humphrey had a phenomenal memory. He stored information like his mind was a computer and had quick recall of what was stored there. One day he was needling me about something, and I responded, in mocking tone, that I had first seen him campaigning in 1943 standing in an oil spot in a garage on Plymouth Avenue near where I lived. They had cleared out the cars and set up a table and chairs, and he stood next to the most corrupt alderman on the council, talking to about a dozen people. Without pause, now a couple of decades later, he said, "Margolis's garage." He had never been back, and Margolis hadn't had the garage for years.

He also remembered faces, a talent that could not have been learned, but had somehow to be in his genes. It must have happened regularly since I heard stories of recognition frequently. Before I got to Washington, I had talked with a Minnesota couple at a ward club meeting. They had been in Moscow as tourists when Humphrey came up from the subway station, spotted them, bounced over to greet them, asked about the guy's parents, and then dashed off with a wave, leaving the couple eager to call home.

Arthur Naftalin introduced his wife's grandmother to Humphrey who saw her a few times before he went off to Washington. Several years later, he was speaking at Claremont College in California when he spotted a little old lady heading down the aisle toward where he stood. He waved and almost shouted, "Hi, Mrs. Healy."

Recently, a friend, Sandy Lerner, told me that in 1944 before Humphrey was elected to office, her mother, Evelyn Karon, invited him to speak to the Duluth Council of Jewish Women. They had not met before and she did not see him after that until 1948 when he was running for the Senate. Sandy and her mother came out of Dayton's department store in downtown Minneapolis to find Humphrey campaigning on the corner. He spotted them, approached and asked, "Mrs. Karon, how are you?"

Humphrey had good foresight as well. During his first term, he woke one morning in 1951 to read in the *Washington Post* that a federal judge in the District of Columbia had died. He didn't know the late judge, and his mourning was brief as he grabbed the phone and called the White House asking to see President Truman as quickly as possible. He was told to come down immediately before the day's scheduled appointments started. Within an hour of his morning ablutions, he was with the president urging the appointment of former Minnesota governor Luther Youngdahl to the vacant judgeship. It seemed a strange request since Youngdahl was a Republican.

Humphrey explained to the president that Youngdahl had once told him that his life's dream was to be a federal judge. He had been a good, immensely popular governor, never partisan and always willing to work with the DFLers. His brother was the prominent pastor of Mt. Olivet, which was large at the time and which became the largest Evangelical Lutheran Church in the United States with over 10,000 members by 1968. The Youngdahl presence was immense.

Humphrey's strange request was not so strange. The governor had been talked of as a possible Humphrey opponent in the 1954 election and would have been a formidable one, quite possibly a successful one. One fewer Democratic judge virtually ensured one more Democratic senator. Youngdahl was benched then. Humphrey was re-elected.

(Youngdahl's son, Bill, was also a Lutheran minister. In 1964 and 1965, serving in the national headquarters of the Lutheran Church in America, he was an ardent supporter and advocate for the civil rights acts of those years.)

Letters and constituents were not, of course, Humphrey's main or sole concern. Legislation was always prime. At any given moment after his early presence on the scene, he might hold in memory dozens of bills that he had developed and stored when they didn't pass. He would personally, or have a legislative aide, adapt an old one, and then he'd reintroduce it. There was never a major bill on any question that escaped his interest. He wanted to be involved, to learn, and to persuade others to his point of view.

In the years before I joined his staff, he had already made his mark on legislation over a broad spectrum of our national life. He is remembered mostly for his civil rights accomplishments, but he was the creator of the Peace Corps (although John Kennedy as president gets credit for it), crucial in establishing Food for Peace and was seminal in matters of arms control and the reduction of nuclear weapons. He cared about working people and authored the Occupational Safety and Health Act. No education bill passed without his input and influence. He was both generalist and specialist, something I discovered and admired immensely when I joined his staff. Going to work every day was exciting even if I stood only nearby to major action.

Because he had long earned a national audience by the time I joined the staff, his press secretary answered the demands of national, as well as international, journalists. Humphrey asked me to look after Minnesota weeklies and out-state dailies, and, on some occasions, Twin City reporters who worked in Washington. It didn't require much on my part since there were few questions or demands from the little papers, and not many more for me from the dailies, but it seemed important and I liked it.

But always more important than what I knew was who I knew—county DFL chairmen, union leaders, farm organization officials, civil rights advocates. And, even more, many campaign envelope stuffers and precinct walkers were friends. That was not something that the bright staff members with a Harvard Ph.D. or other elite university credentials who were attracted to Humphrey brought with them. I was not in their league. But, my years of bouncing around the state were often politically useful and occasionally touched on substantive matters as well.

That was true one memorable day when about 50 Minnesotans came to town in August of 1963 to participate in the March on Washington for Jobs and Freedom. Some were old friends I knew from our working together. Others became friends in a minute. There was excitement in every step, in every word, in every embrace as we gathered.

The entire group along with some ministers from around the country was invited to breakfast in the basement of the First Congregational Church in downtown Washington. We were there because of John Stewart. He and his wife, Nancy, led a small gang of volunteers including Humphrey, Eugene McCarthy, and other members of the Minnesota congressional delegation in preparing and serving a pancake and sausage breakfast. The elected officials and the visitors moved around the church basement in a rare kind of shared joy of purpose and community.

John Stewart deserves special notice. No Humphrey staff person in my time served him better and more wisely. John grew up on Long Island, part of a comfortable family and a Republican one. After an undergraduate degree from Cornell he went to the University of Chicago for his Ph.D. in political science. He came to the Humphrey Senate office as an American Political Science Association fellow, still a Republican, and was asked by Humphrey to stay after his APSA time was up. He ultimately became the chief legislative aide. He put his exceptional intellectual skills to work for Humphrey, seeking social goals for a better society, doing it quietly and unwaveringly. He was devoted to Humphrey, and he soon voted Democratic as he has since.

After breakfast, we marched together from the church to the Lincoln Memorial. On the way, Humphrey saw a mother holding up her daughter to see him. He gently lifted the girl from her mother's arms to hug her. The child seemed bewildered, but her mother in a frenzy of joy snapped picture after picture in the minute we lingered.

The crowd seemed slim when we arrived, but suddenly people came from all directions, growing to about a quarter of a million packed together. No scene of the exciting day has stayed with me more than a fleeting, unplanned few minutes. The delegation from Mississippi, maybe 50, maybe a hundred men and women, suddenly appeared. Far from home, in a strange new world, all of them wore new dark-blue bib overalls, a tuxedo for their day, and as they moved into the crowd, people spontaneously moved apart and made an aisle for them, letting them get closer and closer to the podium where Martin Luther King and other dignitaries soon stood to speak.

There were cheers from us, smiles and nods from them, and if I were a religious man, I would describe it as an epiphany. In Mississippi they were excluded, demeaned, and lynched. That day in Washington they were American citizens as never before. There was a vision reflected in those overalls of a more democratic tomorrow. They belonged up front.

Even before Martin Luther King spoke, the program was extraordinary: well-known religious leaders led prayers, several pioneers and activists of the civil rights movement spoke, and the sound of music lifted us all. There were white singers. There were black singers. Joan Baez, Bob Dylan, Mahalia Jackson, and Marian Anderson who, of course, had been there before. In 1939, the Daughters of the American Revolution had denied her the stage of Constitution Hall, which they owned, because they permitted only white performers and certainly no integrated audiences. Eleanor Roosevelt invited her to the White House, arranged for her to sing "My Country 'Tis of Thee" on Easter Sunday at the very place where we then were. (President Roosevelt in 1938 wrote to the DAR, "Remember, remember always, that all of us, and you and I especially, are descended from immigrants and revolutionists." Mrs. Roosevelt had resigned seven years earlier.)

Myrlie Evers gave a short speech on black women who had been in the fight for civil rights. Her husband, Medgar, a NAACP organizer in Mississippi, had been shot in the back in front of their home and died, just a few hours after President

Kennedy made his televised speech on civil rights. Mrs. Evers and her children had listened with approval to the speech and, ironically, anticipated a better tomorrow. (The Ku Klux Klan member who killed her husband was not convicted of the murder until 1994. Two all-white juries would not convict closer to the time of the murder.)

Each of us was only a speck in the crowd, but felt huge. As King spoke, some wept, many cheered, applauded, and echoed his words. The Kennedys, despite having spoken and acted well on civil rights, had not been willing to meet beforehand with the leadership of the march. They watched the event on television as millions of others did. But, by prior invitation President Kennedy entertained the leaders after the program. A presidential blessing is better late than never.

But epiphanies and emotion and belated embraces don't make law. Doing so would not be easy. Within a year, Humphrey, not single-handedly, but as Senate whip and a major strategist and floor leader for the bill (H.R. 7152), was able to break a filibuster (the word comes from a Dutch word for pirate) and see a civil rights bill that changed America forever once it became law. The lives of almost 20 million black Americans (10 percent of our population then) and their descendants would never be the same.

If not totally and immediately "free at last," they were closer. The scope of the bill was massive. Beyond public accommodations, the access to hotels, motels, and restaurants, it contained sections on equal employment opportunity, disbursement of federal funds, voting rights, and public education. Its aim was simple and great at the same time.

The legislative struggle for a civil rights bill in the years just before had been difficult, sometimes more show than real, and with inconsistent strong advocacy from both John

Kennedy and Lyndon Johnson. Johnson gets a lot of credit for the bills passed in 1957 and 1960, but they were watered down to get votes for what was left. In 1957, for example, he took out the heart of the bill aimed to prevent discrimination in employment. He had been known to use the word "Nigra" even after he was in Congress, (probably to keep his Southern allies comfortable with him as one of them) but he had also embraced some blacks in Texas, a politically courageous thing to do at the time, and that may have represented his gut feelings as well.

In his first speech as president, he said that there would be no greater homage to Kennedy "than the passage of the civil rights bill." The bill had been introduced in the House on November 20, 1963, just two days before John Kennedy was assassinated. To get it out of the House would require 40 to 50 Republican votes, and Johnson did work effectively on House members, particularly Republicans Bill McCulloch and Charles Halleck. They had the power to persuade others and get the votes to send a strong bill on to the Senate. But his influence in the Senate, despite his having been majority leader, was not great nor, in the end, essential. (The best book I have read on this legislation is by Todd Purdum, *An Idea Whose Time has Come*, and I have used it to refresh my memory.)

Support from the Oval Office in 1961 and 1962 for any serious civil rights legislation had been limited and restrained. President Kennedy did react after there were riots in Birmingham and did address the nation on June 11, 1963. Bobby Kennedy, as Attorney General, did send marshals to the South. Crisis brought out their latent support. They seemed to many of us as reluctant to take a political chance, regardless of what they may have felt to some elusive degree. (Teddy Kennedy in his first speech as senator on April 9, 1964, said. " My brother was the first president to state publicly that segregation was morally wrong." He continued, "His heart and soul are in this bill." It was a moving moment with significant impact both within and outside the Senate.)

The House bill finally came over to the Senate at the beginning of May and the filibuster began. It went on for 54 days and only ended because of essential support from Republican Senator (and Minority Leader) Everett Dirksen of Illinois. He delivered votes that none of the Democrats, including Humphrey or Johnson, could.

On the floor and out in the open, speeches filled with bigotry, prejudice, and simple meanness droned on and on. Senator Russell, who led the fight against the bill, lamented the fact that the church and clergy had been vital in soliciting the needed Republican votes. He complained of "priests, rabbis, bishops, ministers, deacons, pastors, and stated clerks" filling the halls and offices of the Senate to lobby for the bill.

I wasn't responsible for their spiritual presence, but I took special pleasure in his complaint. My contribution to the battle was to come up with an idea for a book to be sent to clergy across the country. It was not intended to convince, but to provide material for sermons. It was called *Moral Crisis: The Case for Civil Rights*. The cover showed Kennedy, Johnson, and Humphrey walking together. The book consisted of a few speeches, including Humphrey's speech to the 1948 Democratic national convention that drove the Dixiecrats out of the hall and party and established Humphrey as a national figure. He said then, "The time has arrived for the Democratic Party to get out of the shadow of state's rights and walk forthrightly into the bright sunshine of human rights."

The book reprinted speeches by John Kennedy, Lyndon

Johnson, and Senator Kuchel of California. It also included an explanation of the bill. The book worked. Its words rippled across America many Sunday mornings and a few Friday evenings after sundown. The clergy convinced others as well as themselves if they needed conversion.

Slavery and then discrimination and segregation seemed the Southern way of life without shame or doubt. It was "just" history. The first slave came here in 1525. By 1800, blacks were almost 20 percent of our population. The Southern senators represented the views of most of their white-voting constituents. They stood self-righteously, and morally wrong without question, but performing as the heirs of generations who had cherished slavery, saw the "Nigra" as a lesser creature, and wanted their society to remain as it was.

One leading evangelical preacher, Reverend Bob Jones, bleated, "If you are against segregation and against racial separation, then you are against God Almighty." For his parishioners and their neighbors across the South, bigotry was blessed. What they saw when they looked into the mirror was a devout follower of God's word. On a secular level, they didn't quite deny the existence of the 15th Amendment to the Constitution, but close.

For the clergy, enlisting their senators would not be easy, yet was vital. Success could not depend solely on the liberal voices, but on conservative ones disinclined to vote for civil rights laws. Humphrey needed their votes, and he looked and hoped for help from the religious community.

He barely knew Reverend Martin Luther King and asked John Stewart to arrange for King to come in. John was Humphrey's eyes and ears and essential surrogate both inside the Senate and out. King came, accompanied by two other young civil rights leaders, Reverend Andrew Young, later our ambassador to the United Nations appointed by President Carter; and Reverend Walter Fauntroy, who a few years later was elected to Congress from the District of Columbia.

John and I were also in the meeting. That he was there was understandable. I am not sure why I was. (I had Dr. King sign two copies of the bill for my children.) The meeting was held in the small whip office where my own historic hiring took place. The office had antique furniture and mirrors and paintings. The mirrors lent an odd quality. I could see Humphrey and King not only from where I sat, but with a bit of a twist I could also see their reflections from a different angle. What I saw and heard in that office was unforgettable from any direction.

Humphrey described to King how he would behave in order to keep the debate focused and civil and, thus, make it easier for wavering senators to come aboard. He urged, almost pleaded, that King not say what might be in his heart, but must be kept from his tongue. He should advocate, Humphrey said, but in a manner that would help keep the debate calm and, thus, keep the bill from being amended into nothingness, if not stopped altogether.

Humphrey asked King to try to keep his allies, both inside and outside the Senate, in check. His reason was simple: don't give those on the fence, Dirksen's coterie, reason or opportunity to show outrage and pose as the advocates of good manners, fairness, and reason as they voted against what King and Humphrey were fighting for. Success would come only out of constant and continuing civility, deserved or not.

The count that day had the proponents eight votes shy of what was needed for cloture. Neither Humphrey nor King could get them. Dirksen could. For all his excesses, his bombast and his show-business style, Dirksen was a powerful leader of the Republicans on substance. They listened to him.

What Humphrey asked of King and himself was not easy. The national outrage at the bombing by Ku Klux Klan crazies of a Birmingham, Alabama church in September 1963 was undiminished across most of the country and particularly within the black community. Four young girls at Sunday service died at the hands of those supporting the contrary senators. If these senators were not complicit, they were at least silent most of the time, their silence giving heart to the killers who did not deserve it and should have instead been quickly found, arrested, tried, and jailed.

King and Humphrey talked for about 90 minutes. King ultimately seemed to accept the value of what Humphrey asked, though he certainly could not control everyone who would be speaking out. They agreed they would seek to mute any incendiary words or acts from their allies the best they could. On the floor, Humphrey without visible rancor would demonstrate fairness to the Southern opponents, letting them have their chance to oppose the bill. Restraint was the only way to victory. And it worked.

(Humphrey struggled with his own injunction. At one point he noted, "In Charleston, South Carolina, there are 10 places where a dog can stay and none for a Negro.")

There were some unexpected moments because of the calculated civil tone. Early on, Senator Willis Robertson of Virginia made an impassioned speech in opposition. He and Humphrey had a lively debate on the substance of the public accommodations section. It outlawed "discrimination in hotels, motels, restaurants, theatres, and all other accommodations engaged in interstate commerce." It struck down what Southerners cherished.

Robertson proclaimed his abiding personal affection for

the "distinguished senator from Minnesota." He talked of the Civil War not in anger, but how the "brave men of Minnesota surrounded the brave men of Virginia" and "we could not whip them." When they finished their debate, Robertson walked over to Humphrey, embraced him, and stuck a little paper Confederate flag in his lapel pocket. Robertson was almost a parody of the Southern gentlemanly senator.

Ultimately success was possible, as I have noted, only with help from Everett Dirksen. A Shakespearean actor in his youth, Dirksen had a deep, mellifluous voice, wild white hair, grand gestures, and a sense that he was the current heir of the most distinguished orators of the past. He dripped vanity and self-importance. He loved the limelight and Humphrey told us he would get it every moment of every day. Dirksen could deliver the votes that meant the filibuster would end. Without him, defeat was certain. With him, victory was not only possible, but likely. Humphrey could finally count on the 67 votes necessary to end the debate. It was the first time ever that the Senate had done so on a civil rights bill and 37 years since any cloture vote had been successful.

Credit is often given to President Johnson for the favorable vote. He really doesn't deserve as much credit as he gets. Humphrey has said that Johnson did indicate that he would not accept any weakening of the bill and he did talk to Dirksen frequently, maybe even daily. But, Johnson as an advocate is elusive. He had said positive things about bills in 1957 and 1960, and then caved when it was expedient.

In this case, Johnson had been a strong inside advocate and particularly influenced the bill's beginnings in the House, but he really did not control or persuade anyone in the Senate to vote for the bill beyond those Mansfield, Humphrey, and Tom Kuchel had in line, and the conservatives Dirksen delivered. The president was important, but Dirksen was quintessentially a creature of the Senate and that is where the constant reinforcement was vital. Indeed, had Mansfield and Humphrey followed the President's repeated advice to hold around-the-clock sessions, the bill would have failed to be what it was and become a replica of the '57 and '60 bills: nice, but not enough to do what had to be done.

Johnson had commitments from two senators, Carl Hayden of Arizona and Alan Bible of Nevada, to vote for cloture, the procedure to cut off debate and bring the Senate to a vote, if their votes made the difference. They both voted no when it didn't. But a president inevitably ends up getting credit for whatever happens on his watch while those who fought in the trenches fade away. Johnson deserves some credit, but not nearly what he too often gets.

It is interesting that a greater percentage of Republican senators, with Dirksen in the lead, voted for the bill than Democrats. I think none of that would have happened except for Humphrey's style (and King's ability and willingness to go along with it). Opponents got respectful treatment, even when they did not merit it. Wavering senators finally saw that the Southerners had had their fair shot and that it was time to vote.

One vote was more special than any of the others. Senator Clair Engle, a Democrat from California and just 51 years old, came from a hospital bed where he was dealing with a brain tumor that would cause his death less than a month later on July 30. He couldn't walk; he couldn't speak. He was wheeled to the open area at the front of the chamber below the dais where the presiding officer stands, and close to the clerks calling out the names of the senators. "Mr. Engle of California." The virtually helpless senator pointed, with some difficulty, to his eye. Without pause, the clerk announced, "Mr. Engle votes "Aye." The filibuster was soon over.

Humphrey's senatorial regiment, like the Civil War Minnesotans, stayed strong. It wasn't easy to remain civil as the Southerners gave their valedictory speeches in the final days. Senator Thurmond ranted, "This (sic) so-called Civil Rights Proposals . . .are unconstitutional, unnecessary, unwise and extend beyond the realm of reason. This is the worst civil-rights package ever presented to Congress." By then, Senator Russell, accepting defeat in the offing, leaned over to Humphrey and said, "Hubert, how in hell can we shut up that fool Thurmond? He's going to wreck us all." (In 2003, Thurmond's family acknowledged that he was the father of a child born to a 16-year-old black housekeeper in the Thurmond household when he was 22.)

As Humphrey approached his long awaited moment of success, he carried a personal burden. Muriel had called the previous day to tell him that their son Bob had cancer and that he was in the hospital. Ordinarily Humphrey would have been on the next plane home. But, he was between a rock and a hard place: be with his family as he wanted and jeopardize passage of the bill, or remain. He chose, in tears, to stay.

After cloture, each senator was permitted one hour of talk. When the talk was over, it was time to vote. The final vote was 73 in favor and just 27 opposed. To say victory was sweet is both a cliché and an understatement. After that vote, Senator Russell, bitter and defeated, approached Humphrey, did not congratulate him, but said, "If you had not permitted us the time to make our case, the bill would never have been enforceable in the South. We would have seen to it." (This from a guy who wondered aloud when Humphrey first arrived, how "the people of Minnesota could have sent that son-of-a-bitch to the Senate." Russell was probably involved in another welcoming gesture. Incoming senators usually are given a temporary office. The other new senators in 1949 got one. For 19 days, Humphrey, excluded, worked in a borrowed office in a law firm downtown.)

As Humphrey left the Capitol, a crowd of several hundred people stood silently on the sidewalk, smiling, but soon waving and cheering. Unable to resist an audience, Humphrey gave one more speech. For me, standing by, coming down those steps, it was a March on Washington moment. Our country would be permanently different and better. I had been at least a tiny part of a moral and legislative victory of historic importance and impact.

Now, almost half a century later, many doubts are back, many old hopes challenged, the way forward unclear. I suppose I should not be surprised. The difficulty of change, of where we were and what we had to overcome, was clear in the mail to Senator Humphrey. Here are four samples:

"You are a nigger-loving, kike-loving Communist traitor to the Aryan race."

"I hope and pray there is another Lee Harvey Oswald waiting around some corner for you."

"Get cancer, Mr. S.O.B. Very truly yours."

"Let me ask you this you pig fucker, would you let your daughter marry one of those animals?"

That language and the hate that inspired those letters are publicly rarer today, but the attitude still exists barely beneath the surface in many places and in clear view in others. The Dixiecrats are gone, but the bigots remain. Legislation that might help minorities—black and Latino—is picked at, delayed, and buried when possible in both the Senate and the House. Voting is made difficult, almost impossible, in some states as though democracy was a dirty word.

The moral imperative for seeking a fair society, something that once motivated good people in both parties, has withered, wizened, wasted away in the hearts and mouths of demagogues and self-promoters.

8. Convention Wisdom

From that high, politics took over in a surprising and wonderful way. The 1964 Democratic National Convention raised my spirits and hopes even higher. It ended with Hubert Horatio Humphrey being nominated for vice president of the United States at the Democratic National Convention in Atlantic City in late August.

To be vice president of the United States is not so much an honor as it is a way station. It often gives you a leg up on your party's nomination when the president's term is over, or if the president dies in office you're there. While recent vice presidents seem to have more involvement, more to do, and a greater role as adviser than just a few decades ago, it is still a job in the shadows, a constant dance to avoid stealing the spotlight from the president even as you yearn for glory, praise, and respect. It is a time for public, and even private, silence when you differ from the president's position by even a hair.

Humphrey had been talked of as a candidate for higher office by others as well as himself for a decade or so. He encouraged the talk in subtle, and a few not-so-subtle, ways, even as he proclaimed his pleasure at being in the Senate.

In 1952, two important players, Senator Brian McMahon of Connecticut and James Finnegan, a political power broker from Pennsylvania, who were against Adlai Stevenson strenuously urged him to run. He declined. The next election was different.

In 1956, he thought idle talk had turned into real action. He had a firm commitment from Adlai Stevenson that he would be the vice presidential nominee. At least he and others thought so. But Stevenson backed off and threw the choice of a nominee to the convention itself. All of us were surprised and disappointed by Stevenson's unexpected action, but it provided me a significant role even though it was my first national convention and I was still a janitor.

Freddie Gates, Humphrey's close friend since the mayoral days, gave me a small bundle of cash and told me to find a sign painter who would work overnight to produce catchy signs that said "Stevenson-Humphrey—A Team for America" and creative variations of my choice so long as they spelled the names correctly. The signs would be carried and waved during the traditional demonstration following a candidate's nomination. It was by then a bit of show business made for television, but changed no more votes than it ever had. That did not diminish the honor given me. These were signs of the future and could not be waved without me.

By noon, well before the convention was to start for the day, I sat and dozed in a wire cage in the warehouse space behind the platform, ordinarily used to house commercial products overnight for display in expo booths on the floor the next day—tools and grass mowers and plumbing, dresses and lingerie, desks and other furniture. I may have been the first person in history to sit there for hours guarding material of no commercial value.

As my special moment drew near, Sam Rayburn of Texas, speaker of the House of Representatives and chairman of the convention, decreed there would be no rallying for a candidate, no demonstrations. As a result, signs and sadness surrounded me, sitting in lonely splendor, caged and sniffling. Senator Estes Kefauver of Tennessee, a second-rate senator and compulsive philanderer, got the nomination while I tried to get rid of my eloquent and artistic garbage.

By 1964, things seemed different. There was no Stevenson-like commitment, but a lot of talk and good reasons why Lyndon Johnson should select Humphrey. He was strong where Johnson was weak: in the liberal wing of the party, among blacks and Jews, with the labor movement, all vital components of a victory. With Johnson as president many of them yearned still for a John Kennedy, or at least someone more like him as Humphrey was in terms of both program and style. His support was reflected in a Gallup Poll of 3,000 county chairmen in June. Of the 1,671 people who answered, 31 percent were for him. Bobby Kennedy was next at 19 percent, followed by Sargent Shriver at 13 percent, Adlai Stevenson at 11 percent, and Gene McCarthy at 2.3 percent.

Despite that, the trip to the nomination was not easy and with Lyndon Johnson not inevitable. The choice, as always except for the Stevenson equivocation, was the presidential nominee's and his alone. There is essentially a convention of one person and a unanimous vote is required. The candidate wants someone who will ensure or at least help get some additional electoral votes, be at ease with something close to an obsequious relationship, and still be ready to assume the presidency. (The last is the least in the political calculus. Johnson was a living example. Disliked intensely by Bobby Kennedy, and no favorite of many others, he had been chosen for vice president largely for the electoral votes he would bring from Texas and possibly other Southern states.)

For this convention, I was not only uncaged, but I had been promoted. I was Norman the Doorman for much of the time. I stood in the doorway of the Humphrey suite where he and his closest political advisers waited nervously for a call from the White House and met mostly with super-delegates, primarily office-holders who controlled votes in their states. There was little they could do for Humphrey that they hadn't already done, but their visits filled the nervous hours.

My job was to decide quickly who got in to see Humphrey, who was handed off to someone else, and who was graciously sent on his or her way. It was heavy duty, but I remembered names of people I had never met as well as names and faces of many I had. Among my supplicants, a special familiar face showed up. Saul Bellow, a sudden, resurrected buddy from my university days who would win the 1976 Nobel Prize for his novels, was at the door. For a moment, that he remembered me well after two decades was pleasing and astounding. I had taken a course from him, but because we had a close mutual friend, we three and wives also had had dinner together from time to time. I learned then what great disdain Bellow had for students as well as some of his colleagues and how rude he could be.

One night at the only Mexican restaurant in the Twin Cities, the waitress spoke English, but Bellow insisted on responding and ordering in Spanish. She answered in English. He kept up his Spanish to everyone's discomfort, particularly hers. When he spoke English to us, it was just as bad. He badmouthed other faculty with ease, an act of disloyalty and, since we were not that close, indiscretion. He mocked his own teaching, as well as others' as casting "false pearls before genuine swine." It was a borrowed line, but delivered with obvious self-satisfaction. I found him petty, dismissive, preening. I know not everyone then or later felt as I did, but I think I was right.

Now, at the convention, Bellow greeted me as though I were a special and dear friend he had never forgotten. In fact, someone who was close to both Humphrey and Bellow had told him I was the guard at the door and the great decider. Bellow was so embracing, so friendly, I was momentarily flattered.

Then, he told me, in English, not Spanish, why he was really there. He wanted to follow Humphrey everywhere during the convention, be in all the meetings, listen to every phone call, and then do a book about it all. He had already written a book, published in 1947, called *The Victim*, and I thought he was looking for another one.

I smiled a hypocritical smile, hailed a substitute doorman, left Bellow in the hall, and quickly urged Humphrey that my buddy Saul's request be denied. I just didn't trust him. With permission, I let him into the suite, escorted him in to talk briefly to Humphrey, who turned down his request. We didn't need a political voyeur adding to the unease and uncertainty. I sent him on his way as quickly and graciously as possible with an unspoken, "Adios, Saul." I knew a woman someplace in St. Paul smiled. I make more of it today than I could at the time and I am not sure my advice made a difference. There were more serious things that had been happening.

The lily-white delegation from Mississippi was being challenged by a group of blacks, including people who had been among those wearing the blue bib-overalls that had moved me at the March, and white liberals led by Joe Rauh, a longtime friend of Humphrey. The president, fearing that any resolution that drove an unhappy South out of the convention would doom his election, asked Humphrey, holding credentials with both sides, to try to resolve the issue. Focused on himself as he needed to be, Humphrey asked Walter Mondale to help find a way to solve the problem. Johnson also sent in Walter Reuther of the UAW to work with Mondale. Reuther had better national credentials, of course, but Mondale was in charge as the main negotiator.

While there was no explicit "succeed or else" from the president, the fear that it might be the case and that Gene McCarthy, the other leading contender for the vice presidential nomination at that moment, would be chosen added to the tension. Mondale succeeded in getting agreement for a couple of black delegates at large. It satisfied no one, not Humphrey, not Mondale, not Reuther, but the Southern delegations did not walk out and Johnson had to consider the uncomfortable resolution a success.

Beyond the moment, it spoke to the future. It wasn't easy. It wasn't simple. But it was lasting. Party rules were changed in dramatic fashion and unexpected ways that had a profound and lasting impact on our party. Racial or gender discrimination in selection of delegates was prohibited. The delegation had to reflect the racial make-up of the state. Mondale and Humphrey strongly felt that they had established an important precedent for every convention that followed and they had. By the next convention, Mississippi's voting delegates were integrated, and in 2000 there were 26 African-Americans and 22 whites.

In a real sense, it was an extension of the message and purpose of the Civil Rights Act applied to the democratic process. It deserves to be remembered as more than an uneasy agreement for one convention as the word compromise may imply.

It was a prescription for the future and a bitter pill for the entire South to swallow.

Yet Johnson continued to jerk Humphrey around. That Johnson had reached this point without really having decided on a running mate seems strange, unlikely, and uncharacteristic. After the Mississippi compromise was reached, Jim Rowe, a close friend and confidante of Johnson's, told Humphrey at dinner that he was the likely candidate, but swore him to silence. Then at 1:30 a.m. Jim called to say it could still unravel. It is hard not to believe that he was calling at Johnson's direction, thus adding one more sleepless night and gut-tightening day.

The tension and excitement continued, political hopes and fears alternating. It was hard to find anything to talk about. There was only one topic of interest and we had long since exhausted everything to say. Small talk was fake and almost impossible. We waited.

Then the call came. Johnson told Humphrey there was a plane waiting to bring him to Washington. He left for the airport and the rest of us danced about, smiling, clapping each other on the back, acting a bit like fools.

What we (including Humphrey) didn't know was that Johnson had also invited Senator Tom Dodd of Connecticut. Dodd was a mediocre senator and his presence made a short trip a long one. The press were bewildered; Humphrey was in limbo. Certainty flew out the window and minutes seemed like hours for him, but when the charade was finally over, Humphrey, a little bruised, was the chosen one. I wondered at the time how Dodd felt, used as a political marionette, really having no chance at the nomination for which he had never been mentioned seriously, if at all.

The Humphrey-Johnson relationship had not begun

easily. They both were elected to the Senate in 1948, Johnson by 87 votes in a recount. Each side in Texas accused the other of voter fraud and both were probably right. Johnson's people just stole a bit more. Johnson had been in the House for 12 years, functioned as a "good old boy." In the Senate, he quickly cozied up to Senator Russell and other Southerners to whom Humphrey was, of course, anathema.

It seems that Johnson arrived with the goal of being the Democratic leader as soon as possible and, indeed, even as a freshman, was elected whip, then minority leader, and became majority leader when the Democrats took control after the 1954 election. That he had the support of the Southern senators should indicate how safe on civil rights they thought he was. Humphrey, of course, did not support him or vote for him. He led the liberal forces—four votes—and was clobbered by Johnson who counted votes better than Humphrey. Johnson then adopted and co-opted him as his liberal conduit, and a 10-year productive working relationship was begun.

At the Republican convention in mid-July, the Republicans had selected Senator Barry Goldwater, a conservative whose supporters had booed Nelson Rockefeller, a competitor for the nomination, and prevented him from speaking. It was a spectacle that emphasized Goldwater's undiluted record.

Back at our convention, after Humphrey was routinely nominated, he gave an acceptance speech with a litany of good things that had been voted for or favorably discussed in the Senate and then followed each with "But not Senator Goldwater." It was good theater and smart politics. His audience chanted it with laughter that night and later wherever Humphrey appeared during the campaign. (It is still remembered today when highlights of old campaign speeches are repeated.) That the Republican nominee had once described the atom bomb as "merely another weapon" also helped.

I looked forward to the campaign: many cities I had never seen, large crowds, endless cheering and waving and jumping. Politics. But I got what I thought was a demotion even though it was described as important. I was told that the Senate office must continue to function well and that I was to be in charge and would remain in Washington. It was an empty honor earned by my good work.

Instead of gulping meals and suffering indigestion, there were pressure-free lunch hours and undisturbed dinners. Instead of the fatigue and strange beds in dreary hotel rooms I had hoped for, I slept at home and woke up refreshed and sad. I wasn't really where the political action was. I missed a lot.

During the campaign, Mrs. Humphrey went to Georgia for a reception organized by Jimmy Carter's mother, Lillian, and sister, Gloria. Waiting to enter the hall, Mrs. Humphrey suddenly asked if there were any black women in the group. If there weren't any, she wouldn't be either. Gloria said she would go check, probably knowing well what she would find. She had the waitresses remove their aprons and scatter through the crowd. Jimmy Carter, then in the Georgia state senate, later acknowledged it was the first integrated political reception in Georgia that he knew of.

Carter would run unsuccessfully for governor in 1968 before being elected two years later. His '68 campaign was liberal by Georgia standards, apparently even on race questions which reflected his personal actions, including having black friends in his earlier years. He finished a distant third in the primary.

Despite my isolation in Washington, when the Johnson-Humphrey ticket won, I felt I had made a great and indispensable contribution to the massive victory. It is impossible to describe the exultation that comes when the first television announcement makes victory almost official. It was not a surprise, but it was a breath-taking, heart-pumping moment anyway. The ultimate proof comes when you suddenly notice Secret Service agents next to where Humphrey is sitting and at the doors to the ballroom where we began celebrating

Unfortunately, I did not know then what I soon learned. Lyndon Johnson was a good president, maybe a great one in some historians' eyes, but he was a miserable human being. His behavior patterns were described in a letter to him when he was himself vice president. Jim Rowe, who had known him since 1937 when Johnson was elected to the House of Representatives and a young Rowe worked for Franklin Roosevelt, wrote it.

Rowe was a decent, generous, and politically wise man, maybe unequaled by anyone I have ever met, and had a deep commitment to good democratic, and liberal, government. I assume that as a Washington lawyer, he used his influence on the Hill, but I doubt it was ever destructive to the public good. What I saw when I got to Washington and met him was a rare Washington bird, interested in an improving society and decent laws more than self-interested in profit or status.

Rowe had written to Johnson during the 1960 campaign: "I have not seen you pay one compliment, thank one person. I have seen you do nothing but yell at them.... Maybe you do not know it—I do—the morale of your staff is awful. They are in tears, all of them; they are beginning to dislike you intensely. They cannot do anything right, they don't dare make a decision about where to hang your clothes even, and they bend their heads and wait for the blows to fall—like obdurate mules who know the blow is coming."

He goes on, "It makes me so goddamn mad at you, I'd

like to sock you in the jaw." Rowe had a solution and suggestion: "One day a week, go up and down that plane and tell George Reedy and Bill Moyers and the stenographers... that you appreciate what they are doing for you . . .. I have a feeling that at present you are caught between vanity...and a curious lack of self-confidence about your judgment of men." Then he laments, "This is probably the end of an old friendship. But somebody has to say these things. And I will say one more thing I didn't mean to say—lay off that booze."

I don't know if Rowe's frank talk had any impact, but I doubt it. The inevitable separation of the two campaigns in 1964, keeping the principals apart, each campaigning in different states, meant Humphrey and our staff were beyond any immediate capriciousness from the Oval Office. Separation permitted our hearts to grow fonder. But the election and the succeeding years made it possible to judge, and made my appreciation and respect diminish.

When the 1964 campaign was over, the people had spoken clearly: "Not Senator Goldwater." Goldwater carried his home state of Arizona by about a point, and five Deep South states—Mississippi, Louisiana, Georgia, Alabama and South Carolina—by more. In Mississippi he buried us, getting almost 90 percent of the vote and in Alabama near 70 percent. We expected it that way in those two states and took it less as rejection than affirmation that there were real differences, and we were right.

The election was not close. My work in the office paid off. The popular vote for Johnson and Humphrey was 61 percent to 39 percent. The Electoral College vote, 486 to 52, said landslide. It was beyond a simple election. It seemed a mandate.

9. Working for a Vice President

After the election, the FBI did a full-field investigation of all the Humphrey staff. That meant, as I later understood, multiple agents doing multiple interviews in multiple places where you had ever lived or worked. I should have anticipated that some of my old activities would be noted or already in a file. But, the various sins of my past were far behind me, and I couldn't recall relevant new ones. If I had thought about it, I would have hoped that the FBI had found the guy who sneered at me as a "vacillating bourgeois." But I didn't think much about it.

After a decade in the DFL, I hardly saw myself as a revolutionary or out of the mainstream. I had been a student of Ray Dunne once upon a time and was still a quiet admirer, but I was certainly no longer a follower. The only people who took me seriously as a radical were the FBI agents. Their work reminded me quickly that "long ago" was, indeed, not forgotten.

Soon after the election and before the inauguration, Joe Dillon, then mayor of St. Paul and a long-time DFLer, told me a disconcerting story. An FBI agent who had been a classmate of his at St. Thomas College came to interview him about the

Humphrey staff. Joe apparently said nice things about me. A couple of weeks later, the same agent came back and told Joe what he had learned about me elsewhere. He asked Joe if he didn't want to change what he had said, offering to toss the earlier interview aside as though it never existed, inviting a less favorable assessment.

Joe said he told the agent there were no changes he wanted to make. He stood by his earlier comments. I thanked him and thought how wonderful FBI procedure was to be able to discard the positive statement, solicit a negative one, and all in the interest of national security, thus saving the country from rabble-rousing people like me.

I wasn't done as suspect. A couple of days after Humphrey was sworn in, he got a call from Marvin Watson, a top aide to the president, who asked him to come over. Humphrey, reacting to the portentous tone, thought it was an important call about something vital. He dropped what he was doing and moved quickly across West Executive Avenue, the street that divided us from the White House in more than physical ways. Portentous turned out to be petty.

Watson got immediately to the point. He shoved a file folder across the desk and said, "This guy's FBI file is about five times thicker than any other one on your staff. Do you really want to hire him?" When Humphrey got back, more slowly, he told me, all grins, about his conversation and said, "I just pushed it back without looking at it and said yes." But he added, grin gone, in mock seriousness, "I knew you couldn't come through clean." Then he broke up.

That was not the last of the FBI in our lives. Deke DeLoach, the deputy director and J. Edgar Hoover's liaison to the White House, came around our office from time to time, but never visited me, asked me anything, or noted my existence. I did not expect any relationship and did not miss it. In retrospect, however, with my "background" I might have been a source of information as much as, maybe better than, any of my colleagues. I could have told him how a couple thousand of us SWP fans could have manned the barricades. Or, considering our numbers, a single barricade.

DeLoach seemed to have one continuing mission. He whispered stories of Martin Luther King's extramarital activities. He did not explain how the FBI's sleazy voyeur work protected our national safety or why they spent agent time and federal money in their bizarre pursuit of irrelevant details of a public man's life or even why they were following him. The tomcat label has often been applied accurately to a number of men (including John Kennedy) during their elective careers. Political power is a strong aphrodisiac, but the beneficiaries always take it as personal recognition of their distinctive charm. One wonders whether the white folks had FBI files as big as King's or whether black leaders had a special appeal to J. Edgar Hoover.

My first real moment directly with the agency was educational, of sorts. I went with Humphrey to a graduation ceremony for new agents where Hoover, as well as Humphrey, spoke. I noticed that there was an agent standing next to every light switch in the auditorium. It seemed odd since we were inside the heavily protected FBI headquarters.

I later asked a former agent who had worked in the central office if he knew why the light-switch vigilance. He told me that at a similar event in the same place, someone had brushed a switch and the lights in one area had gone dark. It had apparently scared J. Edgar, and he vowed it would not happen again.

Had I known more about Hoover I might have expected it. I learned then that he was a compulsive nut about inter-office memos. If an error crept in, the memo was returned to the sender with a pink slip attached. That meant that everyone connected to it would be punished in some manner: a note in a personnel file, a pay raise delayed for a penalty period.

The former agent, my undercover informant, said there was a worse tag—a yellow one. If Hoover had a question about a memo, it came back with a tag to call attention to its importance. "Everyone began running around in near panic, sometimes trying to figure out what the question precisely was," my agent recounted.

One story that may be apocryphal is that a memo came back with the fearful yellow sticky on it and a note: "Watch the borders." No one was sure what it meant, but agents were alerted in offices near the Canadian and Mexican borders, even if no one knew why or what to watch for. In fact, there was no national emergency. The memo to Hoover had been typed with the margins too narrow. That my agent told the story was proof enough for me.

I also learned from a journalist that when Hoover spoke at any event, if there was a press table just in front of the podium, each chair was filled by an agent. As a journalist approached, an agent vacated a chair. Too few journalists meant more agents taken from real work. Hoover did not like to speak to an empty seat so close by.

Despite all that, I was still aglow from the inauguration ceremony. I stood in the cold weather with thousands of others in front of the east portico of the Capitol, warmed by the scene. There were no down moments, no time to worry about tomorrow, the future, and certainly not J. Edgar.

At that moment, my focus was entirely in front of me. I felt the ceremony was what democracy was all about—continuity, a better society for all the people, a more perfect world. And I was not embarrassed by the tremor I felt when I heard, "I do solemnly swear..." uttered by someone I knew.

Even the pomp and circumstance were moving. The Marine band played "Stars and Stripes Forever," a black woman, Leontyne Price, sang "America the Beautiful." The Mormon Tabernacle choir, filled with blonde heads and innocent faces, inspired us all with the national anthem. The prayers were tolerable.

Humphrey stood facing Speaker of the House John McCormack, who would swear him in, his hand on the Bible held by his best friend, Freddie Gates, with the president and chief justice nearby. Transcendent is a cliché, but apt. I stood among thousands moved by what we saw and heard, and I could not have been happier or more certain that days of national and personal fulfillment were imminent.

Escorting Humphrey at the Minnesota State Fair, 1966

But the years that followed were not so unambiguously thrilling. Moments of misery intruded, most of them unnecessary, diverting attention from serious work. I have thought that there was a divine signal early on. A traditional dinner for a visiting head of state took place soon after the inauguration. Senate debate had run longer than expected and Humphrey, in his role as president of the Senate, was delayed. When the Senate finally adjourned, Humphrey took a quick shower, dressed hurriedly in his tuxedo, jumped into his limousine for the short trip to the White House. He went upstairs a back way to join President and Mrs. Johnson, the visitors, and his wife for the ceremonial entrance down the stairs. The glamour of the vice presidency took his normal exuberance higher than usual.

At dinner, he felt a little uncomfortable. When Johnson toasted the guests and all stood, Humphrey realized that he had put his undershorts on backwards and was bunched where he shouldn't have been and tight where he wouldn't want to be. He told us the dinner was the longest one he had ever attended.

Discomfort midst ceremony was just beginning. Jim Rowe's Johnson, a willful, capricious, and an unrelentingly angry man, was often present. Humphrey naively thought his independent judgment in serious policy deliberations was why he was there, but Johnson brooked no independence.

Soon after he became vice president, Humphrey spoke at the annual Gridiron Club dinner. The club, founded in 1885, has a limited membership of top D.C. journalists and holds an annual dinner where a prominent political celebrity gives a funny speech. That night Humphrey was the speaker and made a prescient joke: "The president looked at me and said, 'Hubert, do you think you can keep your mouth shut for the next four years?' I said, 'Yes, Mr. President,' and he said, 'There you go interrupting me again.'" Much laughter that night; far less ahead.

Though more than a year had passed since the assassination, Johnson was haunted by comparison with the martyred president. He was not John Kennedy. Lyndon Johnson's speaking style, even when he announced major accomplishments like the War on Poverty or Medicare, was generally pedestrian and ponderous. He seemed to have a voice and a soul without poetry or passion. He drew applause as a president will, but the reaction often lacked real intensity and any affection.

Kennedy, on the other hand, could announce he was going to the bathroom and the crowd would cheer, clap, and a few folks might shed a tear. He moved with grace, he spoke with feeling, real or feigned; he grabbed an audience with his smile and charm. He certainly was often no more liberal than Johnson, but Johnson roared and Kennedy soared. Some of that jealousy may have accounted for the distemper he too often showed to Humphrey. Humphrey, out of loyalty, rarely spoke about what he would encounter and have to endure. He just took off in search of a role.

About a week after the inauguration, he was in Tucson, Arizona, for several public events, one on an Indian reservation, another a visit to a Titan Cruise Missile site at Davis-Monthan Air Force Base in Tucson. I was with him in an elevator that took us up alongside a missile that seemed about 100 feet tall and could reach Moscow, if that were its target, in less than half an hour.

A nuclear warhead sat atop the missile, a bit too far away to touch, but close enough to induce shivers. For Humphrey who was such a proponent of nuclear disarmament to be that close to a warhead that could take out a city and all of its inhabitants was chilling for him as it was for me.

The surroundings didn't help reduce that feeling. It was explained to us that there were two enlisted men and two officers in the underground command post so that one man, in a crazed moment, could not hit a single button and send the missile off. It would take two crazed men to hit two buttons separated and out of the reach of one, or two sane guys following orders. It was unreal in its reality.

The language surrounding nuclear missiles is fascinating. They are housed in "silos," a benign word usually used to describe a farm building for storing grains. They are "cruise" missiles, not deadly weapons aimed at a target thousands of miles away, but seemingly as casual as a boat trip up the coast. The command post is in a "hardened" facility, a description that hardly suggests that it was built to protect the missile and men from incoming enemy explosives.

For Humphrey who had been for years the strongest, and sometimes almost the sole, spokesman and advocate of disarmament and the Nuclear Test Ban in the Senate, it was a reminder of failure to gain lasting support for something that consumed him. The missile was then, as Vietnam was a bit later, a distressing companion to his new role.

Tucson brought another learning experience. The Secret Service came to Humphrey at the hotel to say a man on their list of people to be watched had disappeared from his home with his rifles. They urged Humphrey to move rapidly from the hotel doorway to his car since there was an office building across the street with many rooms and many windows. They had checked it, found nothing, but were still worried.

As we came out of the door, Humphrey spotted a crowd of cheering people across the street. Being who he was, he could not resist. Leaving agents in a sweat, he dashed across the street to shake as many hands as he could before the agents almost wrestled him to the motorcade.

Not long after the Tucson visit, Humphrey quietly raised his doubts about our Vietnam policy. At his first National Security Council (NSC) meeting in February 1965 believing we ought to get out of Vietnam, he opposed our bombing of Hanoi as national security adviser McGeorge Bundy, a carry-over from the Kennedy administration, strongly urged. That was Humphrey's last opportunity for a year to advocate withdrawal, or at least to draw down our troops. The president wanted affirmation, not discussion then or later.

Taking his role as vice president seriously, Humphrey had spoken to both Secretary of State Dean Rusk and Secretary of Defense Robert McNamara ahead of that first meeting hoping for their support. He didn't get it, but thought for a moment that he might not have any opposition from them. He did have two allies in Undersecretary of State George Ball and Ambassador to the United Nations Adlai Stevenson, although I am not sure they were in the meeting. (Humphrey gave the president a memo outlining his opposition to the war dated February 25, 1965, that I have included as Special Section 2.)

Johnson responded with some form of a theme he frequently used, "I have two son-in-laws over there." His reaction was immediate, deep, and angry. It precluded any further questions or discussion. Unfortunately, by making it personal, it ignored a president's deeper responsibility to every son or son-in-law whose lives might have been protected by more discussion. The roles of father and president may be similar, but they are not the same and should not have been confused, particularly with such piety.

A mute Rusk and a silent McNamara spared themselves ostracism or firing. Humphrey's views were obscenities in church to the high priest. I sometimes wonder how different would our policy in Vietnam have been if Humphrey could have made his case regularly and often. A single voice, but a persuasive one, might have saved many American lives and the country much torment.

That he ultimately gave in and became a cheerleader for the Johnson policies was sad. He did say, "I did not become vice president with Lyndon Johnson to cause him trouble." In face of presidential anger, Humphrey internalized his feelings, destructively, I think, knowing it was either ardor or continued oblivion. He intensely wanted to be where decisions were made, to be involved, to offer his views. That had been his life in the Senate and what he had hoped would be his role in the White House. But he knew his isolation would continue unless he mollified one man. It was a bargain with the devil.

Vice presidents' isolation and exclusion were, of course, not new. In all of 1961, Johnson spent about 10 hours alone with President Kennedy and in 1963 not quite two hours. Years later, when Walter Mondale became vice president, he saw President Carter several times a day, often spent hours with the president in the Oval Office. He had unrestricted access to the president himself and access to all of the president's private classified information. Key presidential aides and cabinet members responded to his questions. His opinions were taken seriously even when they did not totally agree with the president, and he was never excluded for expressing his opinions.

In a minor way, Carter also treated Humphrey better than Johnson did. The presidential retreat, Camp David, was a short helicopter ride away from Washington and Johnson's favored guests would go there for a social, but often also substantive, weekend. Humphrey was never invited. Only when he was fighting his fatal cancer and would soon return to Minnesota to die and there was a new president did he savor what had been denied him. Carter, in an act of respect, invited him up for a few days of conversation and friendship.

But Johnson was not Jimmy Carter. The decent gesture seemed to elude him. Difference was disloyalty and a punishable offense. In Humphrey's case, Johnson had politically castrating ways to show his displeasure. Since the vice president is a member, by statute, of the National Security Council,

Johnson held no more NSC meetings to discuss Vietnam, substituting informal discussions or more formal meetings called anything but NSC, if they had any designation at all. Humphrey was neither informed nor invited to important discussions. He was a vice president in proximate exile. A week, sometimes even longer, would often go by without his having any contact with Johnson. Staff took their clues from Johnson. Once Humphrey scheduled a meeting with a top domestic aide, Joe Califano, who was in his early thirties and prematurely arrogant. Humphrey arrived on time, but Califano kept him waiting for almost an hour before seeing him. There was no explanation or excuse. Joe, comfortable with simple rudeness, knew there was no penalty, and maybe joint glee if he told Johnson what he had done.

Johnson did not stop with his arbitrary behavior on Vietnam and other major issues. He took the time to be petty, matters of no consequence becoming his bludgeon of the day. Johnson directed that Humphrey travel in a small jet, devoid of glamour, too small to comfortably carry more than a couple of journalists along. The exit door was small. Anyone Humphrey's height had to bend slightly for a moment to deplane. Somehow the excitement of his arrival was diminished a bit by his posture. In lighter moments of reflection, I have thought he might have won the presidency in 1968 if he had arrived previously in dozens of cities upright and smiling, waving a step earlier to the crowd and cameras. First impressions count. The top of your head is not a good first impression except for your barber. (When Mondale was vice president, he traveled in a Boeing 727. It didn't help elect him, of course, but he didn't look stooped.)

But someone at the White House, if not the president himself, had even less important games to play. We were issued baggage tags soon after inauguration day, possibly by the Secret Service so that they might spot luggage that didn't belong. The tags had your name and "The White House" on them. They impressed baggage handlers, taxi drivers, and your parents. They were suddenly recalled, replaced by a different color tag without the House designation.

The dining room for staff was declared off limits. Entrance to the White House itself was permitted only when the person requesting your presence put your name on an admission list each time. Showing your identification was not sufficient.

Vice presidential cuff links provided by the Democratic National Committee were not expensive, but looked even less so when they were suddenly in a little plastic bag held closed by a staple instead of a box with tissue paper. None of that was important, but did reflect an unspoken, omnipresent, put-down.

Once the election was over, the question of staff, of who would do what, how we would function, was, of course, central and immediate. Many of my colleagues were graduates of prestigious universities with significant experience in some field. Without pause, each followed his expertise into a defined responsibility. I had no claim on any domain.

I learned that the vice president is by statute a member of the National Aeronautics and Space Council. The Council was created when Dwight Eisenhower was president, but he apparently didn't much like it and urged that it be abolished. It was an advisory body, with limited influence, if any. The director, in our years, of the National Aeronautics and Space Administration (NASA), James Webb, cared for it less than Eisenhower did. Both apparently thought it could only be a nuisance and interfere with the real programs. President Kennedy put his vice president in charge, apparently to give him something to do and Humphrey inherited the duty under Johnson.

Our vice presidential payroll was limited, and some staff had to be on an agency or department payroll. I latched on to the Council, parlaying my vast scientific background in a submarine factory and with a thermostat titan. That was more than anyone else could claim on the subject. On the rare occasion when the vice president had to deliver a space-related speech, I drafted it. And whenever he went to a space-related event, I went along. That meant visits to Cape Canaveral to witness the lift-off for several space shots, an exciting adjunct to my normal day. It also brought me an abnormal day.

Just after astronauts James McDivitt and Ed White's flight that involved the first extravehicular walk in space, the Paris Air Show took place. The show began in 1909 and continues today, every odd year, to show off what is new in the air, attracting publicity, buyers, air buffs, and just people from around the world. (In a recent year, 3,250 journalists from 80 countries and about 350,000 others attended.)

A CIA agent attached to our office in a peripheral way came to me and said that the CIA anticipated our being wiped out by a new, huge Soviet plane that would capture headlines and impress visitors, but, he thought, all that publicity would disappear if McDivitt and White could be sent over. We had little time since the show lasted only a week starting almost immediately. He also told me that the policy then was that astronauts would not be used for any purpose except space exploration. James Webb had made the policy and was adamant about it. His men, he insisted, were not public-relations puppets.

When I explained it all to Humphrey, he told me to write a memo from him to the president and that he would give it to Bill Moyers, who was then on the president's staff, as the conduit. The answer was back almost immediately from the president. It was a succinct, unambiguous no. That was on a Monday. On Wednesday, I went back to Humphrey and said we were right and the White House wrong. He told me to draft a second memo. We heard even less this time—no response at all.

On Friday, the president invited diplomats from all the embassies in town to the State Department to see the film of an astronaut floating in space. He also sent word that Humphrey should be there. The film was impressive. Diplomatic reserve disappeared when the astronauts themselves were introduced. There was a long, standing ovation and cheers in many languages.

When Lyndon Johnson followed with a short speech, he announced that the vice president and the two astronauts were leaving the next morning for Paris. No warning. No prior suggestion it might happen. It was a surprise to Humphrey, kept a secret for no good reason. His chain had been yanked and he jumped. I had to jump higher.

I had never been out of the country. I had no passport. I am not sure I had a clean pair of socks, but I suddenly had about eight hours overnight to get ready. We took off by helicopter from the White House lawn, waved away by the dour president and one of his cheerful daughters.

The CIA guy was right. The astronauts' arrival immediately relegated the Soviet super plane to the publicity hangar, out-of-sight and largely out-of-mind. For me, it had already been a breath-taking trip over the ocean to Paris in special company. The excitement was constant and increased when we ultimately got to our seats in the grandstand. Applause sounded at our every step, every nod, every wave.

When we were seated, someone told Humphrey that the Soviet astronaut, Yuri Gagarin, was also in the stands. Humphrey immediately led our astronauts toward Gagarin, only to be stopped by a State Department officer who said he should not do that; it had not been authorized. Humphrey didn't push him, but moved him aside with his eyes. We went down the steps to where the Russian delegation was seated. Humphrey shook hands, introduced McDivitt and White to his new friend, Yuri, and the crowd went nuts with applause and shouts that wouldn't stop.

That night, our ambassador, Charles Bohlen, took us to a posh restaurant where upscale, elegant folks were eating and drinking. When we entered unannounced, they, recognizing the astronauts, were all instantaneously on their feet, clapping and cheering as the grandstand crowd had. It was a spontaneous outburst of sophisticates that I would later describe to my CIA instigator with great, shared pleasure. He had been right, and without him none of that would have happened.

During that difficult first year, Lady Bird Johnson often invited Mrs. Humphrey to lunch or for an informal visit. They had been long-time friends as Senate wives. Now, they bonded more since they were two and not a hundred. Out of that continuing friendship, by December, Mrs. Johnson apparently pressured her husband into mildly resurrecting Humphrey and involving him, although not on Vietnam. Without her, the isolation and exclusion might have continued.

And while the embrace was not enthusiastic, Johnson had Humphrey do what vice presidents do, travel around the world on state visits, often as much show as substance, but in this case a kind of rehabilitation process as well. Anything would have been welcomed. For an activist senator with great expectations who was now sitting on the sidelines, Humphrey's new role as vice president, theoretically a promotion, had been more than tough.

Speaking of his empty honor, although not in those words, he would often get a laugh in a speech by reminding his audience of great vice presidents who had preceded him: Charles Fairbanks, James Sherman, William Wheeler, Hannibal Hamlin, and Garrett Hobart. (Sadly, today when I speak of Humphrey, as I often do, some people don't even know his name. Not long ago, a delivery man needed a phone and I took him into my office where there are pictures on the wall. My daughter, Susan, calls it a "shrine to myself," as it may well be. The guy asked whom I was with in one and I said, "Hubert Humphrey." It drew a blank. I said he had been vice president under Lyndon Johnson. Another blank. Then he spotted someone he recognized. "That's Fidel Castro.")

At the end of the first year, I became press secretary when the man who had held the job was let go, victim of the bottle. I was given the job on a temporary basis. Bill Connell, without whom I never would have been hired in the first place, told me that they didn't want to embarrass the person leaving and would publicly say that we were readjusting and condensing the staff. Our arrangement was that if Humphrey was comfortable with me in the roll and I liked being there, I could remain as the permanent press secretary. My life changed.

Briefing Vice President Hubert Humphrey aboard Air Force Two, 1966

I suddenly became more attractive. I was invited to dinner and parties by newfound friends—journalists of stature or at least well-known. It became an exciting adjunct to my day job. One day Sander Vanocur, a bright and friendly television reporter and star on NBC, invited me to dinner. I asked if I could bring my girlfriend. He said he was sorry, but they limited their dinners to six people, and another couple and a State Department official, my date, were coming.

The other couple turned out to be Nick and Lydia Katzenbach. Nick was the federal official during the Kennedy administration who in June of 1963 faced off with Governor George Wallace of Alabama. Wallace blocked the door of at the University of Alabama that was to be integrated, and Katzenbach led the race-barrier breakers past him. I admired him. Later, he became Lyndon Johnson's attorney general.

His wife came from an establishment family. Her father had served in the White House when Herbert Hoover was president; an uncle had been canon of the Washington National Cathedral. She was used to a kind of glamour and high places and politely ignored me at the beginning, tough to do at a table for six.

At one point, the others were discussing some issue about which I knew nothing. They asked for my view of the (now forgotten) matter, and I said that I did not have an opinion. Lydia said, "I hate people who have no opinion." I was silent, but thought it nice that I had finally made an impression on her.

While we were still eating, the phone rang and the cook in the kitchen answered it. She pushed open the kitchen door, and said, "Mr. Vanocur, it's the White House." Sandy excused himself, and all of us were impressed, although not quite as much as he. In a moment, he was back and said, "Norman, it's for you." I don't remember the meal, but that was a delicious moment.

After dinner, we played a word game. Really. Sandy and his wife had gone through an unabridged dictionary finding words they thought no one would know. We were to write down a definition of the word. I didn't get the fact that it was meant to be serious and wrote silly, funny, absurd definitions. Lydia did not hate me less for my jokes. At least that is my opinion. The game was called, and the evening mercifully ended after a short period.

But, during the day, I was now central, not peripheral. I was the voice, not a whisperer. I had opinions. I took to the role with an almost embarrassing eagerness, but was warned firmly that we could do nothing that seemed to compete with the White House. We were an adjunct and a subsidiary. It was a tight rope I walked with my lips, not my feet, an unnatural exercise for me.

Not long after I began my new role, a major newspaper reporter asked a question that belonged to the White House for an answer. Remembering my instruction not to wander into higher domain, I told him, "You have me confused with George Christian (Johnson's press secretary). I'm Norman Jewish." On another occasion, not involving the White House, Humphrey slipped on a freshly mopped floor in the lobby of his apartment building and broke his wrist. Bill Connell told me to get the story out quickly to prevent any speculation that Humphrey had been drinking. The first reporter I called asked if he would be canceling any speaking engagements. I said, "For Christ's sake, it's his wrist, not his tongue." It was not printed, but moved verbally to other press, and back to Humphrey. The wrist made the news. I did not.

I had a second new role. I got married again. During many of my post-divorce years, I had wanted to be married. I had been single for about 15 years, and I missed the companionship of a wife and a family. I had decided, in the abstract, what that wife should be: good looking, young, smart, and Jewish.

One day, a friend who was a judge in Minneapolis, Howard Bennett, called me to say his daughter had a classmate at Radcliffe College who wanted to work in Washington. He asked if I would meet with her and help her find a job. I happily agreed. When the classmate showed up, I soon knew that she had all four qualities I yearned for. I was not sure where I would find her a job, whether she was worth hiring, but I decided to marry her though I was almost twice her age.

I did get her a job in the Humphrey office and set out to woo her and win her. I was successful, and in a couple of months, we set a marriage date. Before we married, several of my colleagues and friends came to me to say they thought I was making a major mistake, that what I saw was not what others saw and suffered. My quick decision appalled them.

If that were not enough, her mother—my future mother-in-law—added to the exciting time. She declared that she would not come to the wedding if either the vice president or my children, evidence of my earlier marriage and advanced age, attended. I foolishly compromised on the kids—they would not attend the ceremony, but could come to the reception that followed. I held out hope for Humphrey. She, a nasty, unyielding Republican, stood firm, and I was not able to invite him.

One day, after he got his schedule for the coming weeks, he stopped me in the hall outside our office and said, "Norman, your wedding is not on my schedule and you know how quickly it fills up." I said, "Mr. Vice President, you're not invited." He laughed, waved a dismissive hand, and went on to wherever he was headed.

A week later, he stopped me and said again that the wedding

was not on his schedule, and I responded with the exact same words, "Mr. Vice President, you're not invited." Same reaction: a grin and a wave. Another week went by and the encounter was re-enacted. This time, I added a bit. "Mr. Vice President, when I say you are not invited, do you know what I mean? You are not invited." I explained about the mother-in-law and, taken aback, he said he had not intended to embarrass me. I allowed as how it was not he who had embarrassed me. We each laughed a hollow laugh.

Several weeks later as the fateful Friday approached, Evelyn and I had a last heated discussion with her parents. They urged us not to marry. Urged understates it. (Oh, why didn't I listen?) Despite the rancorous confrontation, we were determined to go forward. A couple of days later, the gracious mother called to say it was okay if Humphrey came. I wanted him there. I had insulted him three times. It was the day before the wedding and, indeed, his schedule had filled up.

I spent a couple of hours unable to make up my mind on what to do. I finally went into his office and told him what had happened and that he was now invited, though certainly did not have to come. He did not pause a second. He said, "Tell Ursula (his scheduler) to cancel my afternoon appointments. I'll be there." The ceremony took place in the living room of the house where Evelyn lived. There was a rabbi and a *chupah*, a cloth canopy that stands, with some religious meaning, over the heads of the rabbi and wedding couple.

Humphrey entered, trailed by Secret Service agents who were friends of mine and had been selected on that basis by Humphrey. He embraced the bride, warmly greeted the rabbi whom he knew, then spotted the mother-in-law out of the corner of his eye. He moved in on her, seized her hand, and told her how wonderful her daughter was. I swore I heard the elastic in her underpants snap. She beamed. It seemed, at that moment, she was part of my good fortune. Purgatory had disappeared. I thought.

She remained a periodic part of my life. If the vice president's travels took him within about 200 miles of her home in New Hampshire, she showed up, announced to a Secret Service agent, "I'm Norman Sherman's mother-in-law. I want to see the Vice President." She didn't ask to see me.

Earlier, in addition to the press job, I had lucked out with another assignment. Humphrey asked me to advance his trips overseas. That meant going out ahead of time to make arrangements: where he would stay, whom he would see, what he would do, and equally important, what he would not do. I was asked, in effect, to see strange new places through his eyes. I had to work with our embassy personnel and someone from the host government—all pretty serious people.

I advanced almost two-dozen countries during the vice presidential years. I generally led a four-man team: a State Department protocol officer, a communication specialist, and a Secret Service agent. When the advance was over and Humphrey arrived, I reverted to my press secretary job. It was heady stuff as I worked Vietnam and six other countries in the Far East, five countries in Europe, and nine in Africa. Each country brought unique experiences.

In Vietnam, General William Westmoreland would not see me, although our ambassadors and other top officials in every other country would, some merely as a courtesy, some to work on the schedule with me. One ambassador even picked me up at the airport so we could have more time to talk alone.

I needed Westmoreland, not the ambassador, in a war zone. I had the benefit of counsel from Herbert Beckington, a Marine officer who had been the vice president's first military aide as the result of a Max Kampelman suggestion. Max had gone from conscientious objector about 20 years before to the Marine Corps reserve and had met Herb.

Herb, after a short time, had asked to be reassigned to Vietnam, knowing his future in the Corps depended on his serving there. He was right. He ultimately became a lieutenant general and second in command of the Corps. Without his Vietnam service, that wouldn't have happened.

In Saigon where our planning took place, Herb would suggest a visit to a particular place, explain why we should go there in a rather innocuous way, and I would put it on the schedule. The tentative schedule would go in to Westmoreland, and each time what Herb had suggested would have been eliminated when it came out. After several deletions, I learned from another officer that Herb wanted us to see places where the war was going poorly, despite reports to the contrary. He wouldn't confirm for me what he was doing, not wanting to be seen as disloyal to his duty and position.

So we saw what military brass wanted us to see. Had we been able to follow Herb's leads, I am not sure what effect it would have had. Having just come out of exile, would Humphrey have embraced a point of view or produced a report that Johnson did not want to hear? Resurrected to a vice president's life and role, he would have found it difficult to speak out on his return. The memory of his first efforts to change our Vietnam policies and its consequences for him could not be forgotten.

But even what he did see was tough to ignore. We visited a field hospital where soldiers wounded not 15 minutes before were flown in by helicopter, hauled on stretchers into little emergency rooms with waiting doctors. Some would survive; some would not, and as Humphrey went from bed to bed visiting yesterday's survivors he fought tears and was clearly shaken. He saw bravery and blood, disfigurement and possible death. He couldn't and didn't change his public statements about the war, but having to follow his political brain, not his compassionate heart, was a debilitating burden for the rest of his term.

One day, we were scheduled to fly to the Demilitarized Zone, or DMZ, where the two Vietnams met. The ambassador, Henry Cabot Lodge, patrician and cautious, was scheduled to be with us, but some of our military guides laughed and told me he would come up with a minor illness and would not be able to go. They were right. Lodge had been appointed by President Kennedy, who had beaten him when Lodge sought reelection to the Senate from Massachusetts. Lodge had proposed that South Vietnam become a protectorate of ours, as the Philippines had. It was an idea that died almost as soon as it was spoken.

My group of press and I almost stayed back with Lodge. We were to fly in a second plane just ahead of Humphrey and the military brass and embassy people who were going along. The reporters were gathered around an officer as I came up from dealing with other things. The officer was telling them it was a dumb thing to do: we would be low enough to take ground fire, there was nothing to see except tree tops, and we would come as close as a plane could to a 90-degree turn to get us out to sea quickly and out of danger. The press, as chicken as Lodge, were muttering assent.

I moved through the press up to the officer and said, "Major, I'm in charge here. We're going." It was a bit of braggadocio since I had no authority to decide anything at that moment. We boarded the plane, flew to the DMZ, saw nothing except those tree tops, and got the hell out of there as quickly as possible. The rumor came soon after we landed that we had, in fact, taken ground fire. I denied it, didn't check it carefully at the moment before the stories were filed, but I think it may have been true from what I learned later.

Another evening, the vice president and Ambassador Lodge were to attend a reception with Ky and Thieu, the South Vietnamese leaders. I decided I could pass since I had work I could do and wasn't much for receptions anyway. While I sat at a desk with my military escort nearby, I heard a thump, thump, thump. I asked my expert companion what the noise was, and he said, "Oh, it sounds like out-going artillery." He was right about the cause; he was wrong about the direction. It was in-coming. I took a bathroom break when another officer corrected him.

(Later, I was shown a CIA document from 1964 that read: "Thieu is considered to be loyal to only one ideal – his own personal aggrandizement. It is felt that Thieu will stoop to anything, stop at nothing, in his drive for self-advancement.")

In Saigon, Tom Wicker of *The New York Times*, unable to sleep, wandered down in the middle of the night to the empty press room. He found a pile of press releases intended for distribution on the plane as we left the country. He took one and filed a report. I didn't know what Tom had done until we were airborne and other journalists found out about their being scooped. They would not be able to file their own stories until several hours later after we landed. Suddenly, Phil Potter of the *Baltimore Sun* was standing in the aisle towering over me at about 6 feet 4. He screamed, "You goddamned whore for the *Times*." He continued, clearing up any ambiguity about how he felt. What had actually happened through no fault of mine was no defense. He tried to get me fired.

We also visited Indonesia. On my advance, I met the

ambassador, Marshall Green, who gave me a quick audience and dismissed me into the hands of his top assistant, a guy named Jack Lydman. Green was, I think, a fancy rich dude married to a princess—or least she thought so. I did not meet her until our entire group arrived.

But her presence was felt immediately. My advance team and I sat with Lydman as I worked out the schedule. Almost the only absolute order I got from Humphrey was that I not schedule him doing some social event with other countries' ambassadors. He felt they, with rare exception, were probably not major players in their own countries. Meeting them took time away from the country he was visiting and had no substance or lasting value. It was not part of why he was where he was and a handshake, a smile, and a hello were a waste of limited time.

(Humphrey later explained to me what you did if you were trapped in a receiving line. As you shook hands, you put your left hand on the right shoulder of the person in front of you and gently moved the person along. It was a friendly gesture, the greeting was shorter, and the exercise over sooner.)

Mrs. Green thought the meet and greet was necessary. She was, apparently, a bit of a social butterfly and wanted exactly that kind of event where she was the visible hostess. Lydman suggested a reception, and I said we would not do it. When we were finished with our tentative schedule, he took it into the ambassador. When he came out, the event I had forbidden was back in with a slightly different description. We went through all the changes, and I once again took the event in question out.

Lydman went in a second time and came out with yet another version and tried to justify its presence. I leapt to my feet and almost shouted at him, "Mr. Lydman, I have the sense I am pissing in my own ear." Lydman was smoking and in his shock at my undiplomatic language inhaled in a gasp that made him cough and turn red.

I don't know where the line to Lydman came from. I had never read it, thought it, or said it. I was as surprised as my three serious associates, who tried to keep from laughing. When we left, they all guffawed as they patted me on the back.

Years later, I was at a party in a fancy neighborhood in Washington. Among the guests was a career foreign service officer. We were chatting about something when he suddenly pointed at me and grinned, "You're the guy who told Jack Lydman that you were pissing in your own ear." He had trouble stopping his laughter, and his wife responded as though she had heard the story before. A lasting State Department audience pleased me, an unexpected bit of immortality.

Not all the trips were so unsettling. Europe brought a variety of more relaxed pleasures and experiences. When we were in Rome, clearly Humphrey had to have an audience with Pope Paul VI, and I had arranged it with Bishop Marciniak (formerly of Chicago), my Vatican guide and counselor. Their talk would begin with a private audience of a serious nature, and then Humphrey would ask the Pope if he could present members of his traveling party and his staff. The Pope would say yes.

Humphrey, with one exception, took only Catholics in with him, including Secret Service agents who swapped shifts and duties at his suggestion. As he introduced each one with some details of duties or relationship, they would get a papal blessing and a crucifix. One member of our staff, David Gartner, was as devout as one could be, seeking a Mass on Sunday morning if the schedule permitted anywhere we were in the country or world.

As David stood in awe before the pontiff, Humphrey explained his role in agricultural matters, feeding the hungry, and concluded, "But, your Eminence, I simply cannot get him to go to Mass." The Pope got the joke; David could not as his mind went blank, his protruding ears turned red, and he could only open his mouth as nothing came out. The Pope took David's hand, blessed him, gave him his crucifix, and said in English, "My son, you must go to Mass."

About two weeks later after we had returned, David got a call from his mother who lived in Des Moines, Iowa. She had heard from her local priest that the Pope himself knew that David was a delinquent Catholic. Bishop Marciniak, not blessed with a sense of humor, had heard the exchange, taken it seriously, and called a priest in Chicago, who found the priest in Des Moines, which set the shocking call in motion to David's mother.

But Rome had other, less holy, moments. One night, the Humphreys and the ambassador, his wife, and young daughter went to the renowned Rome Opera. Standing at the entrance to welcome his special guests was the impresario, Angelo Carlucci, rotund, jowly, and formal. He bowed deeply as his guests came near, and as he did a plastic bag of yellow paint was thrown by an anti-Vietnam protestor, one among a group of jeering young people, including some Americans.

The bag hit the wall behind Carlucci, burst, and splattered yellow paint. The Secret Service agents pushed the illustrious party into the building while I did an obstructing dance to keep a *Time* magazine photographer from getting a picture. A Secret Service agent had vaulted the hood of our car in an Olympic move to aggressively grab the protestor who had tossed the paint. With the wrestling over and the picture prevented, I went inside. An agent who never smiled much less laughed, at least when he was on duty, was doubled over with a wide grin on his face. I said, "Walt, what the hell are you laughing at?" He asked, "Did you hear what the vice president said to Carlucci?" Humphrey had asked, "Does this happen to you often?" Carlucci, gesturing with his hands moving up and down, said with an accent, "Not-in-a-thirty years." Humphrey later explained that he was just trying to make his host feel better, and that was what came out.

The scene of an agent manhandling the guy who threw the paint was unique. I had never seen an agent physically restrain anyone, even when there might have been good reason to do so. I grew to like most of the agents and to admire them all. When your job is to take a bullet if it protects a candidate or office holder, no moment is casual. It is pressure every minute while you are on duty with no time to relax. When I wrote an article on the Service in 1974 for the *Washingtonian* magazine, I learned that during the 1972 campaign the presidential candidates made 2,447 trips with 6,163 stops. Agents spent 703,800 man-hours in advance and on the scene. Today with more candidates and more travel, those numbers must be far greater. (Current stories of Secret Service behavior make me wonder where my agents have gone.)

A doctor who had studied agents said they displayed the same symptoms that he observed in combat fighter pilots. He found "mental and physical exhaustion brought on by extremely prolonged periods...under constant tension." Yet they rarely gave in to the pressure. Beyond the angry screams of obscenities and threats, our agents also had urine poured on them on several occasions. One exasperated agent, not on our detail, punched a protester in the mouth, breaking his own hand. He was reprimanded and given some time off to heal both physically and emotionally.

Not every stop was traumatic, although protestors did seem to be everywhere. In Paris, General (and President) Charles de Gaulle hosted a lunch for Humphrey. It was limited, and I did not attend. A guy from the Embassy handed Humphrey his toast to de Gaulle and France just as the group was about to go in to the meal. Humphrey read it hurriedly and didn't like it. It was largely a litany of things the U.S. had done for France. He tossed it aside and ad libbed a paean to France and what it had meant and done for us. He thought he saw the imperial de Gaulle tear up for a moment, moved by the generous *merci* for deeds long past.

(Years later, and after Humphrey had described in his own book what took place, one of my colleagues declared, among other absurd things, that he wrote "both speeches," a pretentious description of a brief prepared toast and a spontaneous one. Done without a desk, without a typewriter, without time, without a place, it would have been a miracle. Self-approval and glorification is a chronic disease in Washington that gets worse as time passes. Skepticism is the reasonable first reaction about anyone's story, except for this one.)

I also met a real king. The King of Belgium hosted a lunch just after we arrived in Brussels. Our visit was the last stop on the trip, and I was weary and getting sick. At our previous stop, I asked the State Department officer traveling with us to take me off the attendee list. He said he would, unless someone of "my rank" was needed for balance.

When we stopped in the palace driveway, others got out while I slumped in the back seat of the car, quite out of it. Suddenly, an embassy officer came dashing alongside the cars, half-shouting, "Sherman, Sherman." When he spotted me, he said, "Get out, get out. We need you." In an indecorous way, I ran up the steps, saw a couple standing at the door, and extended my hand, shook his, and announced, "Hi, I'm Norman Sherman."

When a third person standing nearby said, "Your Highnesses," and led them in, I felt sicker. It was the king with the queen alongside and fortunately just out of reach. You do not touch royalty in a familiar way and never address them so informally.

Later Humphrey, the king, and I were alone together among the crowd before going in to lunch. The king asked what my role was for the vice president. I said, "I'm the court jester." The King smiled. Humphrey didn't and gulped out, "No, no, he's my press secretary." I explained later to Humphrey that I was not applying for a new job, and he said he thought I should consider it.

On that same European trip, we had lunch at No. 10 Downing Street, the hallowed home of British prime ministers. Harold Wilson, prime minister at the time, was an old friend of Humphrey's, and the two them and their wives later had dinner with the queen and stayed the night in Buckingham Palace.

At lunch, I was seated between two titans of British

Vice President Humphrey at television news appearance, 1965, with the inscription: "To Norman Sherman—a man who gets things done and does it with good humor and competence—many thanks, Hubert H. Humphrey"

journalism. If one didn't own the major paper of some town, the other probably did. My companions were Lord Thompson of Fleet and Sir Arnold Goodman. As the meal went on, they began to talk of the selling and purchase of a paper. I was reasonably ignored and finally broke in and asked, innocently, "Since I am literally the middle-man, do I get a commission on this sale?" The response was simultaneous and a definite no.

Europe was like a history class of known places. Africa was not. One day Humphrey called me into his office and said the president was sending him to Africa. As usual, he wanted me to advance the trip that was to be about two weeks long. My advance work would run three.

I told him I couldn't do it, that my marriage was touch and go, and that if I were away for five weeks, it was doomed and certain to end. He asked a couple of questions and then said he understood that I could not go. I felt I was letting him down, but that I had no option. We parted shaking our heads. I was sad on several counts, failing him, missing a new continent and new countries, all of that for an uncertain and unhappy relationship with my difficult wife. He was disappointed because he had come to like my preparatory overseas work.

The next day, Humphrey called again and asked me to come to his office. He said, "What if I brought Evelyn along as my guest? You would be gone three weeks, but she's interested in Africa." Other guests were close friends, titans of industry, people of status in our country, including recently appointed Supreme Court Justice Thurgood Marshall. That was pretty good company. I said I would try the idea on her, suspending any reservations I had. She agreed to that arrangement, I thought, with some delight at the honor. My marriage was saved. I could fulfill my duty. I relaxed.

We were to visit the Ivory Coast, Liberia, the Congo, Zambia, Ghana, Kenya, Somalia, Ethiopia, and Tunisia. The central purpose of the trip was the swearing in of President Tubman of Liberia, a kind of ridiculous man who had served a number of terms. Indeed, a book on the country titled *Top Hats and Tom-Toms* had recently been published documenting his behavior and the country's.

The State Department made all the arrangements for housing and transport. I never had to give any thought to how I would go or where I would stay. But Africa was different from my other trips. It is not only a huge continent, but the countries I would visit were far apart. Direct commercial flights from where I was to where I needed to be were often not available and on the airlines' schedule, not mine. To solve all that, someone at State arranged for an Air Force DC-6 (and two crews totaling 13 men) from a base Germany to fly me around. No one told me.

Coming from the U.S., I landed first in Ivory Coast on a commercial airliner. The next day while I was working in the embassy, I got word that a colonel wanted to see me. When I walked into the office where he was waiting, he threw me a formal military salute and said, "Sir, so long as you are with us, you have the equivalent civilian rank of brigadier general."

I smiled inside at that ludicrous promotion, but said with a straight face, looking as serious as I could, "Well, under those circumstances, I would like to be called general whenever I'm spoken to." He took the "order" with a snappy, "Yes, sir." (How could he not?) After a couple of days with all the crew calling me general, I had to explain that I had not been serious. Not everyone across the world got the word.

When we flew from Ethiopia to Tunisia, we had to refuel in Greece because we couldn't fly across the Sudan and go directly to Tunis. We were at odds with Sudan; no diplomatic relations meant no overflight. On the plane, exhausted from my work and lack of sleep, I tried to catch up. I slept in a T-shirt and rumpled khaki pants. When we landed in Athens,

I was unshaven, bleary-eyed, and a mess. Standing at the top of the ramp to get a glimpse of the country, I saw a car move quickly out from a nearby building and zoom to a halt at the bottom of the steps. A young Air Force corporal came dashing up to where I stood, got face to face with our noses almost touching, and whispered, "Which one is General Sherman?"

When I pointed at myself, his eyes widened in disbelief, but like my colonel, he had to believe me. "Sir, your car is waiting." With me still looking like a bum, we set off to the office where more high-ranking officers welcomed General Sherman with their own higher-ranking disbelief.

My arrival in Tunis was not quite as wonderful, but nice anyway. When I got to my hotel and approached the desk, I saw a board with events of the day. It had only one line: "Cohen Bar Mitzvah—Lower Level." I had an undelivered speech I wanted to give the Bar Mitzvah boy, but wasn't invited.

At the end of my advance when my crew flew me back to Liberia where Humphrey's visit would begin, the crew held a ceremony with mock formality to say goodbye and present me with a one-star metal insignia about 15 inches wide. It was meant to be affixed to the bumper of any car this brigadier general rode in. (I have it yet, but it stays in my garage on a wall, not on a car, and no one salutes it or me.)

When Humphrey's plane landed, I watched as he and honored guests came down the steps. I saw my wife in line a few people behind them all, and as her feet hit the tarmac, I raced toward her with my arms extended for an embrace to make her feel welcome in a special and loving way. As I got close to my anticipated hug, a foot or two away, she barked, "When we get home, I want a divorce."

I put my arms down and said, incredulously, "You came all this way to tell me that?" She said, "Yes," and moved toward the motorcade. I went to look after a small group of press who had come with Humphrey, hoping, I think, that she would die en route to the hotel and I could leave her at the roadside. I was pained, certain to be humiliated in the days ahead, and grossly bewildered.

I went on, doing my job, smiling on the Humphreys and guests and press, spending vital bedtime hours arguing with my hostile companion. It was a trip made in hell, but we all got through it. (Our marriage lasted a year or so longer because I was too busy to end it earlier.)

In Somalia, on my advance, I had located a school a distance outside of Mogadishu where most of the teachers were Peace Corps volunteers. Afgooye, the town, seemed perfect for a visit, super visuals with young faces, hands-on American involvement, appreciative faculty and townspeople. On my way out of the country, I read a State Department description of the village. It was the malaria capital of the universe, and Humphrey had a bit of a germ fetish. It was too late to cancel the visit without embarrassment, so we went, and Humphrey managed to shake hands with dozens in a receiving line virtually without touching. It was quite a feat. No one got malaria and we survived the trip.

Somalia had other charms. On the advance, Glenn Weaver, the head of our Secret Service detail, and I checked out the rooms in the official guesthouse where the Humphreys would stay. The canopied bed had a mattress that sunk down in the middle deep enough that even an able bodied young person would have had trouble getting up and out. I wasn't sure the sheets had ever been washed.

As innocently as we could, we asked to see the best hotel in town. We were taken to their skyscraper, a building of four or five stories. All the rooms had the same window style—open with moveable wooden slats. Before we could make a firm decision, we were told by an American embassy person guiding us that two American businessmen had stayed in adjoining rooms on our chosen floor several weeks earlier. One, getting ready for bed, heard some sounds and then an insistent knock on his door. When he opened it, his associate, in panic, pointed to a bat hanging from his neck. Glenn and I decided we would make the trip a day visit without an overnight.

The Africa trip was hard work, but it was almost a vacation for Humphrey. Heads of state seemed pleased, maybe honored, by his presence and delighted by his embracing warmth. For them, he symbolized America at its best, and he found welcome in both private and public events. There was excitement and satisfaction in being vice president of the United States. The periodic misery and ambiguity of the previous months were far away.

At home, his work as vice president was to carry the message of the administration as defined by Johnson, and that is what Humphrey did with a vengeance. There was one point of view, one idea of success, a focused mission to gather support or acclaim for what had already been decided. That included Vietnam. Inside discussion had proven to be problematic. Outside, differences were unacceptable and unspoken. On several occasions, people working with Johnson quoted him as saying of Humphrey in his Texas drawl, "Ah got Hubert's pecker in mah pocket." Reporting the insult to Humphrey, as some did, brought the whisperers the risk of exile, but they whispered nonetheless.

I have often thought of Eugene McCarthy in that context. In 1964, he was more than eager to get the nomination for vice president that Humphrey ultimately got. Gene knew Johnson well, was dutifully obsequious in the Senate as most everyone was, and hoped that he might be kept in consideration since he had not yet voiced any public alienation from our Vietnam policy. He had disdained John Kennedy openly, but he bowed to Johnson and seemed loyal to him.

Despite his later, almost holy, mission to get us out of Vietnam, I think beyond question that had Johnson selected him and not Humphrey, Gene would have tucked his courage in his back pocket and kept his eye on a more possible presidency. If that required acquiescence, as it did, he would have acted in his distinctive and attractive style, but he would have toed the Johnson line. What was theoretical for him was real for us as the vice president reached for some productive role.

Peckerless or not, there was domestic travel for Humphrey to praise the administration policies, including Vietnam. There was a lot of domestic policy and executive activity to praise and his words came easily and strongly. Vietnam was another matter. He became not an explainer, but a public enthusiast. His need to please Johnson added decibels to his voice. To say the country was filled with anger, distemper, disgust with our war policies understates the visible malaise.

When the administration had raged about a North Vietnamese attack in the Gulf of Tonkin on a U.S. destroyer on August 2, 1964, only two senators, Ernest Gruening of Alaska and Wayne Morse of Oregon, said it was a set-up by our military to invite retaliatory attack. Both Humphrey and McCarthy were silent in the Senate. (Humphrey was not quite mute elsewhere. He gave an intensely hawkish speech in Los Angeles just two weeks after Tonkin, praising the president, justifying American presence in Southeast Asia. While many people heard it, it probably had an intended audience of one.)

The number of troops soon rose from almost 19,000 "advisers" under John Kennedy to several hundred thousand,

and ultimately to half a million "boots on the ground" troops, although Johnson had said, "We seek no wider war." From 1964 through 1968, 35,000 Americans died. In the next two years, under Nixon, over 15,000 more did.

(I think presidents, at least subconsciously, like the title Commander in Chief. Most in our time, except for Dwight Eisenhower, have been governors or senators and being president seems just a career move up. But military authority is different, and supreme authority insidious. George W. Bush, the self-styled "decider," declaring "Mission Accomplished" about Iraq may be the best example of the delusion, but there have been others.)

On our Johnson-Humphrey watch, several people in protest had doused themselves with kerosene and set themselves on fire. Student protests grew larger and more widespread. On a single day, preach-ins, the discussion of the war, on 122 campuses involved 100,000 students and faculty, most of whom would have undoubtedly been Humphrey supporters in another time, but saw him now as nothing more than a mouthpiece for whatever Johnson decreed.

People everywhere in the country grew increasingly disillusioned with our presence in Vietnam and administration explanations. Against that backdrop, Humphrey soldiered on. Political gatherings, state conventions, fundraising dinners for governors, visits to schools and universities, some civil rights meetings took us around the country. He met with editorial boards of newspapers. There were press conferences, but there was never to be any reaching for a new program, a new solution or a new vision that had not come from the White House.

Humphrey internalized whatever doubts he had. I rarely heard a questioning word, even when I knew it must be there.

It is likely that some other policy staff heard more, but the chance I might inadvertently say something to a journalist about his doubts was sufficient, and proper, for keeping me at a slight distance.

Increasingly for Humphrey as he moved around the country, for every smile there was a frown, for every cheer, a louder jeer. Vietnam was more than a distant war; it was a proximate, constant aggravation for many. It overwhelmed anything good happening domestically. We could not escape it. Police would put up barricades not just at meeting sites, but at hotel entrances to keep the protesters at a distance. We were never beyond the angry shouts, the screams of rage, even the throwing of human excrement when we visited Stanford University, an elite college where you might expect booing, but not what we got. No arrival or departure anywhere was easy.

At one hotel, the barricades were much too close together, giving us clear passage of only a few feet. It was a horrid few seconds where contorted faces filled with hate were within breathing distance. When we got upstairs, I saw a smile cross Humphrey's face. I asked why he was smiling, and the grin grew larger; "I got one in the balls with my brief case." That he thought it was satisfying, and I thought it was deserved, says something painful about those years. Lyndon Johnson would have approved, but have asked in a sneer why Humphrey hadn't gotten two or three more.

My work in the vice president's office was often demanding, and frequently repetitious. I rarely felt the excitement I had in the Senate in a lesser job, nor did I sense that good things were happening nearby, or that I had even a useful peripheral involvement. We were parrots, not eagles. We sat in a cage; we didn't fly high. I was not certain I would enjoy another four years, although I, of course, gave no thought to quitting. Routine intruded. And that had to be okay.

For Humphrey, 1967 had been a bad personal year as well as a difficult political one. His brother, Ralph, had died, leaving the family drugstore without anyone in charge, and Humphrey felt he had to be not only vice president, but a part-time pharmacist at a distance. Muriel had spent some time in the hospital, and Humphrey himself had a difficult bladder infection. It was a precursor of the next year. Personal bad went to political worse.

Campaign poster of Muriel Humphrey, 1968, with the inscription: "To Norman Sherman with affection and, yes, great admiration for a loyal and dear friend without whose 'spark' and imagination the way would have been more difficult. Muriel Humphrey"

10. The Year From Hell

1968 began as a year from hell with the Tet offensive. The North Vietnamese scaled the walls of our embassy in Saigon, an embarrassing moment that couldn't be explained away. It was complemented, before and after the year began, by protests across the country, by assassinations, riots, mayhem. To anticipate more years of such turmoil was a nightmare, not just for the leaders, but for the rest of us as well.

The previous three years had been sometimes fulfilling, but sometimes not. Humphrey as vice president looked on with a sense of accomplishment, at least by proximity: the Voting Rights Act, Medicare, the War on Poverty. There were satisfying moments filled with a sense of effectively helping carry the liberal message as he had for 25 years. On the other hand, it was a time of war and civil unrest across the country. It was also living with Lyndon Johnson's style and the near-daily burden that arose from being his sidekick. Real and lasting satisfaction was elusive and rare.

Suddenly everything was different. Sunday, March 31, was a day unlike any other in Humphrey's life, and certainly, by proximity, in mine. The morning began for me in a pedestrian way. I gathered my clothes, my toothbrush and other toiletries, and packed my bag for a flight to Mexico City where Humphrey would sign a Western Hemisphere nuclear non-proliferation treaty.

Humphrey's day began with a bit more excitement. He answered an unexpected knock at his apartment door, and there stood Lyndon Johnson on his way home from church with his daughter and son-in-law. He could have called ahead or had a Secret Service agent do it. But he didn't. Presidents don't often knock on doors, but Johnson did that morning.

For Humphrey, it seemed odd, but nothing more than an unexpected, unprecedented visit, a social call. Johnson quickly indicated that he wanted to talk to Humphrey alone. In the den with the door closed, the president said that he was considering two possible endings for his speech scheduled for that evening and then read them aloud. One would announce that he would not run for re-election, but he wasn't yet sure if that was the one he would use. Humphrey, he cautioned, must not share what they were talking about with anyone, including Muriel.

That he was considering not running was a surprise, but quite understandable. He had come through a difficult primary period. He had not done well in New Hampshire and Wisconsin, barely winning, and the McCarthy campaign had been energized by the narrow margins; then Bobby Kennedy announced on March 16 that he would seek the nomination. Kennedy had tried to get McCarthy to withdraw, but, not surprisingly, failed. McCarthy had long disdained all the Kennedys, including, maybe particularly, Bobby.

In 1960, during the presidential primary in Wisconsin, the Humphrey campaign had printed a pamphlet describing John Kennedy's votes on farm issues. They were not very good for a Midwest rural audience. McCarthy, campaigning for Humphrey, bumped into JFK in a hotel corridor. Kennedy whipped out a copy of the pamphlet and said of the attack, "This is awful." McCarthy, ignoring what he meant, quickly responded, "Oh, it's not so bad for a senator from Massachusetts." I wasn't there, but heard about it soon after from one of the participants.

In 1968, McCarthy and Kennedy primary votes combined would have left Johnson with fewer votes in state after state. Even without that, the anti-Johnson votes seemed certain to bring further political humiliation, if not clear rejection, to Johnson. That would have been insufferable for any president, but with Johnson's personality, it was clearly beyond what he could endure even if he scraped through.

The president knew that Humphrey would be in Mexico and told him to be sure to listen to the radio broadcast of his speech. Then he headed back to the Oval Office, embracing Mrs. Humphrey as he left. Soon after, we took off from Andrews Air Force base as we always did when on official business. None of us knew of the meeting and, thus, not a glimmer of what had gone on or might happen. Nothing in Humphrey's body language, nothing in his behavior gave any of us a sense of something out of the ordinary happening. It was just another long, ho-hum flight.

That night there was a dinner for President Gustavo Diaz Ordaz at the American ambassador's residence, and as the time for the speech neared Humphrey, the ambassador, Diaz Ordaz, and their wives separated from the rest of us and went into the library. Just moments before we all would hear the president's voice on the radio, Humphrey had gotten a phone call from Marvin Watson. His message was delivered succinctly: it was to be the second ending, saying to the country that Johnson would not run again.

All of us were huddled in little groups around the various

static-filled radios set up in several rooms. When I heard the surprising words from Johnson, I took off running toward the library. Another staff guy in another room did, too. We collided breathlessly and without dignity in front of the door, almost knocking each other off our feet in our ludicrous quest to be first at Humphrey's side. When the door opened, Humphrey beckoned me in and gave me orders on what to say and what not to say.

My unexpected moment in the spotlight was brief. The few Mexican and American press with us soon gathered around Humphrey himself. They simultaneously babbled questions about whether Humphrey would run and got elusive answers. The dinner went on as did the treaty ceremony the next day, but it was an extraordinary time. Our dreams of glory could have kept the plane in the air on our flight home.

Monday night we were back in Washington, greeted at Andrews by three cabinet officers, Dean Rusk, Willard Wirtz, and Orville Freeman, and a few other excited Humphrey friends. Rusk's presence was odd. He was not as close to Humphrey as Freeman and Wirtz, who were long-time friends and liberal political activists. I have thought it might have been expiation by Rusk for his muteness when Humphrey by memo and in a National Security Council meeting raised questions about our Vietnam policy.

An exuberant, but also restrained, Humphrey was soon off to his apartment. Six of us—Bill Connell, Bill Welsh, and I of our staff, Max Kampelman, Gus Tyler from the AFL-CIO, and Dick Maguire, an old John Kennedy hand—spent a couple of hours talking about what Humphrey should say immediately, what he would ultimately do. Some thought he should announce without hesitation that he would be a candidate. Others shared his inclination to delay. To move too quickly might make him look like someone dancing on Johnson's political grave, thus inviting his living wrath. The meeting ended where it began: no irrevocable decision, and thus no immediate announcement.

We had to decide what each of us should do during the following days. Inevitably I would be barraged by press inquiries and would need to be informed, disciplined, and careful to say nothing that would offend the president. I was to duck and dodge, regret the president's decision even as I silently applauded it. I tried and, I think, succeeded. It wasn't easy. Humphrey might not want to dance on the grave, but I did.

(Humphrey's loyalty was not reciprocated. In a biography of Nelson Rockefeller published in 2014, historian Richard Norton Smith wrote "Nelson and Happy were smuggled into the White House for a private dinner with Lyndon Johnson, who strongly advised Rockefeller to abandon his coy stance and become an active candidate." Rockefeller said, "He told me he could not sleep at night if Nixon was president, and he wasn't all that sure of Hubert." That took place in April, less than a month after the host of the evening withdrew from the presidential race.)

Our euphoria was short-lived. On Thursday, April 4, Humphrey was to be the main speaker at a major fundraising dinner for the Democratic National Committee. The hotel ballroom, sporting bunting and signs, was packed with a thousand well-dressed, noisy, political people. It was a jolly gathering, just a little tense so soon after Johnson's withdrawal, but with rhetoric that looked forward, not back. It was exciting for the audience, and even more so for me. Humphrey, uncertain, couldn't announce his candidacy, but that couldn't keep the audience from thinking they were probably seeing their next Democratic candidate for president.

I was at a table far from the podium with other

non-contributors when a Secret Service agent appeared and asked me to come with him. We went to the back of the room, and he quietly said that Martin Luther King had been shot and was in critical condition and not likely to survive. He thought my telling Humphrey would be less noticeable or attention getting. At the head table in sight of everyone, I whispered the news so no one else could hear. Humphrey asked me to prepare a statement for him in case the worst came to be. I was hardly back in my seat scribbling words when the agent came again to tell me that Dr. King had, indeed, died. I carried the news to Humphrey along with my quickly written draft.

When the death was announced, the noise stopped, people spoke to each other quietly, if at all. A few cried, but not the Alabama businessman who was the chairman of the event. He had worked hard to gather people and money, and saw no reason to adjourn the dinner. Everyone should get his or her money's worth. Humphrey stepped around him to the microphone and announced the evening over, giving the short statement he had written when he found my draft inadequate, not quite what he wanted to say.

(Later at home, I thought of the day when President Kennedy was shot. I had a lunch date with a reporter for a St. Paul paper. When she called to say she couldn't make lunch, I went alone and coming back overheard a conversation on the elevator that didn't make much sense to me. When I walked into the office, I learned what had happened. Everyone was crying and all the phone lines were ringing. They continued to ring until well into the evening. People from Minnesota needed to talk to someone and tried to speak to their "Hubert." Shock needed comforting and several hundred callers seemed satisfied to talk to staff.

Everyone needed comfort. Long after, I read in Orville

Freeman's diary that he, as a cabinet officer, visited the new president shortly after the assassination. Johnson complained that the Kennedy family "had paid no attention" to him.)

The day after the King assassination, Humphrey was scheduled to give a mid-day speech to a business group on Long Island. In the late afternoon as we approached National Airport on our return, the pilot told us that the airport, already under military guard, was to be closed as soon as we landed and asked us to come to the cockpit to see why. Heavy smoke billowed from Anacostia, a largely black ghetto, and from downtown. To see the city burning as we made our final approach was surreal. The riots that followed in Washington and other cities around the country were tearing the country apart. It was no time to start a political campaign, but we had no choice. We had to move. Exactly when was the problem.

There were constant questions from the press. There were frequent urgings from political people. Potential donors like things settled so they can plan where they will contribute. We offered neither a yes nor a no. It seemed like indecision to some, but it wasn't. It was a calculated dance. Our confidence, and delay, was founded on numbers. We were certain at that moment that we would have all the convention votes needed unless something untoward happened. A state primary defeat by McCarthy or Bobby Kennedy might damage or even destroy our lead.

We had support where it mattered. Most governors were for Humphrey and were usually able to determine how most, if not all, of their delegates at the convention would vote. Beyond that, the two major public opinion polls at the time had Humphrey clearly in the lead among rank-and-file Democrats, but too close for absolute political certainty. The Gallup poll had Humphrey at 40 percent, Kennedy at 31 percent, and McCarthy at 19 percent. The Harris poll had Humphrey at 38 percent, Kennedy at 27 percent and McCarthy at 25 percent. Both polls showed only 10 percent undecided.

We had other favorable numbers. A Gallup survey of Democratic county chairmen, people at the grass roots, showed 70 percent were for Humphrey, only 16 percent for Kennedy, even fewer for McCarthy, just 6 percent. That was a vital measure.

It made no sense for Humphrey to take a chance on the primaries, particularly remembering his embarrassing, unsuccessful 1960 run against another Kennedy. Humphrey did not have the Kennedy mystique and aura, the possible fuel for being overtaken and suffering a Kennedy come-from-behind victory if we goofed up or Bobby Kennedy took hold. By waiting, we also saved money that was in short supply, saved energy by skipping a constant dash around the country, and avoided any even minor possible misstep that might harm our chances, including somehow offending a sensitive Johnson.

With the country as shaken with riots as it was, any campaigning was tough. On a trip to Cleveland, the white mayor, Ralph Locker, was a special problem. He had gone to black neighborhoods a couple of days after the riots in an armored car and just drove through without getting out of his car. When Carl Stokes, a black leader intending to run against the mayor in the next election, set up a church-sponsored rally for Humphrey deep in the ghetto, the mayor first objected and then sent in mounted police to protect us.

Stokes had an agreement with the more militant blacks, the Black Panthers, not to cause us any trouble and just to stand by without being hassled. The horses were sure to inflame and cause trouble. That morning I got a call from the Secret Service agent in charge asking me, with some desperation, to get the horse patrol cancelled because it could only inflame those who had agreed to silent protest. Before I could get that done, he called back to say he had taken care of the situation by telling the police captain in charge that if the horses weren't removed within the hour, he was going to start shooting them.

Stokes had also arranged for a Cub Scout troop connected to the church to stand in a greeting line. It was a tiny bit of peace and welcome; the kids were dressed in their uniforms, their smiles and excitement unambiguously welcoming. I had dropped back to accompany Mrs. Humphrey as I often did. I spotted one kid up the line whose uniform was in disarray, cravat off center, shirt creeping from his pants, and his glasses somewhat askew. As Mrs. Humphrey shook his hand, he said, "Hi. Miz Kennedy." Mrs. Humphrey almost hugged him as his error relieved the tension a bit.

During that same period, I had lunch with Mel Elfin, the Washington bureau chief of *Newsweek* magazine, at The Assembly, McCarthy's frequent lunch restaurant. Gene was sitting up at his regular place at a table on a riser along the wall. He waved when I came in and sat down with Mel. After a bit, Elfin asked me, "If you had one word to describe McCarthy, what would it be?" I thought for a silent moment and then said, "Mean." He was also silent for an awkward moment and then asked if I knew Frank Mankiewicz, my counterpart in the Kennedy office. I said I had met him once, but that was the extent of our "friendship." Frank later became a friend, but at that point, we hadn't really talked about anything. Elfin said he had asked Frank the same question the previous day in the same place with McCarthy at his nearby table. Frank had answered, "Mean." Suddenly, for a moment at least, "Clean Gene" became "Mean Gene" by unanimous vote.

Humphrey finally announced his candidacy when it was too late to enter any of the primaries. As he described his vision for the future, he talked of the "politics of joy." It was a natural expression of his exuberance, his own pleasure in the political process and governing, but it seemed to many as inappropriate considering the chaos of the year. It haunted us when our political world, and America's, suddenly got worse. Humphrey was to give the commencement address at the Air Force Academy on June 5, the day after the California primary. It was a moment above the political fray. He was speaking as the vice president to officers who might soon be in Vietnam. We stayed in officers' quarters the night before. Tired and no longer needed, I went to my room in a building next door to Humphrey's.

I had barely fallen asleep when there was a loud knock at my door. Our advance man, D.J. Leary, opened the door, bounded in, breathlessly shouting, "Bobby Kennedy has been shot!" I leapt from bed, got dressed, and dashed over to Humphrey's room where he like much of America was watching TV. Shortly, through the Secret Service switchboard, he was on the phone talking to Pierre Salinger, a Kennedy aide, in Los Angeles. Tears rolled down his cheeks as he learned how dire the situation was. Soon after the first call, Pierre called back to ask Humphrey's help in getting an Air Force jet to fly a neurosurgeon from Boston to Los Angeles.

Humphrey called the Pentagon and told the duty officer what he wanted. The officer responded, "Sir, under what authority are you ordering this plane?" Humphrey shouted, "I'm Vice Commander-in-Chief." It was an office that did not exist, but it worked. The doctor was soon in the air, but he arrived too late to help.

The next morning Humphrey had visitors, responding to his decision not to give the speech, but to take the podium, congratulate the graduates, and then stop. The secretary of Defense, the top general at the Academy, and a couple of other officers made brief speeches calling on Humphrey to change his mind. Their argument was that these were soldiers on their way to Vietnam to defend our country and deserved Humphrey's encouraging words. If there was an ounce of human emotion in any of them about Kennedy's murder, it was not apparent. Humphrey was visibly bereft, but they continued until he, politely, but firmly, sent them on their way.

Days of mourning led to a suspended campaign and sapped the joy and drama from the pursuit of the nomination. Presidential ambition had driven Humphrey for a long time, and now the pursuit seemed almost inappropriate. The "politics of joy" became an albatross, not a rallying cry. It now seemed fatuous.

Though he had the nomination in hand by any count, he suddenly seemed a diminished victor by the death of his chief rival. Bobby Kennedy and he had not been close friends early on, but Humphrey respected him and understood his political glamour. In an interview in late fall of 1967, he had told a reporter that if Johnson were to die and he became president, he would ask Robert Kennedy to be vice president. He also said that, assuming a second term for Johnson and Humphrey, he thought 1972 was Kennedy's year. "Bobby has everything going for him. He's young. He's got the name. There is what he has done in his own right." All that was now moot.

After a couple of weeks, Humphrey asked his friend and Kennedy's campaign manager, Larry O'Brien to join us as ours. They had gotten to know each other well during the John Kennedy presidency when O'Brien was on the White House staff, visible always, and respected. Their friendship grew when O'Brien became a member of Lyndon Johnson's cabinet.

Some old Humphrey hands wanted the job and only

begrudgingly accepted the appointment, but O'Brien was a national figure of great political skill and experience. I did not know him and was surprised by his selection, but it was a sensible choice and a good one for our campaign.

After several weeks of mourning, the campaign began again. Nixon was enough to get most Democrats everywhere going, and we had a long way to go if there was to be a Democratic victory. Our campaign went smoothly for much of the time, but sometimes not. Shouted interruption, dramatic and noisy walkouts, signs of rage and distemper were inescapable companions to the good times. (One read, "Hitler, Hubert, Hirohito.") We looked forward to the national convention as a welcome moment of affirmation.

The convention was held later than usual since the date had been set when it was assumed that Johnson would run again. He, as a sitting president, didn't need, or want, too much time in a candidate's role. At his direction, the convention was scheduled to coincide with his birthday on August 28. Regardless of the date, it should now have been an exciting time for Humphrey and his supporters.

But the repeated misery and devastation for the Kennedy and King families made politics ugly and difficult for political survivors as well. None of that was avoidable, but holding the convention in Chicago was a disaster waiting to happen. Several strikes, involving both telephone workers and taxi drivers, were scheduled for maximum impact during the convention. Communication is vital, but it became difficult and sometimes impossible. We had hoped, in fact, to get the convention moved at the last minute to Miami where the Republicans had been and where necessary infrastructure was still in place.

Walter Mondale, as co-chair of the campaign, called

Chicago Mayor Richard Daley, a curmudgeonly and difficult man inordinately proud of his city. It was a holy site in his eyes. Mondale suggested the move with little hope and he was, of course, right. As a fallback, he suggested that special activities and places be provided for the protestors. Daley immediately refused the move and said to Mondale of the expected demonstrators, "We will give them every courtesy." His sneer was almost visible over the phone.

The convention took place in the midst of chaos. Grant Park, across the street from our hotel, was filled with antiwar protestors, both young and old, exhibiting a variety of attitudes and behaviors, from peaceful and prayerful to shouting, threatening, belligerent, all of them irritating and indistinguishable to the already hostile police with their dogs and batons, unrestrained anger, and paddy wagons

Some of the demonstrators were pacifists, deeply antiwar, carrying signs, satisfied that their presence was sufficient testimony to their beliefs. Some were hippies, determined to put on their show of the absurd, particularly when one of the abundant television cameras aimed their way. Many were angered by the Johnson-Humphrey administration's bellicose behavior in a far-away land. Newspaper estimates at the time said there were 1,000 National Guardsmen on the street and 5,000 demonstrators in the park. There were another 4,000 guardsmen elsewhere, all called up because the governor anticipated "tumult, riot, or mob disorder."

The demonstrators all looked the same to the protectors of the peace who were sometimes out of control in what was later described as a police riot. For most of them, with their parochial view, it was all a continuing affront to their city, their own patriotism, their belief in the war as an extension of American virtue. Smacking a demonstrator with a baton was in their eyes not a brutal, but a responsible, act. If they couldn't hit them, they shoved them around. Sometimes while mounted on their huge horses, they would swing hindquarters into the crowd. Over 100 people were injured in Grant Park alone, 25 of them policemen. At the convention site, *The New York Times* reported that there was a mile long chain link fence with barbed wire at its top. Manholes in the area were tarred shut to keep out non-existing bombs. Of the 3,000 protestors who marched on the hall, 150 were arrested.

At one point, the vice president leaned out of a window in his suite, smelled a whiff of tear gas, saw the entire surreal scene from on high—tiny figures moving around, jumping one way and then another. If it hadn't been so appalling, it could have been a cartoon scene of turmoil. Voters in their homes saw the same scene, up close and vivid. Humphrey shook his head in dismay, unable to speak as we both saw the election going to hell on horseback and at the end of a stick.

Our main problems were major and visible, the consequence of Daley's anger at the protestors, but there were less visible ones, too, growing out of the petty vindictiveness of Johnson. Humphrey's son-in-law, for example, had to get in line with the general public to get tickets for the family, except for Muriel, for the nominating session that night. Johnson's minions, still in charge of the convention, were apparently doing his bidding, or at least what they thought he would like.

A more serious demonstration of Johnson's presence and influence had come earlier on Humphrey's effort to find a Vietnam peace plank that would start to heal the party and country. Humphrey knew he needed acceptance by Kennedy people (which he got with significant help from Mondale's lobbying Ted Kennedy), McCarthy people, and more enthusiasm from others who only begrudgingly supported him. The peace plank was a vital way to get them, maybe the only one. He cleared the language he wanted with administration representatives and felt we were on our way to consensus, even if a fragile one.

There was opposition from friends. The AFL-CIO with whom Humphrey had worked closely for years said they would not support the effort. Congressman Hale Boggs chairman of the platform committee, originally supported the plank, but worked over by Johnson folk (maybe by the president himself) showed up in the suite, well-oiled from a few too many drinks. He told Humphrey soberly that our peace plank would not get out of his committee. There was no negotiation possible; the decision was firm, final, and beyond discussion. He staggered off leaving despair behind.

What we didn't know at the time was that President Johnson had been thinking seriously and incredibly of jumping back into the race, in part because he thought the convention might reject both Humphrey (an odd surmise for a shrewd vote counter) and the Johnson Vietnam policy (much more possible). He told his close staff with him in Texas that he was going to do it. Some of them probably thought it was a nutty idea, yet remained silent. The president called Mayor Daley.

Tapes of their conversation were recently released. (Strangely, I read of it only in a British Broadcasting Corporation release.) Johnson asked if the presidential helicopter could land safely on the Hilton Hotel roof and whether Daley thought there were enough votes to be had to beat Humphrey. Daley apparently assured him that both were possible—the votes were there and the roof was sturdy. He may have known about the roof, but he was not a national vote counter. He was not someone Johnson, in normal circumstances, would have turned to, ignoring his own long-time political advisers and better national politicians on site. In retrospect, it would have been ludicrous, a final act of humiliation and rejection of Humphrey if it had come to pass. Daley may have been sure of the votes, but I certainly don't believe Johnson could possibly have won.

Johnson also congratulated Daley on "his handling of the protests." That Johnson taped all that duplicity is incomprehensible. (The tapes are in the LBJ Library.) The only reason he didn't go was not political, but practical. The Secret Service told him they could not guarantee his safety. That apparently kept him home when loyalty, decency, and good sense would not.

On a less cosmic level, my own life was a victim of the chaos. I couldn't deal with the press in a normal fashion. I couldn't get from our part of the 15th floor, protected by the Secret Service, to a room fit to hold a press briefing. A place and certain time for a calm presentation, beyond interruption or distraction, were just not possible.

But keeping the press informed was obviously vital. I had no choice but to use the space in front of the elevators that opened on three sides leaving a fairly large area for the press to gather. It was a mob scene of a hundred reporters, maybe more, pushing and shoving one another to get closer. I stood on a low table, part of the elevator-well furniture, with the noise of elevator doors opening and shutting, people coming and going. Questions had to be shouted and answered in the same way. It was beyond difficult, a bellowing conversation in the worst of circumstances.

On the day when the convention would vote, I was in my place, had said my prepared piece, and answered serious questions when a final joking question from someone I couldn't see was shouted out. "If Hubert gets the nomination tonight, will he ask Lyndon to be his vice president?" There was laughter and I responded, "Lyndon who? And that's off the record." There was even more and louder laughter, and I got down from my makeshift podium pleased with myself.

Then one reporter, a good friend, came out of the crowd and spoke, close to me and quietly. It was the chief Associated Press reporter, Harry Kelley, and he said, "One reporter says he is going to file the 'Lyndon who' answer because you said, 'It's off the record' after, not before, you spoke the line." I elegantly said, "Screw it. Who cares? I suppose it was the *Toledo Blade* guy." My thinking was why worry about a tiny audience in an insignificant town somewhere in the boonies. Harry said, "No, it's my AP colleague, Carl Leubsdorf." Carl, I learned later, had been told long before by his editors that nothing was off the record if many reporters heard it.

I shrugged a bit and was momentarily troubled that it was going everywhere in the country, but I gave it little thought while I continued chatting with other reporters, answering their remaining questions, anticipating the nomination which was only hours off. Suddenly, there was a Secret Service agent at my side. He whispered that there was a call for me in their command post.

With the phone situation as it was, I was not totally surprised that a call for me should come to them. I was surprised when he said it was "from the Ranch." I could not remember when I last had a call from the White House and certainly never from Texas.

The Secret Service room was filled with a switchboard and agents, unsmiling and under great pressure, and I was an intruder. I was handed the phone and was delighted to hear greetings from George Christian, the president's press secretary, and Loyd Hackler, his assistant with whom I had a pleasant, if distant relationship. They said that they had just read the AP wire and that it had a spelling error—I was identified as the "pees secretary."

George said, in his Texas drawl, "Nohman, what's a piss secretary?" For a few minutes, we talked about nothing important, but I wallowed in my recognition by people I might soon replace. As soon as I hung up, I headed for Humphrey's suite. When I opened the door, Humphrey was right there hanging up his jacket in the closet. He wheeled and barked, "Did some son-of-a-bitch just say 'Who's Lyndon?'" I brilliantly responded, "You've got the right son-of-a-bitch, but the line is 'Lyndon who.'" I grinned; he did not.

He, too, had just gotten off the phone. Arthur Krim, the head of a major Hollywood studio, a New York moneybag, probably our most effective and important fundraiser, and a close friend of Lyndon Johnson, had called. He and the president were together at the Ranch and, like Christian and Hackler, had just seen the wire story. Krim's message was curt and unambiguous: "If you have people on your staff who are disloyal to the president, I am through raising money for the campaign." It left Humphrey shaken. Later, when he calmed down some, Humphrey said he could hear the president breathing and listening silently on an extension. It was a stumble we didn't need on the way to the nomination. I should probably have been fired.

Humphrey was determined not to play games with his selection of a running mate, but there were differing opinions among his closest advisers. For many, the most important, maybe the only, criterion was residence: how many electoral votes would the nominee bring. Governor Richard Hughes of New Jersey was eager to be chosen and had strong advocates among those close to Humphrey. His state had 17 electoral votes. Senator Fred Harris of Oklahoma, with fewer votes, but young, liberal, and attractive, was another one. Humphrey raised the idea again of Sargent Shriver as an accomplished member of the Kennedy clan even though word had come earlier that the family did not approve. Terry Sanford of North Carolina was also considered. Other names floated around.

Eventually Humphrey ignored everything but his gut. He chose Senator Ed Muskie of Maine, a state with three electoral votes. Muskie was a liberal who was a friend, bright, serious, and a hard worker. Humphrey thought he could be a good president if that were to become necessary. The assassinations of recent times could not be ignored. And he thought they would work well together as they had in the Senate.

Just before the convention, *Newsweek* said Humphrey was only 32.5 votes from the majority he needed. Had Bobby Kennedy lived, even with a narrow California primary victory, he knew he was second and had told Humphrey that he would support him after California if he didn't win by a substantial margin.

As early as May, several months before the convention, a month before the California primary, Kennedy had Kenny O'Donnell, a long-time family political operative visit Humphrey. He made a *pro forma* request that Humphrey withdraw and support Kennedy, knowing that Humphrey would not. He then told Humphrey that if Bobby did not do well in California, he would withdraw, as he had promised, and immediately support Humphrey. A squeaker meant goodbye. Kennedy beat McCarthy by four points, 46% to 42%, hardly a game-changing landslide.

Despite the facts, the idea that Bobby Kennedy would have gotten the nomination persists, a popular, lasting, maybe growing, myth, over the intervening years. The Kennedy name, in all its deserved glory, is iconic and certainly stands alone. Losing presidential candidates like Humphrey melt into the mists of ancient history, forgotten names with forgotten accomplishments. Myth is more enduring.

Bobby's relationship with Humphrey had become friendlier than it once had been and, while he denigrated Humphrey's support of Johnson's policies in Vietnam, they had shared other liberal views. He knew that Humphrey, after being beaten in West Virginia, had been of great help to his brother during both the 1960 campaign and the presidency.

It seems crass, even now, to say that the assassination, after which the nation mourned, was a living disaster for Humphrey. The month-long hiatus in the campaign sapped for a while the spirit and momentum from our efforts. And a lot of our promised money dried up. Wall Street folks who could not get close enough to Humphrey before took a walk into the sunset, reneging on their promise of millions of dollars we desperately needed. They disliked Bobby Kennedy more than they liked Humphrey. They no longer answered our phone calls, and, our paychecks bounced for a couple of weeks.

When we started campaigning again, Johnson was a continuing burden we couldn't shake. Humphrey was incessantly asked, "When are you going to be your own man?" It was tough to answer. To do so meant he admitted the import of the question, something he couldn't do. Almost any answer might offend Johnson, inviting his wrath once again.

As early as March, only 36 percent of Americans supported Johnson's war policies, but a public fight would have been disastrous. Johnson's approval ratings had withered all over the world. As students took over San Francisco State University, students also rioted in France, England, and Germany in the first three months of the year, and more riots soon followed in

Belgium and Mexico. Nightly news, it seemed, could hardly break for commercials. If Johnson was the target, Humphrey was the reasonably innocent victim standing too close.

Beyond that, we were dealing with other matters out of our control. Teddy White, the esteemed journalist and historian, wrote, "The main feature of the August 29 NBC Morning News was a poetic montage of the previous day's convention highlights." He noted that NBC cut back and forth between "convention hall celebrations that followed Hubert Humphrey's first ballot victory" and footage of protesters "being beaten, clubbed, maced, and gassed by hordes of clearly enraged, out-of-control policemen." He finished, "The events were not going on at the same time. . . . NBC liked the dramatic effect." Phony drama was more important to them than simple truth, and it was devastating for us.

(Later, during the campaign, we were in Atlanta where we were greeted at our hotel by a raging group of protestors. NBC and CBS filmed the demonstration as one would expect. The ABC crew had wandered off and did not get the scene on film. As the protestors disbursed, the ABC crew arrived and raced down the street to get protestors to return. They shouted and wave their signs long after Humphrey had passed so ABC was not scooped.)

Inside, things were calmer. On the first ballot, Humphrey got 1,760 votes. McCarthy; George McGovern, who had also become an anti-war candidate; and several other token candidates got a total of 880 votes. Even some of those delegates had told us that they would switch to Humphrey if he needed them.

When the convention ended, Humphrey, emotionally drained, had no time to sit and savor his nomination. There was a campaign to plan and define. He headed for Minnesota. His lakeside home at Waverly was a quiet and soothing place to plan after Chicago. He could stand on the dock and look at clear blue waters, not police and protestors. The sound of a distant outboard motor was a lullaby replacing shouts and screams. After the chaos of the convention and before the constant and enervating rush of a national campaign, it was secular heaven—scenic, refreshing, peaceful.

But planning is not a picnic. There are a thousand questions to be answered quickly: where to raise the necessary money; what themes to emphasize; how to treat Vietnam; how to stay on the good side of an irascible and easily angered Lyndon Johnson; where to go to get the electoral votes one needed. It seems odd that no one had done so before, but the immediate demands of the moment, even in a campaign where you are ahead, take precedence over the future. Today and tomorrow are now; next week is far off and election day out of sight and almost out of mind.

Humphrey had gathered eight of us: three from the staff, Larry O'Brien, adding his valuable Kennedy experience, and two of his associates, plus Orville Freeman and Max Kampelman. Humphrey had already asked Larry to be the campaign manager, as I have noted, with Fred Harris and Fritz Mondale as co-chairs of the Humphrey-Muskie ticket. Larry had become a special friend and there really was no second choice. He was an accomplished political strategist and manager, and carried the glamour of both John and Robert Kennedy.

We planned as well as one could in anticipation of the social unrest that would be our companion for the next eight weeks. We seemed ready for endless travel, crowds, heckling, speeches, applause, sleepless nights, exhaustion, and hope.

11. Hopes Dashed

Plans for a campaign are partial and tentative. You can't predict what will happen the next day, much less the next month. But we came away from Waverly feeling good about what we had accomplished in terms of staff selection, where we would concentrate our efforts, and who among those opposed to Humphrey might come on board.

Humphrey took upon himself to continue dealing with McCarthy and McGovern. McGovern, his next-door neighbor in Bethesda, Maryland, had been immediately, wholeheartedly, and publicly for Humphrey at the convention. McCarthy, in a meeting before the convention, had told Humphrey he would support him, but said again that he had to delay his endorsement for a bit so that his most ardent supporters had time to get over their disappointment. McGovern's equally committed supporters apparently healed and got over their disappointment faster.

McCarthy took a vacation in Europe not long after the convention, dilly-dallied when he came back, and ultimately provided a mushy endorsement. Even after Humphrey made his speech on Vietnam saying he would stop the bombing of the North, Gene remained distant and indifferent. Humphrey had helped McCarthy whenever he was needed over the years, but all that was clearly forgotten or ignored.

Years later, in 1996, at his 80th birthday celebration to which Ginny and I were invited, Gene spent much of his talk getting even with people, belittling, vindictive, still angry. It was a few minutes of extraordinary bitching and moaning, without an ounce of real or heartfelt appreciation for those who had stood at his feet several decades before, worked passionately for him, and were still there that evening. For an immensely smart and attractive person with much broader intellectual and literary interests than most, maybe all, of his congressional colleagues, it always amazed me that he wallowed in such excursions of distemper. It was a sad waste.

Back in 1968, I had had a special role beyond being press secretary, or so it seemed for a while. Humphrey told me early on that he and McCarthy had agreed that I should be their liaison, the contact through whom significant words might be exchanged. I am not sure who suggested it, but I would guess it was McCarthy. (Gene said from time to time to a reporter that I was the only one of Humphrey's staff that he would want on his own. It brought no applause from my colleagues.) I was impressed with myself, and my new role. McCarthy called once while Bobby Kennedy was still alive, and I arranged a meeting at his request with just Humphrey and him. I was not in it, but the conversation, as reported to me, was odd. He complained about the Kennedys and their money as though that were new. Then he acknowledged he could not win the nomination, but wasn't going to get out. He also indicated that he would support Humphrey, as I've noted, when the convention did choose Humphrey. After weeks of his silence, I got a second call.

I was exhausted one day while we were on a tough trip, and

I needed a couple hours of rest. I took off one afternoon and was sound asleep when my phone rang. I grabbed it and a voice said, "Hi, Norman, this is Gene." In my fog, I said, "Gene who?" When he identified himself, I puffed up anticipating an important message. He asked, "Did you see my article in *Life*?" I said I had. It was on baseball, not the war, and not the campaign. Then he asked if I had noticed anything special about the pictures. I had not. He said that the only movement was a ball going over the fence and an outfielder standing still and looking up. He explained to my puzzled silence that that was the trouble with baseball: it was more than slow; it was static. A minute later he said goodbye, and I didn't try to get back to sleep. What was the call all about?

In its emptiness, it seemed a bit of a putdown, not to me, but to Humphrey, and I recalled an earlier conversation with Gene. He spent nine months as a novice in a monastery aiming to become a priest, but the monk in charge rejected him for the sin of intellectual pride. When I blinked in ignorance of Catholic theology, he explained it almost as a virtue, not as a character flaw. I looked it up: "Pride in the sinful sense has been defined as: desire to be more important or attractive than others, failing to acknowledge the good work of others, and excessive love of self."

It was sad that the man who had provided a necessary voice for those who were vehemently against the war and distressed with Johnson and Humphrey couldn't get over his ego games, early and late. I had long thought that Gene disdained any peer group he was in. He dismissed his colleagues at St. John's as intellectual bumpkins. He had no more respect for St. Thomas faculty despite having several of them as advisers and having taught there himself.

In the House, he was not a leader and, to the best of my

knowledge, never passed a bit of legislation distinctly his. I thought his verbal, gratuitous dismissal of his senatorial colleagues ignored the good ones as he heaped them all together. I had heard him speak well of only one other senator, Phil Hart of Michigan, and I had the sense that Hart was the only friend he had or wanted among his peers. I believe that other senators knew where they stood in his estimation. Had he ever been nominated for president, his support from them would have been minimal and begrudging.

But there wasn't time or energy to spend on him. We were on an inescapable marathon. In the nine weeks between the convention and election day, we flew almost 100,000 miles. We were on and off a plane in three or four or even five cities in any working day. A moment alone, short of bedtime, was almost impossible. Virtually every waking moment carried with it the opportunity for misstatement or other blunder. There were only a few rare moments of relief, of real joy, of sustained pleasure.

One night, after an exhausting day of rallies, speeches, and handshaking across the country, we landed well after midnight in Oxford, Mississippi, far from where we had started. Humphrey was exhausted and asleep on the plane. As we taxied toward the small terminal, a crowd of several hundred people, mostly white, were cheering, waving signs, jumping up and down. His eyes immediately sparkled, his sagging skin tightened up, and he bounded off the plane like it was the first stop of the day.

We hadn't noticed that a smaller crowd of young blacks stood to one side, hooting and waving protest signs about the poverty program's inadequacy. The irony of Mississippi whites cheering and Mississippi blacks booing was startling.

As Humphrey worked the crowd, I walked alongside a

reporter who asked a woman in the throng what brought her to the airport and what kept her there for a couple of very late hours. She said, "No plane this big has ever landed here. We thought it might crash." That apparently would have made it an exceptional day worth waiting for.

Each day of campaigning was much like yesterday's and tomorrow's. Baggage outside your hotel room door or in the lobby soon after the crack of dawn. About the only variation was that some days you stayed where you were for meetings virtually all day without a break. Other days, there was a breakfast meeting with a crowd of some sort gathered by a local supporter, a motorcade to the airport, a flight to the next city, which had to be an hour or two away. You needed the time to prepare for what was ahead; a nearby city was too close and too soon.

You landed to a crowd, mostly friendly. Another motorcade, another rally, another city. Sometimes, just an airport event almost taking less time than the final approach itself. If you were going east to west, it was two or three more landings, each time following the same script. Light moments were rare. Once in Chicago, comedian Jimmy Durante, a local boy, introduced his good friend Humphrey as Herbert Humphries. At another rally where a small plane hired by the locals to pull a banner behind also spelled his name wrong.

Every visit, brief or long, required a relatively modern creation, an advance man, to avoid errors like the banner, if not like Durante, and to make things go smoothly. Ours were generally volunteers. They came from different professions and were different ages, but the good ones had something in common—a political sense that anticipates problems and solves them so everything from bathroom stops to microphones to platform guests makes the visit go smoothly.

They must make sure there is no possible embarrassing moment for the candidate and that every event is a positive one: crowds "bigger than expected" by playing down expectations; a meeting hall big enough for the crowd, but not so big that empty seats were likely; an occasion for a public embrace and "photo opportunity" with a governor or mayor, good or bad, enthusiastic or tepid. They must massage the local press so they feel as important as the big names soon to arrive.

I first met two of the best during the 1964 campaign. They were exceptional and have remained good friends. One was D.J. Leary, a Minnesotan with an extraordinarily creative political mind. When I first met him he worked for a mercurial entrepreneur and major contributor, Jeno Paulucci, who manufactured pizza rolls, but also Chun King Chinese food. (Occasionally, during Minnesota winters, I would find a frozen box or two at my door when I opened it to pick up my morning paper. I got the news then and heartburn a bit later.)

D.J. went on to become a television commentator on a regular weekly show and a sought-out political strategist in Minnesota politics. His admiring audience didn't know of the pizza rolls or that he had earned a living for a time promoting midget wrestling around the state.

The pressure didn't seem to get to him. He was always in good humor and tireless. He is notable for a number of singular moments, but one delights me specially since it was quick, off-the-wall, and fed the press. Humphrey was behind schedule in arriving at a town in Wyoming and a local reporter asked D.J. why Humphrey was late. D.J. had an immediate response. With a straight face, he said "There were antelope on the runway," thus delaying the arrival. The local reporter who should have known better repeated the story as fact to the national press who arrived with Humphrey. And the word went forth across the land, the truth never catching up to the speedy creatures.

On another occasion in 1968 D.J. called me from Cleveland to say there was an immensely popular afternoon kids' show featuring a ventriloquist and a dummy and Humphrey could get on it. I politely told him that I thought he was out of his mind, that the press would ridicule Humphrey in their stories. But, as a courtesy to D.J., I told Humphrey of the offer. He loved the suggestion and did the show. He explicated the Pledge of Allegiance, teaching the dummy and kids watching at home what each word meant. It was a mini-lecture on country and patriotism. The photo of Humphrey and his two companions ran the following day on many front pages across the country. It turned out that I was an off-camera dummy.

A second advance man came to us as a stranger. The thought of Barry Goldwater as president drove Jay Schwamm into volunteering. Jay had become the president of a small Wall Street bank when he was 28 years old. His father who had run the bank had died in a plane crash off Nantucket. Jay was a Princeton University graduate, Phi Beta Kappa, magna cum laude, and a graduate of the Harvard Business School. He was a New York City sophisticate. He was Park Avenue.

I met him in the Sheraton-Ritz hotel in downtown Minneapolis, where Bill Connell had invited us to lunch. As I approached the booth where they sat, Jay stood up, we shook hands, and he said, "I've heard a lot about you. You're a smart ass." I said, "I've never heard anything about you." I figured that I won the exchange.

Jay had a superb political eye and sense and a totally independent judgment since he wanted no job after election day, no reward but victory. He told me he found the job exciting and fulfilling, and it showed. In 1968, getting out of his advance man's role, he urged the campaign to find ways to help George Wallace carry some Southern states, keeping electoral votes from Nixon. (Wallace won five states, getting 10 million votes, but only 46 electoral votes.)

One nameless and shameless advance man made one advance too many. Working in Salt Lake City where Humphrey announced what his Vietnam policy would be if he were elected, the advance man worked closely with the most powerful force in the state. Utah, of course, is the headquarters of the Mormon church. The chief apostle liked and supported Humphrey, though the other eleven apostles did not.

Several days before we arrived, the advance man had invited a secretary in the main office to have dinner. After dinner he proffered another invitation, which she also accepted. When he called his wife several days later to say he had contracted a venereal disease, she suggested he stay on the road until cured, and maybe longer. And maybe try prayer at the Tabernacle.

Advance men, good and not so good, made the way for all of us easier. But, for me, the challenges of the campaign not only increased a bit; they multiplied in many ways. The number of press grew tremendously. I was now faced with the top reporters, smart, experienced, tough, and ever present.

Dealing with the top-level press corps is both a constant challenge and pleasure. There are no rookies. They are all experienced, some sent to Washington because they excelled back home, or were grabbed from another job because of recognized skills. Some conservatives then and now regurgitate endless disdain for the press. "They are birds on a wire; when one flies they all fly." "They are "parrots of the left," and thus secret purveyors of a dangerous ideology. In fact, almost no one in my experience then fits those descriptions. The worst of them were still professional, granting me no liberal room for error, misstatement, or obfuscation. They might intend to vote for Humphrey, but they didn't intend to help elect him. To protect their sense of objectivity, some didn't even vote for president.

The conservative reporters, who were not going to vote under any conditions for a Democratic candidate, seemed as balanced. Hostile questions did not inevitably lead to distorted reporting. Only one reporter, a McCarthy acolyte, among all who traveled at one time or another with us, violated his professional responsibility as best I could tell. (He later apologized to Humphrey on his evening newscast with me as his guest. Guests are rare on a news program and an apology even rarer.)

The journalists were never off duty; if one got a story, they all had to, not as birds on a wire, but as responsible, thorough reporters. Meetings, early and late, had to be covered. Breakfast with a governor was news. No breakfast with a governor was also news. I inevitably had to comment on everything they thought of, except the weather. It was exhausting and exhilarating.

The anti-Humphrey demonstrations were reported over and over again. Protests might be repetitive, but each one had to be treated as unique and reported with dramatic words. Deadlines of papers or stations were scattered across time zones creating a perpetual frenzy for my assistants and me. As a result in those less electronic days the most frequently asked question was, "Where's the telephone?"

We carried the horde in two or three 727s behind the candidates. The print press and on-camera reporters rode on the second plane and mainly television crews and photographers on the third, called the "zoo plane" by the other journalists.

Numbers varied from trip to trip, but we often had an entourage of 75, occasionally as many as 150. We carried two guys to handle the press luggage. A lost bag was a bad story.

Even the motorcade was pressure. A lead car of Secret Service agents, then Humphrey with whoever met him, a backup agent car, a wire service car, (something that began after President Kennedy's assassination), two or three press buses, a string of local hangers on, motorcycle cops along side.

A good number of reporters had a recessive gene that caused them to whisper advice to me for Humphrey. They became for a moment or two a surrogate campaign manager. I learned to nod and keep a serious look of interest on my face.

The press traveling with us developed a kind of subculture of their own, or at least it was new to me, with rules and habits affecting their own fraternity. Jack Germond of the *Washington Star* (and later a talking head on television) established the Germond Rule. When they ate together, the check was divided by the number of people present, regardless of what anyone ate or drank. *The New York Times'* Warren Weaver also had a rule: last one into a cab paid for the ride.

Television reporters were more demanding than print journalists. Being on camera seemed to make them stars of a different dimension. Some were idiosyncratic. Martin Agronsky would somehow misplace his luggage, lose his hat, move like a hyperactive child when others walked. He once raced up to me having bounced off the hotel elevator, shouting, "Where's the bus? Where's the bus?" I said, "Martin, it doesn't stop in the lobby."

I liked my press secretary role immensely, but as election day approached, I told Humphrey that I didn't think I should be the White House press secretary if he won. I didn't think a flip remark would get us into war, but I did think it could get us into trouble. He smiled and said I had the job until I made my first major mistake. It might have been a short career.

There was one vital part of the campaign that we couldn't

assess or depend on. That was Lyndon Johnson. Humphrey hoped for his unambiguous, even enthusiastic support. It was an idle hope. It didn't happen. Johnson was sorry he had with-drawn and pouted in the Oval Office for an act that couldn't be undone. It wasn't always what he didn't do, but what he did as well.

Johnson cancelled meetings at the last minute, including one when Humphrey, returning exhausted from a campaign trip, arrived at the White House for a scheduled, but secret, meeting only to be told that the president had just left for Camp David, the presidential retreat. The reason for his petu-lance and disappearance was like a child's foot-stamping anger.

A reporter, Andy Glass of the *New York Herald Tribune*, had asked one of my associates, Jack Limpert, at a rally in a Washington suburb whether there was "a lid on," the journal-ist's phrase for there being no more news that day. Jack, in an attempt to be honest, fuzzed the answer. Andy divined that there must be a private meeting with the president and called the White House to check his supposition. Told of the call, Johnson, in pique, took off.

When Jim Jones, a top aide and later congressman from Oklahoma, met Humphrey in the driveway and told him the meeting had been cancelled, Humphrey asked Jim if he would take a message to the president. "Tell him to kiss my ass." It is probably the only time during the campaign that Hum-phrey spoke up angrily. Whether the invitation was delivered is unclear, although it is unlikely since Jones remained on the staff.

Johnson was no better when a crucial, substantive moment in the campaign came along. Humphrey later wrote, "For weeks, I had delayed a definitive statement (on Vietnam), which my campaign badly needed. Virtually any statement that dif-fered even a hair from administration policy would have been played as a break with Johnson and would have jeopardized the Paris peace talks. I could not do that. Now, the chief negotiator, Averell Harriman, no longer raised that objection. . . . I could do what was long overdue: tell the American people what I proposed to do on Vietnam, if elected. I could speak out without damaging negotiations."

Getting to the proper words was not easy, and the final drafting came following an awful night in the campaign. Seattle's Central Arena was filled with 8,000 people and more outside were trying to get in. There was enthusiasm in the crowd not often seen before. The spirit was palpable and juiced up Humphrey. It was precious because it had been so rare. But it did not last.

To the right of Humphrey in the balcony, there were about a 100 protestors, maybe more, who must have come early enough to get those seats close by and together. They seemed like every one else until Humphrey got to the podium. Then they exploded with shouts amplified by a bullhorn. Murderer, fascist, baby killer were among the politer accolades. Humphrey stood with his face contorted in despair, shaking his head in disgust, impotent in dealing with noise that made his own words impossible to be heard. The local police, encouraged by the Secret Service, forcibly moved the protestors out. It was ugly.

One television reporter, David Shoumacher, apparently had been told ahead of time what was planned. He stationed his film crew where they could film it easily and closer than other networks. As the chaos began, he put his thumb and forefinger together in the sign of approval and smiled.

Back in the hotel, drained far more than usual, Humphrey said that he figured he was going to lose, and in that mood started on his speech that was set for delivery on Monday in

Salt Lake City. He would stand alone without a studio audience. What Humphrey ultimately said did not come easily or quickly. He labored over the precise phrasing for a day and night and through endless meetings. Staff worked on it offering ideas and words, outsiders from Larry O'Brien to George Ball criticized it or made suggestions. Humphrey listened, argued, balanced the different views, and revised. Then the process would start again.

Getting the proper tone and content was hard. The end position was clear in Humphrey's mind, but finding the right words remained a challenge. Anything he said was politically risky with the voters at home and an audience of one in the White House.

Humphrey described it all in his autobiography. "Ted Van Dyk appeared with a handful of speeches, and he and I and Norman Sherman sat in a dining alcove in the suite talking about the various suggestions." The basic draft had been cleared with Averell Harriman, still in Paris trying to negotiate an end to the war, but Humphrey found that it was not what he wanted to say or the way he wanted to say it. None of the variations struck him as on target, either.

He sent Van Dyk off with his suggestions and comments scribbled on the pages with the job of drafting an essentially new speech. But even that, as good as it was, didn't satisfy him. At one point, ten of us, staff and political operatives, gathered to discuss it.

What flowed around the room was a mishmash of useful ideas, words, and attitudes toward the war, but there was no possibility of consensus or clarity of statement. Humphrey described the situation: "One by one, people left—hungry, tired, or simply wanting a change of conversation and scenery. Finally all were gone except for Connell, Van Dyk,

Welsh, and Sherman. (Bill Connell had been his chief of staff since 1960, Bill Welsh a legislative assistant with long political experience, and Van Dyk, primarily a speech writer.) For them, loyal associates, hunger, boredom, fatigue could be set aside . . ." Humphrey did the final draft himself, and it was typed while we flew on to Salt Lake City.

Once in the Salt Lake studio, he called Johnson. It was September 29. Humphrey later wrote, "I told him what I intended to say, and he said curtly, 'I gather you are not asking my advice.' I said that was true, but that there was nothing embarrassing to him in the speech and certainly nothing that would jeopardize peace negotiations." That was still too much for the president. He responded coldly, "You're going to give the speech anyway. Thanks for calling, Hubert." End of call.

Humphrey didn't get the chance to read his words to Johnson, but the people listened. What Humphrey said in a few minutes changed the campaign from hopeless weeks behind us into an exciting month of hope ahead of us. He said to the American people, "As President, I would stop the bombing of the North as an acceptable risk for peace because I believe it could lead to success in the negotiations and thereby stop the war. This would be the best protection for our troops. In weighing that risk—and before taking action—I would place key importance on evidence, direct or indirect, by deed or word, of communist willingness to restore the demilitarized zone between North and South Vietnam."

But, the peace talks in Paris that seemed to promise success in ending the war were derailed with the help of two people: Henry Kissinger, then freelancing, and Anna Chennault. Kissinger was able to move from Rockefeller to Nixon during the course of the year while also offering Humphrey some help. While he was still working for Rockefeller, he offered

Humphrey their files on Nixon. When a Humphrey adviser called back a few days later, Kissinger had gone to work for Nixon and the files were no longer available. Kissinger was a political acrobat without equal. He knew all the moves.

Madam Chennault, a Chinese charmer, had married a World War II American general and hero. She apparently was bright and beautiful. She was also a major fundraiser for Richard Nixon and omnipresent, serving as co-chair of a number of his committees.

Kissinger arrived in Paris as the talks were coming to agreement and somehow learned from friends, Averell Harriman and George Ball, that success was imminent. Kissinger called John Mitchell, Nixon's campaign manager and later Attorney General, who set Chennault to work on Thieu and Ky, the Vietnamese leaders. The FBI taped her conversations.

To believe for a moment that Nixon did not know what she was doing is hard to accept. Teddy White later wrote that she "had undertaken most energetically to sabotage (the peace talks). In contact with the Formosan, the South Korean, and the South Vietnamese governments, she had begun early, by cable and telephone, to mobilize their resistance to the agreement—apparently implying, as she went, that she spoke for the Nixon campaign."

Mrs. Chennault was successful. The South Vietnamese president repudiated the agreements. Eleven Vietnamese senators went further, declaring their support for Nixon. They couldn't vote, but they were determined to affect the election.

As the campaign drew to a close, Humphrey would not speak of anything that wasn't public knowledge about the negotiations. There was some question about whether he, even as vice president, should have been told anything about what was being done to undermines the talks. But he did know what had gone on, and so did I. I begged him to let me tell all of this to the press. I was certain that Americans of both parties would be outraged and that we would get the final boost we needed.

I told him that if it rebounded against him, he could dramatically fire me as the unauthorized leaker and regain the high ground and his virtue as he said a muttered, hopefully temporary, goodbye to me. But Humphrey said that if Nixon were elected president, he shouldn't begin with the burden of what he had, in fact, done. (Looking back after the election, Humphrey agreed that the Nixon sabotage was "my best chance of winning the election" and that he should have been tougher and more outspoken.)

Teddy White also described this moment. "Fully informed of the sabotage of the negotiations and the recalcitrance of the Saigon government, Humphrey might have won the Presidency of the United States by making it the prime story of the last four days of the campaign. He was urged by several members of his staff to do so. And I know of no more essentially decent story in American politics than Humphrey's reluctance to do so."

While the Salt Lake City speech did not get Johnson's approval, it made a difference with the voters and contributors. The crowds everywhere changed after Humphrey said he would stop the bombing of North Vietnam. On a trip days later, one sign held by a former protestor who would have been screaming at us before read, "Hecklers for Humphrey. We came back." Another one said, "McCarthy Supporters for Humphrey-Muskie."

Lyndon Johnson was not among those enthusiasts, and may never have been. Later stories said Johnson had considered supporting Nelson Rockefeller early on and then Richard

Nixon. Humphrey did not want to believe them despite John-son's erratic and often hostile behavior. In any case, if he did think about deserting Humphrey, he got over it. He finally came around late and as election day approached had his peo-ple organize a huge rally in the Houston Astrodome on the final weekend. About 40,000 people bussed in from all over the state, apparently at Johnson's direction, cheered the two of them as they walked the field. The roar was overwhelming. As I walked in a small bunch of aides and Texas politicians behind them, I thought we would win. That feeling was still there on the night before the voting.

One of the gimmicks of the time was a telethon on election eve. The candidate took questions phoned in. The answers appeared to be *ad libbed* and unscripted, although most questions were anticipated and answers prepared. An essential ingredient of the show was an illustrious host who would deliver some show business spark. A California friend, Gene Wyman, who served as state Democratic chairman, suggested Paul New-man, who was a client of his law firm. Newman had what we needed and wanted, but he had been anti-war and a delegate to the convention for Gene McCarthy. When approached, he said he would consider doing the gig, but first had to interview both Humphrey and Mrs. Humphrey. Some of us thought it absurd that Humphrey had to meet *his* standards, but Hum-phrey shrugged, smiled, and agreed to a meeting.

Mrs. Humphrey promptly developed a migraine headache as soon as she woke on the interview day. At the appointed hour, there was a knock at the suite's door in our Los Ange-les hotel. I welcomed our interrogator with false warmth and something close to genuflection. His response was formal, stiff, and unsmiling. He and Mrs. Humphrey talked, and she passed her examination. Then I escorted Newman into a room where Humphrey waited. He greeted Newman, and they sat down at the opposite ends of a table with me at one side.

Newman asked his first question from a memorized script. "Why did you give that 1948 civil rights speech in Philadelphia, not in the South where the message had to be heard?" The implication had only one meaning: Humphrey was a coward and hypocrite to do what he did up North. Humphrey's eyes caught mine as if to ask, "Is this a trick question?" But he was silent for only a second as he said to Newman, "Well, that's where the convention was."

I resisted laughing as a quizzical look covered Newman's handsome face. He was not quite struck dumb, but was silent for a moment before going on with other questions. Humphrey, as his wife, passed the exam, and Newman accepted the invitation. Mrs. Humphrey's migraine disappeared, and Humphrey, in his regular style, made Newman feel like the most important man in our world. Newman was an effective presence who brought glamour and excitement to the show and learned a bit of 1948 history in getting there.

When Humphrey said goodnight to surviving listeners, the campaign was over. (The Republicans had twice as many listeners and their moderator was a college football coach.) Exhausted, we flew to Minnesota from Los Angeles and our mob soon descended on the Marysville Town Hall, a tiny voting place near the Humphrey home in rural Minnesota. Local voters were outnumbered by press, but pushed to be closer to a beaming couple who were their neighbors Then it was collapse, needing to talk to each other, but afraid to do so. Before there was anything to learn, we watched TV. Before there were definitive results, friends and political allies called with quasi-information.

By the time we headed off to dinner at the home of Dwayne

and Inez Andreas, a smile was a burden, a clear thought close to impossible. We dined on boned pheasant in a cream sauce, thinking of a possible meal in the White House when our spirits were up and McDonald's a moment later. We left the comparative quiet and real elegance for the Leamington Hotel, a second-rate hotel owned by Bob Short in downtown Minneapolis. Several thousand people jammed the lobby, the ballroom, the halls. They were all eager to see the next president. We didn't know whether to cheer with them or run away.

Election day and evening were inevitably an emotional roller coaster set in the let-down fatigue that envelopes you. For months, virtually every waking minute brought pressure and stress. The occasional day off was no real relief. If your body wasn't moving, your head was.

Now, there is nothing to do but wait and listen to the wind for messages of good turnout and long lines of voters in favorable districts. You reach for hope, repeating reasons why victory is ahead. And there were some.

Polls before the election showed Nixon not moving. He was slightly over 40 percent at the beginning of October and still there as election day neared. The two major independent pollsters, Gallup and Harris, in their final polls had us neck and neck, one in our favor, one in Nixon's.

While Nixon had remained where he was, we had gained from the lows following the convention. In late September we were at 28 percent to Nixon's 43 percent. You knew that winning the popular vote was ultimately irrelevant, but the necessary electoral votes might follow.

Then the polls close. You tabulate electoral votes as they come in. Inconclusive is torment. Well after midnight with most of the results in, victory was still possible, defeat more likely. Just after 3 a.m., Humphrey spoke to the press, but made no concession statement. When all the results were in soon after and 73 million votes had been counted, Humphrey had lost by about half a percentage point, 43.4 percent to 42.7 percent. If we had been able to switch about 125,000 votes of nine million cast in Missouri, Illinois and Ohio, Humphrey would have been elected president.

I went early the next morning to the Humphrey suite, let myself in without knocking, and found Humphrey sitting alone in the room with the television set on low. There wasn't much to say without crying. Soon, he said he wanted breakfast, and I asked if he would like me to order it. He said he would do it himself. We waited and waited for it to arrive. It took forever and when the room-service waiter finally arrived, he apologized. It was his second trip. His tray had tilted as he got off the elevator the first time, dumping Humphrey's breakfast to the hall floor. Humphrey smiled a sick smile and said to me, "Well, that's what happens when you lose."

Others wandered in and we made idle talk. You couldn't avoid what had happened, but talking about it was hard. While we stood around, Humphrey himself composed a telegram of concession and congratulations and sent it off to Nixon. Then he had to face the mob of press who were waiting in a basement room. I preceded him to announce that he would be down in a few minutes to make a concession statement and that there would be no questions. Dreams of glory were gone.

Soon after that, we were all back in Washington, in a semi-catatonic state that comes with loss. There was virtually unrelenting sadness. It was a time when you wanted to cry thinking of Nixon in the Oval Office, of how a day or two more with the momentum ours might have made the difference between loss and victory.

Condolence mail had begun to pour in, and each one was

to be answered in standard Humphrey tradition, even though we were all on the way out. I read a letter from a young woman who was blind and depended on a seeing-eye dog. She wrote from Boston that she had gone to the Humphrey headquarters to volunteer and was enlisted to stuff envelopes. After a bit she asked to make phone calls. Her letter was to thank Humphrey, through his candidacy, for letting her be a part of something ordinarily denied her—a social and political role and treatment without regard for her handicap.

I took the letter in to Humphrey hoping it would cheer him up. He read it, smiled an appreciative smile, and without pause asked, "Why don't you get her on the phone?" When I told her who was calling, she gulped and could hardly speak. She found her voice in time to have a conversation with her political hero and benefactor. I had hoped to cheer him up. He had hoped to cheer her up. We both succeeded.

(I recently learned, again in Richard Norton's Smith biography of Nelson Rockefeller, that the weekend before the inauguration, Lyndon Johnson took off from the White House lawn with his wife and guests. They were headed for Camp David, the presidential retreat less than an hour away in the Catoctin Mountains. It, of course, would be his last time there. His guests were not the Humphreys, as one might have hoped, but Happy and Nelson Rockefeller.)

I learned another lesson of a less cosmic nature. The unwritten rule for gifts for staff on the Hill was, in theory at least, if you can eat it or drink it, a gift is okay and acceptable. The Christmas after Humphrey was elected vice president and before he was sworn in, I received three bottles of whiskey. The next year, I got seven. The third Christmas, I hit 13. I took it as a personal tribute for my public service. For someone who drank almost not at all, that was a ten-year supply so I gave most of the bottles away. The Christmas of 1968 eliminated that burden. I got none.

While I was adjusting to my new and reduced status, other folks were at work or at play. The president-elect was relaxing in Florida when he learned through Dwayne Andreas that Humphrey was soon on his way down, too. When Humphrey landed at Opa Locka airport just north of Miami, there stood Nixon. With little pause or ceremony, Nixon said, "I want you to be my Ambassador to the United Nations." If Humphrey would do that, Nixon would also let him clear any appointment to a regulatory agency that required a Democrat. To top it off, Nixon said, "If I have to lose to a Democrat in 1972, I'd like it to be you." Humphrey turned down the offer.

Before the inauguration, Nixon called Humphrey and told him that he was going to provide a military plane to take him and Muriel home to Minnesota. The generous offer came out of nowhere, and when Humphrey began to thank him, Nixon quickly explained why he was doing it.

He said when he left Washington after his eight years as Eisenhower's vice president, he and his wife, Pat, were left to their own devices, hauling their personal belongings to Union Station to take the train to New York. He told Humphrey he thought it was demeaning and he didn't want Humphrey to feel the way he and Pat had.

When we got on the plane, there was an impressive bouquet of flowers with a note signed, "To Hubert and Muriel, with our best wishes. Dick and Pat." It was a thoughtful, if unexpected, send off, but it brought little solace. For all of us, no divorce, illness, or death in the family had the persisting misery a loss in a race for the presidency inspired. For me, even as a relatively minor cog, it was a recurring nightmare. I had once thought I would have four more years of a

Johnson-Humphrey second term, a mixture of political pain and satisfying pleasure. Then there would likely be a run for president in 1972.

All of that had disappeared in the reality of the past eight months and I could only look back on a rollercoaster of "should have done" or "might have happened." No day was without moments of depression, even physical ache. Internal musings were not something to share even with friends and co-workers who had themselves been involved as much as you, who must feel as you did. Isolation was more curative than communication.

You think it couldn't get worse, but every Nixon appointment, pronouncement, public appearance added an angry, stomach-tightening dimension. You hope to get over it, but here I am almost 50 years later still occasionally wearing a psychic black armband. I am not alone. When, some years after his unsuccessful race for president, Walter Mondale asked George McGovern who had lost the presidential election in 1972 how long it took to get over a loss like theirs, McGovern said he didn't know, but it hadn't happened yet.

Loss haunts. You cannot escape the recurring "what ifs." What if Johnson, even as unpopular as he was, had been consistently helpful as one would have expected? He could quietly have encouraged large donations of money that we desperately needed. He could have accepted our peace plank at the convention instead of blocking it. If he had, the constant question of "when are you going to be your own man" would have disappeared. He could have permitted Humphrey, after the convention, some distance from the war policy in disfavor with many of our traditional voters without whom victory was far more difficult.

What if Gene McCarthy had found a generous and

forgiving and appreciative heart in his body? He could have helped diffuse the anger and animosity that dogged us. Nightly television would have been good for the campaign, not an endless filmed burden of protests.

What if Humphrey had decided earlier to articulate a new Vietnam policy? That was a tough call. If Johnson blasted him, it was a disaster. But, if we lingered as we did, Humphrey looked wishy-washy or just weak. Was there any way to escape his "politics of joy" pronouncement which became not a rallying call, but a tool for ridicule while people died far away and their deaths were memorialized close at home in towns across the country?

What if Humphrey had blasted Nixon for using Mrs. Chennault to derail the peace talks? If Johnson could have been relied upon to support him, I think that alone would have elected him.

What if we had run a better campaign? We had structural problems. Old staff hands who expected to run the campaign were joined, if not superseded, by volunteer committee co-chairmen, Senators Fred Harris and Walter Mondale, and by Larry O'Brien. There was resentment and only uneasy cooperation.

What if? I still don't have the answers.

12. Out of Politics

But, life did go on, as the cliché has it. Everyone else on the staff found another Washington job or looked for a haven in academe. I went back to Minnesota (leaving my soon divorced wife behind) with Humphrey to work as his entire professional staff when he took up teaching at Macalester College and the University of Minnesota, something less than he had been doing for the previous 25 years. (Some political science faculty at the University opposed his appointment on the basis that he was not a Ph.D. and was "out of touch with the field.")

He made speeches around the country from time to time, including as chairman of the board of the Encyclopedia Britannica (which was owned by former Senator and friend Bill Benton). Mostly, he stayed home and healed in a familiar place among people he loved. He also set out to write his autobiography, and I was there for that.

During 1969, we recorded hours of interviews about various parts of his life, and he also reminisced alone on tape. In January 1970, I carted the first part of his recollections to a cabin in northern Minnesota near Aitkin, a town of about 1,500 people. The lake was surrounded by cabins filled in summer with families of fishermen, boaters, water skiers, vacationers, and the noise of children at play. In winter, the cabins were still since virtually no one was ever there. And that, of course, is what I wanted, still walking heavily in my post-campaign mood. A year had gone by, but the noise was still in my ears, the ache in my political soul.

My winter vacation required me to snowshoe in about a mile from where I could park my car. I carried a backpack filled with my week's food. The house had no dependable winter plumbing so I used an outhouse. After a bit, the snow and ice froze its door open, and I had my only religious experience there. When it dropped to 30 degrees below zero, I knew God meant for me to do quickly whatever I was going to do. I gave it up in March to return to tropical Minneapolis.

Meanwhile, as I continued work on the book, a friend, Jack Valentine, and I had started a business appropriately called Valentine, Sherman & Associates in 1969. He was a campaign junky and a graduate student in immigration history at the University. He had developed a system for combining registered voter lists with phone book names and numbers gathered inexpensively by women, often volunteers, working at home, who then entered them on the computer. Preliminary calls found other information; including party preference.

A campaign could focus on get-out-the-vote efforts with greater ease, saving time and money, as well as being more effective than usual. It was an innovative use of volunteers and the new technology. After the 1970 election, the *Minneapolis Tribune* reported, "They have applied computer technology to the old time-consuming task of canvassing prospective voters to find those sympathetic to the candidate, getting them registered to vote and then getting them to the polls on election day."

Our success drew a lot of attention. Among other papers, both the *Wall Street Journal* and *The New York Times* printed long pieces. The *Journal* noted our successes in Minnesota and North Dakota: " . . .Dems picked up 204 state legislative seats across the nation; 61 were in Minnesota and North Dakota." In both states, senatorial candidates did significantly better than expected. In Tennessee, we worked in only one large city for Senator Albert Gore, Sr. He won by a substantial margin there. His campaign manager lamented "If we had done this in three other cities, Gore would have won."

But, since neither Jack nor I had any real business or technical experience, we had a few stumbles along the way. One of our early clients was Senator Claiborne Pell of Rhode Island. We managed to print thousands of letters signed "Clairborne," a name not on the ballot.

Despite that, we became the political fad of the hour. In a couple of years, we had gone from renting time on someone else's computer, a common practice at the time, to owning one. The computer became an expensive artifact that had a nervous breakdown regularly. Valentine sought help from my family. When my father felt a headache coming on, he would, in a peasant's wisdom, bind a white handkerchief tightly around his head to ward off the pain. Sometimes it worked, but usually by morning, when he slipped off his binding, his head throbbed, confirming his premonition. He hung the knotted handkerchiefs on his bedpost, and I would see them there regularly. One day, Jack called me and asked plaintively if I had any of Louie's handkerchiefs that I could send to tie around the giant IBM that was giving us so much trouble.

We went from paying someone to solve our problems to creating them ourselves. We got our own computers and had to hire programmers and other employees. We couldn't distinguish between competent and con in their resumes. We just hired.

With their help, we occasionally managed to wipe out information and find no way easily to recover what had disappeared. From time to time, our company slogan was "garbage in, garbage out." But soon good work outpaced the errors. We were on our way to becoming a million-dollar-a-year business.

Our growth was startling. The manager of the small bank that gave us our start-up loan was so impressed with our rapidly increasing deposits that he talked us into hiring him. He turned out to be a better banker than business manager. Despite or because of him, we bounced from bundles of money to scarcely any and occasionally to virtually none. We understood finance as well as we did technology.

We ultimately had other troubles. In 1973, Jack and I were indicted by the Watergate special prosecutor's office for a misdemeanor violation of the Corrupt Campaign Practices Act. The part of the Act under which we were convicted is no longer on the books. We were the token Democrats to balance all the Nixonians during the Watergate scandal. I wrote an article about the experience that appeared as the cover story of the *Washington Post* Sunday magazine. I was pictured on the cover, my hands and head in old-fashioned stocks, surrounded by the faces of the Nixon staff and cronies.

We were accused of using corporate money from the American Milk Producers Incorporated (AMPI) in political campaigns. The lawyer we hired had assured us that the arrangement in which we had provided AMPI with actual product that they could use in their business made it legal. The prosecutors didn't see it that way. We were convicted and paid a fine of $500. (We later discovered that our attorney was on AMPI's payroll. He was later convicted on other charges and sentenced to four months in jail and a $10,000 fine.) All of that hastened the demise of our company. I have included the article I wrote for the *Washington Post* in 1975 that describes the ordeal in detail at the end of this book. See Special Section 1.

But until that, it was a nice venture. Our first client was Hubert Humphrey, who had a name we could spell. As the election of 1970 drew nearer, Gene McCarthy decided he would not run again for the Senate. The Republican candidate had given up his certain congressional seat to run against a bruised and theoretically beatable McCarthy. Surprised and doomed by McCarthy's decision not to run and Humphrey's decision to do so, Clark McGregor might not have wept in public, but he must have shed a tear in private.

The campaign carried me beyond politics, An old friend showed up. Ginny Chambers and I first met at the University of Minnesota in 1959. A history professor, Clarke Chambers, and I had become good friends despite my miserable performance in his year-long graduate seminar in American history. Discovering then that I had a taste for knowledge, but no real appetite for it, I went to Honeywell, but Clarke and I had remained friends.

One day, Clarke called to invite me to dinner to meet his cousin from the country. Ginny had grown up in small towns around Minnesota and was still an undergraduate. Our backgrounds were quite different. Her dad had been a county extension agent and then worked for a Guernsey cattle association; her mom had been a high school home economics teacher before their marriage.

I was taken with Ginny, and I soon invited her out several times for what I thought were romantic, wooing dates. I later found that she thought they were just occasions when that "nice Mr. Sherman" took her to dinner or, more likely, to ward club political meetings. She was about 20; I was about 30, and I soon, reading signals, gave up my courting, which she hadn't recognized for what I thought it was anyway.

When she graduated from the University, she moved to California to teach and married. I kept in touch from time to time, mostly sending her junk mail that came into whatever office I was in. Anti-vivisection literature was a big hit. A bigger hit was vanity press sheet music. She can still sing "The District of Columbia Is My Home Town" and does.

What kept us close was the Vietnam War. After dinner and a bit of wine, Ginny and her cousin and their husbands would call or send a telegram urging me, on the Humphrey staff and the most powerful man she knew, to end the war and get the hell out of Vietnam. I continued to hear from them from time to time, but mostly a welcome silence prevailed even as the war went on. In 1970, she returned from Hawaii with a master's degree and sans husband to visit her family in Owatonna, a town about an hour south of Minneapolis. She called me on the advice of a Minneapolis cousin who was active in the DFL and knew I was around. Since the war still raged, we talked of other things, including Humphrey's campaign to return to the Senate.

The "nice Mr. Sherman" invited her to lunch, and she accepted. We ate at Sheik's, a fancy restaurant near the Humphrey office, and when we finished, I asked how she was going to get to the Greyhound bus terminal, a dozen or so blocks away, for her trip home. She said she intended to walk. In a demonstration of *savoir faire*, I insisted, over her strenuous objection, that she take a cab. I hailed one, put her in it with a flourish, and waved goodbye without giving her or the driver the fare. I later learned that she had almost no cash with her and that my grand gesture was both a pain and a drain.

Despite that new and inauspicious beginning, at the urging

of her politically liberal dad, she called wondering if there might be a job in the Humphrey campaign. I suggested she volunteer, but fortunately our secretary, Humphrey's younger sister, Fern, quit, a great relief to me and an even greater opportunity. Ginny replaced her, providing me the chance to make up for past political meetings, cab fares, and lost time. The campaign was a success and so was I. Humphrey drew almost 58 percent of the 1.3 million votes cast to McGregor's 42 percent. (The Socialist Workers Party candidate got almost half a percent.) When Humphrey won, I could have gone directly back to Washington with him, but I had his memoir to finish editing. While I liked being in Minnesota, Ginny preferred a warmer climate. I convinced her to move with me to St. Croix in the Virgin Islands where there was indoor plumbing and temperatures significantly above zero.

We spent about six months there working on the Humphrey book in a house on a hilltop. We could see the Atlantic out front and the Caribbean out back. Ginny typed up the recorded interviews, and I continued editing. When I had done all I could on the book and Humphrey was too busy to dictate more or read what I had done, Ginny and I decided reluctantly to leave our Virgin Island idyll and eagerly get married at her parents' home in Minnesota, then move to Washington. We settled in Chevy Chase Village, one of several similar suburbs bordering the north edge of the District of Columbia.

Still thinking I would be rich from Valentine, Sherman's success, we bought an expensive house on the basis of wealth that was only on paper in company stock we couldn't sell for a number of years. Living there was vastly different from where I began. It was home to a fair share of the Washington elite—mid- to high-level government jobholders (including members of the Cabinet), journalists, doctors, lawyers, lobbyists, foreign diplomats, and other movers and shakers. It ran the whole economic spectrum—from merely comfortable to affluent. I thought that some people spent more on lawn care than my family, with adjusted dollars, had spent on food in my early years.

Our village had neat tree-lined streets, nice parks, fine restaurants nearby. The schools were excellent and filled with a vibrant atmosphere flowing from a student body enhanced by diplomats' children. (One of daughter Lucy's classmates returned home to become "The Bagel King" of Hungary.) Only natural events seemed to intrude. Once a microburst hit us after George H.W. Bush had been elected. It knocked trees across the soon-impassible streets. A neighbor with whom we had had dinner a couple of times came striding by, dodging around fallen trees, head down, brief case in hand, car abandoned several blocks away, and clearly angry with God. I said, "Hi, George." Never turning his head, his only words as he continued down the block were, "This never would have happened in a Reagan administration." Even if it were a joke, and I am not sure it was, George Will remained loyal to the past, as was and is his inclination. He had had lunch with Nancy Reagan regularly, but he never saw Barbara Bush.

I served a term on the village board of supervisors, fortunately running unopposed. We had a tiny police force and garbage pickup service, but not much that required an involved board. We seriously discussed how close to a neighbor's property line someone could put up a basketball hoop, how widely a driveway could be broadened, and whether a tree could be removed. I declined to run for additional years.

A more compelling effort was helping with a fruit and vegetable co-op inspired by one started by Joan Mondale in her neighborhood. One family would be responsible each week to

Reliving this in the village?

212

go to the Eastern Market on Capitol Hill and haul back what was timely and fresh, and the other families would soon appear to pick up their share. It was "Minnesota nice" transplanted. We dropped out when eggplant became a weekly bargain our kids would not eat. We lived in Chevy Chase for almost thirty years in that big house with a pool, a quiet haven and life style I had never really known. Valentine, Sherman was still struggling along, and I earned enough for a while from it to pay our bills. We had two young kids, Lucy, just under two years old, Susan, a newborn, and mortgage payments when that income vanished.

The Humphrey memoir lingered close to finished, but was not published until 1976. I was too old to be a totally free sprit, and too young and poor to retire. And I had a new family who provided me the most personally fulfilling and comfortable time of my life. I wanted to be with them as much as possible and not in some office or lobbying in congressional halls. Whenever a job interfered with my making school lunches and kept me from reading bedtime books to my kids, I moved on. But they did have to eat.

So, beginning then and continuing during the next several decades, I largely lived the life of a ghost, doing three memoirs beyond Humphrey's and writing books and speeches for a wide variety of people. When there were no speeches or books, I did annual reports and newsletters, and an occasional press release. It was an odd career, but I had developed a talent for writing in the voices of others. The books were for quite different people and described their quite different lives. The speechmakers spoke to a wide range of audiences, peddling material things for today, or ideas for tomorrow, or a vision for a distant future. That may be a bit grandiose because I also wrote about paper-box manufacture, municipal bonds, rental cars, and other equally earth-shaking matters. It was a good life. I depended on no single source for income; I had no boss or bureaucracy to serve; I usually worked at home.

Speech writing depends on several things: quick study (and faster forgetting), an ear for the cadence of the speaker, and words that seem natural for him or her, often with some inspirational spirit or purpose, all without being pretentious. Almost everyone feels the need to offer something light or funny to start. I was better on humor than inspiration, but I managed generally to reach both. Somewhere along the way, I was taught that every speech had three parts in which you "tell the audience what you are going to say, say it, and then tell them what you said." That seemed to work.

In later years, I developed a peculiar specialty. I was regularly called on to draft or revise eulogies. It was an odd talent, but the word got out. I helped Skip Humphrey when his mother, Muriel, died. One frequent user of my sad, but inspiring, words for grieving families and friends was Warren Spannaus, who had been attorney general of Minnesota and had run unsuccessfully for governor. He was a caring person, easy to like, and many people justifiably thought of him as friend. He was often asked by appreciative families to deliver a eulogy for a loved one. One day when he called and said, "Hi, this is Warren," I responded, "Who died?"

When Walter Mondale was elected vice president in 1976 and left the Senate, Wendy Anderson, who had been governor and a long-time friend, replaced him. Despite my Watergate conviction that I thought would make me politically poisonous, Wendy, without pause, asked me to help on speeches. That was my first job, and a political one, after my double debacle of Watergate and the Valentine, Sherman failure.

I was not intimately involved in Mondale's campaigns, but I cared about his success. I was surprised to learn that Gene

McCarthy did not like Mondale and did not support him in any way when Mondale's name was floated as a potential vice presidential candidate. Indeed, he disparagingly said of Mondale, "He has the soul of a vice president." I found that a bit of hypocrisy since he had so ardently sought that nomination in 1968.

Several decades of DFL work in common cause and Mondale's support in Gene's own congressional campaigns seemed to mean nothing. Humphrey told us that McCarthy not only opposed the Carter-Mondale ticket privately to the end, but had indicated that he might publically support the election of Jerry Ford. He later called Carter, who subsequently won the Nobel Peace Prize, "the worst president we have ever had." For someone who lived through Watergate and the Nixon resignation, his comment was bizarre.

He must have known Humphrey would tell Mondale and that Humphrey would ask himself whether Gene might have voted, with more immediate ego involved, for Richard Nixon in 1968. In 1980, McCarthy endorsed Ronald Reagan, not Mondale.

McCarthy ran five times for president, getting just under 31,000 votes of the 91 million cast in 1988, running behind candidates from the Libertarian, New Alliance, and Populist parties and a percentage point ahead of all write-in votes. Earlier, in 1982, at home in Minnesota, he was beaten 69% to 24% in a senatorial primary. Beyond his cardinal sin, he is hard to understand or explain.

Writing for others remained my major occupation, but I was open to most anything that sounded interesting. And something that was exciting came along. President Ford was my benefactor, and he enabled me to have a personal moment with another leader of a country—Fidel Castro (and his kid brother, Raul).

When Ford was president, there was talk within the State Department and in Cuba about restoring trade relations. Cuba was permitted to open the equivalent of an embassy in Washington. It was called an "Interest Section," and while its top official could not be called ambassador, he functioned as ambassadors do. It is still there, and we have an equivalent presence in Havana. (That is changing now.) I first learned about this from two people with whom I shared office space. One was Frank Mankiewicz. The other was Kirby Jones, who had worked with Frank in the 1972 McGovern campaign. All of us had been stricken by presidential defeat at one time or another and called ourselves "the government in exile." (One day, Frank asked if I wanted to meet a Southern governor who was coming in to see him. I had long since had my fill of Georgia crackers and told him no. It was, of course, Jimmy Carter.)

Frank and Kirby had little work and little income. In a creative and desperate moment they came up with the idea of interviewing heads of state who had not been on American television for a long time, if ever. They were able to arrange an interview with Golda Meir of Israel, borrowed money to buy film and hire a photographer, and were preparing to leave when she stepped down from her office.

They now had debt, film, and no hope until they thought of Fidel Castro. With the intercession of a left-wing filmmaker, Castro agreed to the interview. They went to Havana and waited. Several days went by and nothing happened. In despair, certain there would be no interview, they aimed for a final dinner together before leaving empty-handed. Mankiewicz, who grew a heavy face of stubble each day, was in the bathroom in his shorts, his face foamed up, and a razor in his hand when there was a knock at the door. Just as he was, he answered the door, and there stood Fidel Castro and an interpreter. (It is a picture that breaks me up even now.)

Castro said he understood they wanted to interview him, and arrangements were made to do so the following day. When Frank and Kirby got home with their treasure, no network would buy the filmed interview.

With Ginny and Kirby Jones joking with Fidel Castro during visit of the Minneapolis Chamber of Commerce to Cuba in 1977

If the networks hadn't done it, it just wasn't journalism. It could be propaganda.

But a reprieve came. CBS said they would buy it if Dan Rather could meet with Castro so they could combine his film with theirs. Frank and Kirby arranged for the meeting and it all aired on CBS as the Dan Rather interview. When the first filming was over, Castro had taken Frank and Kirby aside to tell them of the likely renewal of trade relations. He also said Cuba was not set up for a stream of salesmen showing up one at a time with their sample cases or literature about their products. He asked if they could bring groups down.

Mankiewicz opted out, but Kirby started a company, Alamar Associates, and asked me for help. I was able to get the Minneapolis Chamber of Commerce to sponsor a visit. I contacted a friend I had met while I was a janitor at the Minneapolis Tribune, Bower Hawthorne, who was Chamber president that year, as well as the Trib's editor. He gathered a group of about 100 executives and wives, including some from major corporations—General Mills, Honeywell, and Pillsbury.

Smaller businesses, including one that specialized in pork bellies, completed the group. Their plane stopped in Washington where Humphrey greeted them and wished them well. He was not the last high-level office holder they would meet.

After we had spent a few days visiting hospitals, housing projects, and schools, a session was scheduled with Cuban officials who would be the buyers of various things. Kirby and I were told privately that Castro hoped to come over, meet the visitors, and answer their questions. We were forbidden to tell anyone in case there was a change in his plans, but at the appointed hour, he came unannounced through the door behind the head table.

The Minnesota capitalists were instantaneously on their feet applauding their new favorite communist. He wowed them with his thorough knowledge about everything they were interested in and answered questions for an hour. When Bower asked for a final question, the vice president of the Minneapolis-based Billy Graham Evangelical Association stood. Quoting the Bible, he asked something about Cuban society and religion. It was not overtly hostile, but had an edge. Castro, without missing a beat, responded through his interpreter with another quote from the Bible. He had studied long before at a Jesuit school. It was short of a second coming, but the Graham soul just shook his head in disbelief, and, I think, admiration. He had brought a couple dozen Bibles with him for a Christian church that still existed. He thought he would have to sneak them somehow to the congregation, but the Cubans supplied a car and driver when we asked.

On a later trip of Chicago businessmen and some of their wives, Ginny and I witnessed several smooth performances. One beautiful, smartly dressed wife wobbled up to Castro, grabbed the side of his beard, and uttered, "I have always wondered if it was real." Castro assured his new alcoholic friend that it was.

Later Ginny and I were standing with Raul Castro and his wife, Vilma Espin, who had been in the mountains with the original revolutionary band and was leader of the women's

Ginny and me with Raoul Castro and his wife, Vilma Espin, in Cuba, 1977

movement in Cuba. Raul wore a plain khaki military uniform without medals or stars. A farm equipment salesman came up; we introduced him, and he asked, "Why do you Latin American dictators wear such fancy uniforms?"

Cubans do not think of themselves as Latin Americans; they do not like to be called dictators; and the uniform was, as I have noted, plain and unadorned. Castro smiled and said, "I am head of the armed forces."

We made a few more trips, ultimately taking several hundred corporations from New York, Chicago, Baltimore, Los Angeles, Atlanta, and Miami there. Visiting Cuba was exciting. From the Bay of Pigs to Old Havana, to Ernest Hemingway's house, there were historic sights to see. Meeting Fidel and Raul Castro was unexpected and even exciting. I thought I had embarked on a new career. But, the election of a more liberal president unexpectedly derailed the anticipated changes. Zbigniew Brzezinski, the Carter foreign policy adviser, considered Cuba only a bargaining chip in our relations with the Soviet Union and blocked the rapprochement that would have been valuable for both Cuba and us.

The embargo remains, almost 40 years later, a sieve with some companies dealing for a time through an overseas division. A law making that impossible was passed around 2000, sponsored by a Democratic senator from New Jersey, Robert Torricelli. He was playing for votes from his loudest Cuban-exile constituents. (After leaving the Senate, he was accused of misusing about $2,000,000 in leftover campaign contributions.) Today, once again, normal trade relations and a relaxed diplomacy are being talked about by President Obama.

We made friends with the Cuban diplomats in Washington, several of whom lived nearby, and continued to see them socially for many years after. (Since the business escort service ended, we have taken two trips to Cuba—one in the late 1980s with our children and recently to identify and count birds.) But, the Cuba trips were only part-time and did not provide a steady income, so I looked for more writing jobs.

I was recruited by Bob Herbst to work for him in the Game and Fish division of the Department of the Interior. Bob was head of the division and had earlier run the Department of Natural Resources in Minnesota. I did all of his speeches and a few for Secretary Cecil Andrus. Different from most of my speech writing, the subject matter was one I cared about.

Toward the end of the Carter administration in 1979, I was asked by Doug Bennet to be director of public affairs at the Agency for International Development (AID), which he then ran. That was a more substantial job supervising a staff of 50 people in a field that was new to me. I might have stayed a long time, but Jimmy Carter was not reelected.

Shortly after Carter lost, a guy from Chicago whom I did not know called and asked to see me. I got a chance to become an intellectual almost overnight. My caller explained that he worked for Richard Dennis, a young commodities trader who had started with a borrowed $1,600 and was now, just a few years after he began, worth over $200 million.

Dennis wanted to underwrite a liberal think tank, and when we met he sought my advice on who should run it, topics to study, resident fellows to hire, a possible name to define it. I was incredulous that he should ask me, but remained silent, looked serious and thoughtful. It was a good act and they apparently asked no one else (which bewilders me to this day). I suggested Doug Bennet to run it. The word came back almost immediately from Chicago that they had checked him out and wanted him. When he was hired, he hired me.

The Roosevelt Center for American Policy Studies found space on Capitol Hill. My first significant and memorable moment came soon after we began and I was exposed to my first personal computer. I had spent several hours working on a speech when suddenly a message scrolled down the screen: "fatal error, fatal error, fatal error." I learned how fatal it was. Nothing was left of my eloquence. I was speechless.

I stood in the doorway of my office and yelled, "Does anyone want to see an old man cry?" The cheering throng included young scholars and serious thinkers, very bright and knowledgeable people, most of whom became in later years high-ranking members of Democratic administrations, faculty at universities, and scholars at other think tanks.

One, Barry Blechman, was an expert on nuclear non-proliferation; another, Bill Lynn became Deputy Secretary of Defense. They are still today sought out and quoted. Another useful hire was Nelson Polsby, who gave us instant credibility. He was a distinguished professor of political science at Berkeley, an expert on Congress, and on sabbatical. He had one other appealing quality. He had been my landlord. Before going to the

University of California, he and his family had been living in Washington where we had met at the home of a mutual friend. When Berkeley called, he suddenly needed to sublet his house. I moved in, and our friendship grew each month with my check, although it almost ended when I sent their belongings to them and Nelson angrily accused me of keeping a broom.

But my most delightful and wise hire was a young woman fresh out of college looking essentially for her first professional job. Tina Rosenberg somehow found us, having already had a job offer from one of the weekly news magazines. Nelson Polsby convinced her to come work for us, explaining that she would be a flunky in a news bureau, getting coffee for the stars and sharpening their pencils. With us, she would be surrounded by ideas, invited to not only listen, but participate.

She came to us and thrived. When we lay dying as an institution with diminishing support, she wandered off to Central America, sang in a Mexican nightclub, and within a few years won a MacArthur Fellowship, a Pulitzer Prize and a National Book Award for non-fiction. She has since been an editorial writer for *The New York Times*. I suppose she would have made it without us, but we were a good place to start.

Besides Tina, I helped two other people in their careers. Newt Gingrich and Richard Cheney were relatively new congressmen, having been elected in 1978. I gave them a mini-platform. I had developed a Sunday evening TV debate program for CSPAN. Brian Lamb, the creator of the public affairs network, was a friend and needed to fill the air since they had just begun. My format was to pit a Democrat and a Republican against each other on a topic before Congress. The congressmen jumped at the chance for an audience of hundreds.

The Center did not last much longer, although not because of my association with it. It was funding. Richard Dennis decided he had had enough of us. Just then, Frank Mankiewicz resigned as president of National Public Radio. While it had nothing to do with his leaving, I learned from smiling staff that Frank had interviewed a Minnesota comic and rejected him because his humor was too regional. Garrison Keillor, despite that, began his career on American Public Radio, a kind of competitor, and continues today. With Frank gone, my role as employment agent surfaced again. I had the chance to suggest Doug Bennet as his successor. When he got the job, I followed him there to an ill-defined job as his assistant.

NPR had an exciting atmosphere of immediacy, civic importance, and serious product. I got to know the on-air personalities whom I had listened to and liked. The *troika*, as they were called, of Cokie Roberts, Linda Wertheimer, and Nina Totenberg were excellent reporters, pleasant people and stayed on the air when I went off, with my normal frequency, to another job.

My favorite Republican of all time, David Durenberger, had started a foundation, Americans for Generational Equity, when he left the Senate after two terms of representing Minnesota. He asked me to write for it. (I was not his first Sherman employee. He had hired two of our kids to work in his Senate office.) Ahead of its time, the foundation focused on the excessive burdens that might be left by our generation for succeeding ones.

Millionaires with a social conscience or concern about some aspect of American life seemed to find me. The Roosevelt Center for American Policy Studies, The Benton Foundation, the Hospice Foundation all had an underwriter with a small or substantial fortune, earned or inherited, and a larger heart than most. They wanted to do something useful and lasting.

For a time, I headed the Benton Foundation until my lack

of academic expertise on communication matters coupled with my continued irreverence made my departure inevitable. One day, our funder came in with a band-aid on his temple. I asked, "Cut yourself while shaving?" He said "No, I've just been checked for skin cancer."

Charles Benton, son of the advertising tycoon and U.S. Senator William Benton, cared about communications and quality journalism as an essential part of democracy. Richard Dennis, an unpolished guy with a fortune made in the stock market, wanted a place where ideas were honed and debated and would become a goad or inspiration in law-making. Jack Gordon, a successful savings and loan executive, had accumulated more savings than loans and cared about end-of-life matters and the grieving that followed death.

Each job had its pleasures, but one provided a special and lasting experience for me. At the Hospice Foundation, I put together teleconferences on "Living With Grief" that attracted huge numbers of caregivers across the country each time. Our guide and moderator was Ken Doka, a professor of gerontology and expert in the field of death, dying, and bereavement. (He was also a Lutheran minister, although I didn't know that when we sought him.) We added moderators to the teleconferences to lend some glamour to a tough subject. Cokie Roberts, former congressman Hale Boggs' daughter as well as a friend from National Public Radio, moderated one. Rosalyn Carter introduced another and helped in other ways.

Our third in 1996 reached thousands of grief counselors, social workers, even some clergy, in 120 towns and cities. Alaska was the state with the most places per capita where it could be seen, and a community health worker wrote after the teleconference, "I live and work in Deering, population about 600 . . ..In the village here everyone is related by blood or marriage. When a death occurs in any one the villages, the whole region feels the loss."

She asked if we could come to Kotzebue, a town north of the Arctic Circle, to train people working with the bereaved. I set up a week-long trip with Doka, and he and I flew across the tundra in a single-engine bush plane to several other villages. At one point, we were 600 miles from Anchorage, 2,000 miles north of Seattle, 4,000 miles from D.C. and just 200 miles east of Russia.

Doka was a star. The native people of Alaska we visited are stereotyped as silent and undemonstrative in public. One woman whose year-old daughter had died had refused to talk about it even with her family. They insisted she come. And she wept as others talked about it and her. By the end of the meeting, she was able to talk about her feelings and even smile a bit as she asked for more counseling.

A woman who talked, probably for the first time in public about her mother's decline and death, sobbed and was embraced by others of the "undemonstrative natives." A woman talked of her four children dying in a house fire. The rest of the audience knew once a fire started there was neither water nor fire department to stop it. In the winter, temperatures were too cold to do anything. Ultimately, everyone seemed to have a story to tell.

A young man described his father falling through the ice, ripping off a glove at his last minute and throwing it up and out on the ice to show them where he had died. Another talked of "disappearances." Someone goes fishing and never comes back. Someone on a snowmobile goes hunting and neither man nor machine is seen again. I think I learned more about community and caring and mutual need there than anywhere else or anytime before or after.

After a stint at a Blue Cross Blue Shield HMO, a woman I met there, Lisa Rubarth, and I started a newsletter called *Women's Sports Pages.* She provided the sports knowledge and she and I wrote the articles. We had a handful of enthusiastic subscribers, but too few to keep us going. I added expertise on Title IX, the sex discrimination in educational institutions part of the Educational Amendments Act of 1972, to thermostats and nuclear submarines as subjects I could write about with aplomb and without much background.

After that, I went back to a new dimension of ghost writing. I turned from speeches to books. I had no guidelines for book writing. Books are long and hard to make coherent and interesting. The memoirs I worked on were by distinguished people with very different backgrounds, education, and accomplishments. One was *Entering New Worlds* by Max Kampelman, my early nemesis on the Communist Control Act and soon after a good friend. He had worked for Humphrey for five years beginning in 1949 and later stayed close as a friend and important adviser until the end.

Max was a bit of an anomaly. His family had fled pogroms in Russia and Romania. He became a Jewish conscientious objector during WWII and had volunteered for a starvation diet project housed under the stands of the University of Minnesota football stadium. He started at about 160 pounds and ended at 120. He met Humphrey when the experiment was over and he stayed on at the University to work on a Ph.D. After he gained a little weight and finished his course work, he taught at Bennington College before joining the first Humphrey staff in Washington.

Strangely, through subsequent years, he was less partisan than some of the rest of us, and often belittled as a "neocon" by some around Humphrey. He interrupted his legal career (he already had a law degree when he arrived in Minnesota) to serve successfully as President Reagan's ambassador and negotiator on arms control, forging an agreement between the Soviet Union and the U.S. that diminished the danger of nuclear war. (He first held the job under President Carter.) For one day during the Reagan administration while Secretary of State George Schultz was away, Max was acting secretary of State. It was quite a career for the son of a New York kosher butcher.

Earlier, President Johnson told Humphrey he would like Max to join his White House staff as counsel replacing a "Kennedy man." Max turned it down, in part because a neighbor, the wife of long-time Johnson staff man, George Reedy, described LBJ as "a cold, conniving, demanding, cruel, and mean person." George himself later wrote of Johnson, "As a human being, he was a miserable person . . .a bully, sadist, lout, and egotist. His lapses from civilized conduct were deliberate and usually intended to subordinate someone else to his will."

Another book was for an exceptional and exceptionally rich woman, Mary Marvin Breckenridge Patterson. She was the granddaughter of industrial titan B.F. Goodrich and married the son of a founder of National Cash Register. She was a descendent of John Breckenridge, vice president under President James Buchanan.

In 1929, at the age of 24, she became the first female aircraft pilot in Maine. The next year, she wrote and produced a film on the Frontier Nursing Service, which a relative had founded and funded to serve poor, isolated women in the Appalachians. During the Second World War she worked in Europe for CBS News. Her boss was the preeminent journalist of the time, Edward R. Murrow. She was one of very few females in the trade, and became one of Murrow's "boys," as the team was famously called.

Mrs. Patterson liked to describe herself as a "decollector" and said she would rather work at her desk giving away property and money than go to lunch with friends. I once escorted her to a black-tie dinner at the Library of Congress. It was one of the places to which she made significant donations in her share-the-wealth policy. I bought a tuxedo for the event. I have worn it once since and it does not need pressing if the opportunity for preening comes again.

She introduced Ginny and me to her "village" in York, Maine where she lived on the banks of the York River at Goodrich Point (property later decollected to Bowdoin College). Among her social and economic equals was a lady about 80 years old who joined us for lunch at the York Yacht Club. Knowing of my political background, she talked politics. She told us she would not be voting for George H.W. Bush (who also lived nearby in the summer) for a simple reason: he supported a measure that would prevent her from having an abortion if she needed one. That declaration was later published, with her permission, in *Newsweek* magazine, resulting in a family outraged at her breaking out of their closed world.

Silence apparently was a dominant quality in their village of old wealth. Ultimately, relatives of Mrs. Patterson found her finished book "too honest," particularly about her two adopted children and her relations with them. Sadly the family thought she shouldn't publish it, and she gave in to them.

I worked for several years on another memoir that was not published. It was for a Humphrey friend, Dwayne Andreas, an Amish farm boy who grew up on a tiny Iowa farm and ultimately became head of Archer Daniels Midland (ADM), the agribusiness giant that focused on soybeans and corn. By the time I met him, he was a multi-millionaire, a generous contributor to Humphrey, and a major fundraiser for many years. His company attorney for a while was Thomas Dewey, the Republican candidate for president against Harry Truman. Some Humphrey staff and associates figured he gave money to both parties and was an opportunist. He never hid what he was doing, was selective in whom he supported, and Humphrey never questioned his loyalty or friendship.

Dwayne was more than a money-bag; he was sophisticated in the ways of the political world, cared about programs for feeding the hungry, and was so close to Humphrey that we all, as I've noted, had election night dinner in 1968 at his home. Dwayne's completed book was canned when his son, Mick, was convicted of a relatively minor offense involving their business. Mick went to a minimum-security prison for a time, and the manuscript went into a file drawer. I was sad about both.

The most satisfying memoir, and my first, was, of course, *The Education of a Public Man*, Humphrey's life story. I spent many hours interviewing him and he spent more recording additional thoughts. I turned the oral work into written material still clearly in his voice. One reviewer said he didn't know how much help Humphrey had, but that every word sounded like him. That could make a ghost editor smile. After Humphrey died, the University of Minnesota Press published a paperback edition and asked me to add an *Afterword*.

I also reached beyond memoir writing on one occasion. I helped a psychiatrist friend, Steve Hersh, write a book called *Living With Cancer*. When I started on it, I wasn't sure I would enjoy something so different from the other books, but by the time the book went to press, I thought I had a medical degree and had made some lives more tolerable.

I ended my working career in 2001 after two years as a professor of political communications at Louisiana State

so did I !

University. I had been asked by the dean of the journalism school, then a friend, with whom I had worked at AID to join a faculty committee as an outsider to judge candidates for a chair just funded by a generous outdoor advertising family. I did my work seriously, and, when the faculty deadlocked and rejected all others, someone suggested that I be asked to come to Baton Rouge. It was a wonderful two years of eating the local Cajun cuisine, bird watching in new places, and teaching eager young people.

When my professorial career was up, Ginny and I chose to live in Arizona, not for its politics that are generally awful, but for its weather and natural life that are generally superb. We have liked walking in the mountains, finding both endemic and migratory birds, growing cactus, and relaxing. I have learned local wisdom: do not back up in the desert and do not hug saguaros. It has been a good 14 years.

13. Politics and Public Service

You frequently hear "politicians" heaped together in a negative way as though they are a sub-species and all the same: greasy palms, stuffed pockets, a price tag on a sleeve, grown fat at the public trough, serving the interests of contributors. Some people in public office, of course, are corrupt, panderers, kept men and women. But not every elected official deserves disdain, and the bad ones have many cousins in banking, business, education, and the church.

Politics is a process, not a sin. You find politics at work in the College of Cardinals when a pope is elected, in universities when a new president is chosen, in the boardrooms of big business before the annual statement is written, in the Rotarians when a chapter head is selected, and in student councils in high schools.

Along with some negative definitions, Webster's dictionary says politicians are "experienced in the art or science of government." They are "concerned with the making of, as distinguished from the administration of, public policy." Most politicians are really there to serve, at least most were in my day, and I think most still are. Honor is cherished. Public purpose and service are real. The driving force for a large majority, from alderman to president, is making our democracy work for more people. The traditional Republican party of Abraham Lincoln, Teddy Roosevelt, even Dwight Eisenhower has been in that mainstream. From Franklin Roosevelt, Harry Truman, Hubert Humphrey and beyond, I think we Democrats are even "more so."

Democrats everywhere are battered by the endless conservative chants that government is too big and run by incompetents. But most Democratic politicians know that government can, and should, be dedicated to improving lives as much as we can. Small is not a virtue; service is.

That's why I have proclaimed without apology that I am a politician. And Minnesota is and has been a special place to be one. From all I've seen, Minnesota politicians in both parties (except Michelle Bachman and Jesse Ventura) are often better than what you find in most other states and are more deeply committed to honorable service. That may be excessive self-praise, but is still essentially true. In any case, my years in the DFL were exhilarating because of the people I met and worked with and for the sense of purpose that motivated them. Beyond policy, my satisfaction, my pleasure has come from knowing good people trying to do good things.

Some political associations begin deep and grow stronger, but some don't last, and occasionally are not much more than a passing fancy. Even with seemingly close friends, permanence is elusive. People move and it is tough to stay in touch. Some friends and colleagues rise above you; some sink out of sight.

Two friendships that began when I was first attracted to mainstream liberal politics survived and are special. Those two politicians shared little in background beyond being Norwegian, but they shared much in goals, commitments, and service that I liked. That's why I include Karl Rolvaag and Walter Mondale in this memoir. They were not blood brothers, but they were brothers of another, and precious, sort. They thought and acted on their belief that a good society was not chimera, but something that could be approached if we wanted it and tried.

Karl became a friend when he was DFL party chairman in the early 1950s and stayed one until his death in 1990. He was elected lieutenant governor, then governor, and served as the U.S. ambassador to Iceland. Place and position never affected our sense of common interests. Other than coming from immigrant families, our early years could not have been more different, but that was never an impediment.

That we shared liberal beliefs and attitudes was only the start. We bonded, ex-Wobbly, ex-Trotskyist hanger-on, in a manner somehow different from others in my political life. We enjoyed each other's company. We fished together on the boundary waters out of International Falls on the Minnesota border with Canada. We talked about people and policies everywhere. When Ginny and I married, he and his wife, Florence, drove down to Owatonna for the ceremony. Toward the end of his life, we started working on his autobiography, but could find no one interested in publishing it.

Karl grew up in Northfield, a small Minnesota college town where his father, Ole Rolvaag, had become a professor and novelist. His novel, *Giants in the Earth*, a story of Norwegian immigrant life on the prairie, was one of the Book-of-the-Month Club's early selections. He was later nominated for a Nobel Prize in Literature, although he didn't win.

Ole, as a young man, was a fisherman near the Arctic Circle, leaving that to join the large Scandinavian migration to our Midwest. He arrived in the United States knowing little English. He learned it while working on a farm in

North Dakota, leaving the land for college, then teaching, and writing. Karl grew up in an intellectual household while his dad taught at St. Olaf College. One guest led the family in folk songs. It was Carl Sandberg, the distinguished American poet, visiting and strumming his guitar.

Unfortunately Karl's dad developed heart problems, and the local doctors (named Mayo) urged him to leave Minnesota winters for the warmth of the South. The family went to Biloxi, Mississippi, when Karl was 15. It didn't help Ole's health much, but it had a fateful influence on Karl. He learned about "stump likker." You put a quarter on a stump in the woods nearby and after an hour or so found a Mason jar filled with homemade whiskey where the quarter had been. After the first quarter, he was hooked. At first, he successfully hid his new habit from his family, a skill he honed and used in later years. As an adult, Karl would sometimes use a Mountain Dew bottle to disguise his vodka from those around him, and on Sunday mornings when he had run out of whiskey and the liquor stores were closed, he gulped Nyquil and Formula 44.

Two months after his father, still in his fifties, died in 1931, Karl took off for the West, living as a bum for six years. Much later, he described those years as "drifting, drinking, whoring around the United States." He worked as a field hand, fruit picker, and lumberjack, spent time in soup lines and hobo camps.

He joined the Industrial Workers of the World (IWW), a radical group of socialists, communists, and anarchists who had been around for about 30 years and was past its prime, but still present and active. He emerged from all that filled with an intensified drive for social activism.

As World War II approached, he became president of a local anti-war group, but, soon, putting aside his pacifism when war began, volunteered and ultimately won a Silver Star for bravery and a Purple Heart when he was severely wounded by both enemy and friendly fire that hit his tank. He spent much of two years hospitalized for wounds to his face and body. For his bravery after our invasion in Normandy, the French awarded him their *Croix de Guerre*. He fought on the beaches there and described for me his gagging at the smell of the decaying dead. It didn't make him a pacifist again, but he saw war clearly.

When I asked about his Silver Star, he explained his "bravery" with a smile. He was sitting on the ground leaning against his light tank, when a higher officer came up, glared at him, and said, "Lieutenant, mount up and move ahead." He did and the Germans fled. He felt it was more their cowardice than his skill that brought his award.

While he was still in uniform and still far away, Democratic leaders in southeastern Minnesota asked him to run for Congress. In the heavily Republican district, he lost. According to Karl, he had three qualifications for the office: he was Norwegian, Lutheran, and a veteran. He claimed nothing much beyond that and knew it was a hopeless effort. He ran again two years later and lost again, but losing didn't discourage his commitment to liberal politics and his urge to serve in public office. He was there as the DFL grew, not in the first tier of leaders, but close.

In 1954, he ran successfully for lieutenant governor on the ticket with Orville Freeman at the head and served there until 1962. The last two years were after Freeman lost in his race for a third term. (At the time, the lieutenant governor ran separately from the governor, and, as a result, they could be from different parties.) Karl was solid but not glittery, and when he wanted to run for governor in 1962, there was some opposition within the DFL.

Before his nomination, he asked me to draft a crucial

speech to be given to the State Central Committee, folks who influenced many of the votes at the state convention. It was a successful presentation. It was a near-eloquent oration in a dingy basement room in a St. Paul hotel that lit up the audience and brought an enthusiastic standing ovation, something he did not often get.

The wife of an English professor with whom I had studied was among the listeners and not for Karl before or after. Shirley Unger strode up to me, shook a finger in my face and barked, "You just won the nomination for him and you will regret it." I smiled at the implicit praise, infuriating her even more. I don't know how she felt when he was elected. As governor, he faced a conservative legislature that blocked most of his initiatives, although he did succeed in doing good things in education, particularly for state colleges, in mental health, and in housing.

I did not see Karl often while he was governor since I had moved to Washington, but we talked regularly, still mostly about politics and people, but sometimes about what he was trying to do as governor. Booze too often intruded. Once, when he was in northern Minnesota fishing with some buddies, there was an almost deadly moment. They tied up at a restaurant's dock and the others went in for something to eat, but he had passed out so they left him. In a few moments, he woke, started the boat's powerful motor without untying from the dock. The boat lurched forward only a couple of feet and he threw the motor into reverse, and repeated it all a couple of times until he pulled the pilings off the dock and roared from shore dragging them along. He ran into another boat, tossing the occupant into the water. Fortunately, the man was not injured and complained to no one other than Karl.

When Karl got back to St. Paul, he proclaimed "Boat Safety

Week," using his own sanitized experience as an example of the need for care on the water. He recognized it as an empty gesture, but did it anyway in his guilt and hope to defuse any bad publicity that might come. It was a classic case of political preemption.

He didn't do any better inside. At a dinner where he and his wife Florence sat apart at the head table, he quietly asked the waiter to bring him a triple martini, but put it all in a water glass and when he set it down to say loudly, "Here is your water, Governor." Florence looked over approvingly until she saw three olives floating in the glass.

Karl summed up most of the years of his life: "I had an alcohol-induced heart condition, a bad knee as a result of a drunken fall, and no spleen because of a drunken automobile accident. That was only the physical part."

When he counseled others, he told them of a night in the governor's mansion. Starting up the stairs to bed, drunk and exhausted, he remembered that he had some papers to read for an early morning meeting. But he was tired and torn. He couldn't decide whether he should go up to bed or down to his work. He burst into tears.

I have always felt guilty about Karl and Florence's increased drinking. It got worse in Iceland where they would not have been without my intervention. Karl wanted to be our ambassador to Norway, his ancestral home and whose language he spoke. There was a vacancy, but President Johnson believed that Karl had attacked his Vietnam policy at a governor's conference and would not name him to the post. The president's reaction was excessive. Karl had expressed his feelings about the war very carefully and in a limited way, certainly not wanting to embarrass Humphrey, much less challenge the president.

Bill Connell had persisted with the White House, and

they finally agreed to send Karl as ambassador to Iceland as a compromise. Bill called me one day to share his excitement at the success. I asked if he would like me to call Karl with the news. He said "Hell no." He wanted to carry the message. About 10 minutes later, my phone rang again and a hyper Connell rasped, "He turned it down."

Bill, unnerved, instructed me to call and convince Karl to take the job. I researched Iceland from the nature of the government to temperatures year-round, precipitation, and the size of the embassy staff. I called and persuaded Karl to accept the offer. I don't know if he and Florence would have drunk less in Norway, but I have always regretted that I helped send them to Iceland.

After they came home, Karl dried out with professional help and quit his drinking entirely. Tragically, Florence wasn't able to do so. She went several times to Hazelden, the alcoholism treatment institution where Karl had sought help. The last time, she and they thought she had her alcoholism beat. A few days later she started to drive to Texas to visit family. She drove off the road and died. She hadn't won the drinking battle. She lost her life alone, divorced from Karl and a sober life.

I think Karl's determination to serve well in his tank at Normandy remained every day in later life in his public service. When those who babble about government being our problem, I think they certainly didn't know or understand guys like Karl.

Another special political friendship began even before I worked in the DFL. Gerry Dillon introduced me to Fritz Mondale at lunch. We picked Fritz up in front of Fraser Hall, named after Don Fraser's father, who had been dean of the Law School, and recently renamed Mondale Hall. I didn't know for a time that Fritz's name was really Walter.

Mondale was still a student, but he was already an experienced political hand. He had been active in DFL campaigns virtually from its beginning. Still in his teens, he helped build the party in its infancy, and he apparently exhibited competence in everything he did. When we met, he had earned a bachelor's degree in political science and was working for the law degree he received in 1956. He was thin, wore an old pair of khaki pants and a short-sleeved shirt, a casual sartorial disguise that initially hid his very serious nature from me. Periodically, we three would have lunch again, and by the time Fritz and Joan Adams were to marry, I was close enough to be recruited for an essential job.

They were married in St. Paul a couple of days after Christmas at Macalester College where Joan's father was the chaplain. The student union, the site of the ceremony, was not elegant or festive. To jazz it up, Fritz and I toured the Twin Cities to collect unsold Christmas trees heaped in piles in now-vacant lots. They were worthless and an unattractive nuisance to get rid of. We served a useful role for the absent owner and for civic beauty. We would fill Mondale's car trunk with a few trees, yank them out at the wedding site, and set out again. We decked the hall with boughs and he married Joan who brought a special charm and joy to their long marriage and was an effective political partner.

After he graduated with honors, Fritz practiced law for a short while, but his heart was in political work and public service. He may have learned all that from his minister father, who served churches in small towns in southern Minnesota. But, it was more his natural leadership ability and his integrity that earned him immediate respect.

So it was not surprising when Fritz, just 33 years old, was

appointed in 1960 by then Governor Freeman to be attorney general, replacing an erratic Miles Lord who had resigned. There was a vacancy on the Minnesota Supreme Court and Miles leaked to a reporter that he was the leading candidate for it, hoping to pressure Freeman into appointing him. He was not on the list and Freeman, not someone to be toyed with, was angered by the ploy and encouraged Miles to leave. Without Miles' loony gambit, the Mondale career would not have started then and he likely wouldn't have succeeded Humphrey in the Senate.

Mondale looked his age. On my first visit to his office, he told me he was not going to smile in public, wanting to look serious always, never frivolous, and, thus, maybe appear older than he was. I thought his wonderful sense of humor disappeared, overwhelmed by his statesman-like pose. But it worked. He was immediately popular and respected for his mien, but even more for his creative work, particularly fighting fraud and abuse.

One case that brought him immediate respect was charging and convicting executives of a local and beloved charitable organization, the Sister Kenny Foundation, with fraudulently milking it through kickbacks. Sister Kenny was an Australian nurse who came to Minnesota to fight a polio epidemic with some distinctive techniques and was held in near awe. The chief thief was the former mayor of Minneapolis whom Humphrey had defeated.

Later, when Humphrey was elected vice president and would be vacating his Senate seat, I became a Mondale advocate and ally in the Humphrey office, although the decision was certainly not determined by my support. The other replacement possibility was John Blatnik, the congressman for almost 20 years from the Iron Range and Duluth in northern Minnesota. He had been a good congressman, was a strong liberal with significant labor support. He had a certain charm, but he was not really close to Humphrey or to Rolvaag who would make the appointment. Mondale quickly became the inevitable choice. In his two terms in the Senate, he was thoughtful and successful and recognized by senators much his senior as someone special. I didn't see him often, but despite his new status, every contact we had was as collegial and relaxed as earlier ones.

Humphrey was delighted when Jimmy Carter chose Fritz as his running mate. He gave Fritz a simple bit of advice: "Take the nomination only if you have a commitment from Carter that you will have your office in the White House." (Others, oddly, have taken credit for that caveat, but only Humphrey had been vice president.) No vice president before Fritz had enjoyed that proximity to the president, and Humphrey knew it would make a huge difference.

A president could not easily ignore someone underfoot. His staff couldn't erect a wall between the two men if they were physically close. The process of decision-making, out-of-sight if you were across West Executive Avenue, was impossible to hide. Real estate transformed the vice president into a visible presence and real influence.

During Humphrey's vice presidency, I was in the White House no more than a few times in the four years. Twice I went when Humphrey invited me to lunch with him in the Mess where I could not normally go. Johnson's press secretary asked me to come over one day. When we went to the Paris Air Show, I was on the lawn briefly before the helicopter took off. When Johnson was in the Bethesda Naval Hospital, I went there with my boss. At one point, Johnson looked at me and seemed to be thinking, "Who the hell is that?" Our

staff's isolation and separation may not have made any difference considering Johnson's personality and style, but in some
little, but possibly significant, ways it might have. The White
House was a walled city for us, but not for Fritz.

After Fritz became vice president he would invite me to
have lunch with him alone at his new home on the Naval
Observatory grounds (which he was also the first vice president to occupy). I suspected, although he never said explicitly, that some minor irritation with staff, or possibly with the
president himself, was bugging him. Talking about Humphrey and Johnson's relationship seemed to help.

At one point after I had been asked to do something (I
forget what) and was in his office, I said with a straight face to
his secretary, an old friend from Minnesota, that I heard from
Fritz only when he wanted or needed company and counsel at
lunch. I complained that I had never been invited to the vice
presidential residence for a state or formal occasion for dinner. A couple of receptions had been all. I meant my whine as
a joke since you don't invite yourself to dinner, but Penny took
our private conversation seriously and reported it to Fritz.

My impertinence turned quickly into an embarrassment.
A couple of days later, when I got home from work, Ginny said
there had been a call from Mondale. I said, "You mean from
his office?" She assured me it had been Mondale. I immediately called the number he had left. He answered the phone
and invited us to dinner two nights later, explaining that he
had been fishing, caught some walleye, and would cook them
himself, since the staff would be having a night off while Joan
was away. I thanked him, but said we couldn't, that we had
visitors from California, old friends of Ginny's. We hung up.

Soon the phone rang again. It was Fritz saying that we
should bring our guests. He had enough fish, and the staff

agreed to stay to help out. It was, indeed, a social invitation, and walleye fixed right is delicious. I accepted for us all.

We were a little vague with our guests about where we were going, but as we approached the Naval Observatory grounds where the vice presidential mansion stood atop a hill, we explained what was up. We stopped at the guard shack, gave our names, and proceeded up the hill to the house where Fritz stood outside in greeting. We, and our surprised, awestruck guests, had dinner at a table, with an elegant white table cloth, on the lawn just outside the house, the neat grounds sloping away.

Just as we were finishing our meal, a Secret Service agent approached, apologized for the interruption, and asked if the Mondales were expecting a grandfather's clock from Dayton, Ohio. Some relative of Joan's wanted her to have a family heirloom. The agent said the driver had asked if he could deliver it immediately since that would permit him to drive back to Dayton that night, saving the cost of a motel room. Fritz said that would be fine.

After dinner, Fritz said he wanted to take us upstairs to see a renovation to the house that Nelson Rockefeller had made. Rockefeller, selected as Gerald Ford's vice president, had not moved in, but had expected to. What Fritz showed us was a Rockefeller modification he had made when he thought he was going to continue as vice president and move into the mansion, a step up even for him. The four of us followed Mondale into a small room that served as a library and office, down the hall from the master bedroom and next to a guest room. Fritz opened the closet door and then, grinning, moved a sliding door where a solid wall had once been. While Happy Rockefeller was asleep at one end of the hall, Nelson, ostensibly studying for a next-day meeting, maybe with the president, could slip into the guest bedroom for a discussion, or something.

Mondale was a good vice president. He served a decent president, but a Washington novice, with solid private counsel. He worked the political circuit effectively. He carried off both ceremonial and serious duties overseas well. (He did once describe Washington as 67 square miles surrounded by reality, but he liked being inside those boundaries.) He earned the honor of the Democratic nomination for president in 1984 and it is a pity he lost to an empty suit.

His wife, Joan, was also special. She was an accomplished potter and a devotee of the arts. While Fritz was vice president, she led a successful effort to get the National Park Service gift shops to carry the work of local artists. When they went to Japan, she, the ambassador's wife with a common touch, delighted the Japanese with her interest in their artists and pottery. She earned, both here and abroad, her affectionate nickname of "Joan of Art."

My most special moment with Fritz was filled with sadness. Humphrey, his patron, his colleague, his close friend had died. It was not unexpected, of course. Humphrey dealt with his fate honestly, publicly, and without self-pity. Toward the end, his family had arranged for a long distance line so he could make calls to friends and former staff across the country. When my phone rang one evening there was a chatty Humphrey who talked of many things, but not himself. When I hung up, I said to Ginny, "He's called to say goodbye." He died January 13, 1978, just a few days later.

Shortly after he died, my phone rang again. Fritz was calling from his plane that was soon to land and said he was to give a eulogy two days later in the Capitol Rotunda at the service where President Carter would also speak. He asked me to come to his house to help him draft what he would say as Humphrey lay in state.

When I joined him and Al Eisele, his press secretary and former reporter for the *St. Paul Dispatch and Pioneer Press*, we talked and then began, unsuccessfully, to reach any real eloquence. We struggled; we tossed what we had written, and then repeated the process until Mondale's fatigue and emotion overwhelmed him. Al and I went to my house to write what we three had not yet been able to do. Even that didn't work and Al eventually left.

I stayed up most of the night and produced the eulogy with some of Al's words and with Mondale adding a favorite quote from Shakespeare and a bit more. Ironically, when I arrived in a motorcade for the ceremony, I found that my name had been left off the admittance list prepared by my colleague and the pope's friend, David Gartner. Dave and I had never managed a close relationship, much less friendship. Because of his mean spirit, I listened to the ceremony on the radio standing next to a cortege car in front of the Capitol, some of my own words leaving me close to tears, outside but proud.

Unlike most people in high office, Fritz immediately gave me credit in public and in print for what I had contributed. He certainly didn't have to do it. I had not expected it, since ghosts for the most part remain humbly, or quite self-satisfied, in the background. But he made me a participant at a very special moment of my life. The *San Diego Tribune* reported, "Afterward, when Humphrey's sister went up to Mondale in tears to thank him, he said: 'Yes, it was beautiful. . . . Norman Sherman wrote it.' "

Some political people forget you quickly when they don't need you anymore. That has not been the case here. We exchange emails, he often answering mine faster than I do his. We have lunch or meet when Ginny and I are in Minnesota. In 60 some years he has never disappointed me in public policy or personal relationships.

Here is an example. A couple of years ago, when he was going to be in Oslo, Norway, where he is a known and popular Norwegian-American, I asked a favor of him. He stayed at the hotel where the Nobel Peace Prize is awarded. I told him that Ginny's niece and her husband were chefs in the hotel and I asked, half facetiously, if he would stop by the kitchen to say hello from us. He did, loudly asking once he was in the kitchen, "Is Ronna O'Toole here?" She was not, but her husband, Patrick, was. His cooking may not have improved, but his status did.

Fritz and I, (he a bit farther than I) have traveled a long way since our first lunch. I have met or worked for people I have respected and liked, people who have done good things for our country, but I have never known anyone of greater decency, integrity, and friendship. I regret deeply that he did not become president. The country would have known him as I have. Now, here is the eulogy that he delivered to the brightest star in our political galaxy.

• • • • •

Dear Muriel, the Humphrey family, and guests:

There is a natural impulse at a time like this to dwell on the many accomplishments of Hubert Humphrey's remarkable life, by listing a catalog of past events, as though there were some way to quantify what he was all about. But I don't want to do that, because Hubert didn't want it, and neither does Muriel.

Even though this is one of the saddest moments of my life and I feel as great a loss as I have ever known, we must remind ourselves of Hubert's last great wish: that this be a time to celebrate life and the future, not to mourn the past and his death.

But, Muriel, I hope you will forgive me if I don't entirely succeed in looking forward and not backward because I must for a moment.

Two days ago, as I flew back from the West over the land that Hubert loved and to this city that he loved, I thought back over his life and its meaning, and I tried to understand what it was about this unique person that made him such an uplifting symbol of hope and joy for all people.

And I thought of the letter he wrote to Muriel over 40 years ago, when he first visited Washington. He said in that letter: "Maybe I seem foolish to have such vain hopes and plans. But Bucky, I can see how some day, if you and I just apply ourselves and make up our minds to work for bigger things, how we can some day live here in Washington and probably be in Government, politics or service. I intend to set my aim at Congress."

Hubert was wrong only in thinking that his hopes and plans might be in vain. They were not, as we all know. Not only did he succeed, with his beloved wife at his side; he succeeded gloriously and beyond even his most optimistic dreams.

Hubert will be remembered by all of us who served with him as one of the greatest legislators in our history. He will be remembered as one of the most loved men of his time. And even though he failed to realize his greatest goal, he achieved something much more rare and valuable than the highest office. He became his country's conscience.

Today, the love that flows from everywhere, enveloping Hubert, flows also to you, Muriel. And the presence today here, where America bids farewell to her heroes, of President and Mrs. Carter, of former Presidents Ford and Nixon, and your special friend and former First Lady, Mrs. Johnson, attests to the love and respect that the Nation holds for both of you.

That letter to Bucky, his Muriel, also noted three principles by which Hubert defined his life: work, determination, and high goals. They were part of his life's pattern when I first met him, 31 years ago. I was only 17, fresh out of high school, and he was mayor of Minneapolis. He had then all the other sparkling qualities he maintained throughout his life: boundless good humor, endless optimism and hope, infinite interest, intense concern for people and their problems, compassion without being compromising, energy beyond belief, and a spirit so filled with love, there was no room at all for hate or bitterness. He was simply incredible.

When he said that life was not to be endured but, rather, to be enjoyed, you knew what he meant. You could see it by watching him and listening to him. When Hubert looked at the lives of black America in the forties, he saw endurance and not enjoyment, and his heart insisted that it was time for Americans "to walk forthrightly into the bright sunshine of human rights."

When Hubert looked at the young who could not get a good education, he saw endurance and not enjoyment. When Hubert saw old people in ill health, he saw endurance and not enjoyment. When Hubert saw middle-class people striving to survive and working people without jobs and decent homes, he saw endurance and not enjoyment.

Hubert was criticized for proclaiming the politics of joy, but he knew that joy is essential to us and is not frivolous. He loved to point out that ours is the only nation in the world to officially declare the pursuit of happiness as a national goal.

But he was also a sentimental man, and that was part of his life, too. He cried in public and without embarrassment. In his last major speech in his beloved Minnesota, he wiped tears from his eyes and said, "A man without tears is a man without a heart." If he cried often, it was not for himself, but for others.

Above all, Hubert was a man with a good heart: and on this sad day it would be good for us to recall Shakespeare's words:

"A good leg will fail; a straight back will stoop; a black beard will grow white; a curled pate will grow bald; a fair face will wither; a full eye will wax hollow; but a good heart is the Sun and the Moon; or, rather, the Sun and not the Moon; for it shines bright and never changes, but keeps its course truly." Hubert's heart kept its course truly.

He taught us all how to hope and how to love, how to win and how to lose. He taught us how to live and, finally, he taught us how to die."

• • • • •

Those words moved people across the country, some who had voted for Humphrey, some who had not but recognized his unique qualities. Some belittlers said he had more solutions than there were problems and he took that as praise. Working to make life better for everyone didn't seem a sin to him. His credo was simple: "Life is to be enjoyed, not endured." Just after he died, a cartoonist drew an angel in heaven speaking to God. "I have a Hubert Humphrey ... with a list of reforms."

Several months before he died, the Senate, for the only time in its history, held a session to honor a living senator.

They saw him up close for many years, and bipartisan affection grew. The Senate Historical Society quoted an Associated Press story, not related to his dying. The AP had polled 1,000 congressional administrative and legislative aides, asking them to select the most effective senator during the preceding fifty years. They chose Hubert Humphrey.

Humphrey, Mondale, and Rolvaag devoted their lives to reaching for a good society that benefited as many people as possible. Today, many conservatives in the Congress and some Republican candidates for president appear to me driven in another direction. With Ronald Reagan's "Government is the problem" as their mantra, they seek to shrink government, cut taxes, loosen regulation on finance and business, gut social programs for the middle class as well as those at the bottom who desperately need the safety net. And they do this in a manner lacking comity as they obstruct policies they don't like instead of seeking real compromise.

I wish they had known Hubert Humphrey, listened to him, and understood what drove him. He said, "The moral test of government is how it treats those in the dawn of life, the young, those in the twilight of life, the elderly, and those in the shadows of life, the sick, the needy and the unemployed."

14. Name Droppings:
Famous People Who Have Met Me

I got the idea for this chapter from an unlikely source who was not a friend, but probably would have hoped to be. He is the inspiration for what follows, which I humbly call "Name Droppings: Famous People Who Have Met Me."

For many years, Howard Cosell was the most visible sports announcer in the United States. A sporting event took on cosmic significance by the tone of his voice. He was a star and blessing to the nation, particularly in his own eyes.

On one of our visits to Cuba, a friend, Bill Mead, who had recently written a book about the St. Louis Browns baseball team, traveled with us. When Ginny and I walked into the gift shop of our Havana hotel, I spotted Cosell and approached him to say that there was someone in our group who had written a baseball book. He extended his arm, put up a hand to interrupt me, and said, "He has already met me."

A Texas friend of Lyndon Johnson and our ambassador to Australia, Ed Clarke, also influenced this chapter. When asked about someone he might know, he said "We howdied, but we ain't shook," Some of those whose names follow I have shook. Others, well, we just howdied.

My standards are high for these people to claim my friendship. They must at least have said, "Hello," or seized my hand as I passed in a line. Just a nod does not qualify. Touch is important. A word or two helps. (For those I have left out because of space, please accept my apologies.) Here are a few of the famous people who have met me.

Eleanor Roosevelt, Harry Truman, Nelson Rockefeller, William O. Douglas, Harold Stassen, Frank Sinatra, Nancy Sinatra, Paul Newman, Sammy Davis Jr., Chubby Checker, Gregory Peck, Edward G. Robinson, Jacky Robinson, the Duke of Windsor, Pablo Casals, Eugene Istomin, Isaac Stern, Carl Eller, Alan Page, Dean Chance, Harmon Killebrew, Bill Moyers, James Reston. Jimmy Durante, Haile Selassie, Sonny and Cher, Ferdinand and Imelda Marcos, Abba Eban, Mary Hartle Larson, DeWitt Wallace, Ted Williams, Francis Cardinal Spellman, King and Queen of Belgium, Martin Luther King Jr., Adlai Stevenson, James McDivitt, Ed White, Joe Biden, Willy Brandt.

I hope I've spelled all these names correctly. They are part of my experience as a political butterfly. You deserve to know them better, as well as a bit of vital information about some of them and a few others.

• • • • •

One day, Humphrey was in Dwayne Andreas' suite in the New York Waldorf Towers when the phone rang and I answered it. A voice said he was calling from Frank Sinatra's suite, that Sinatra was a great fan of Humphrey, and wondered if he could drop by for a visit. I covered the phone and relayed the message. Humphrey almost shouted "yes" in his excitement.

Shortly, Sinatra and Mia Farrow showed up with the guy

I had talked to. Sinatra and Humphrey hit it off immediately, talking of Sinatra's early tours through South Dakota as a young and little known singer. While they chatted, the Secret Service quickly decided the third visitor was a bodyguard and possibly armed. They quietly asked him to leave while Humphrey and Sinatra continued uninterrupted in their story telling. At one point, Sinatra told Humphrey that his mother had been a Democratic Party precinct worker in New Jersey, and that sealed the bond as Humphrey took her phone number.

From time to time after, Humphrey would call her to chat, and he and Frank (he called me Norman) kept in touch. While Humphrey was on another visit in the same hotel suite, Sinatra called and invited himself once again. This time he brought his daughter, Nancy, with him. By chance, we soon had other guests. A politically important Southern governor called and was invited up. He arrived with a small entourage, all of whom, including him, had had a bump or two.

The near-drunks surrounded Sinatra like breathless teenagers. I intervened, extricating the Sinatras from their new fans. When Frank and Nancy were leaving, Nancy embraced me and whispered in my ear, "I love you." It was a special moment overheard by a member of our group, who took it seriously and spread the word. Nancy was thanking me for my protective move. The eavesdropper thought it represented something more. He soon enhanced my reputation with his loose lips. Many years later, I wrote a letter to Nancy and never heard back. She didn't love me anymore.

My final visit with Frank came just after Humphrey had lost the 1968 election. There was a dinner in Los Angeles the following February for the astronauts. Several of them had gotten to know Humphrey from our visits to launches and events they were involved in. They liked him and asked the new president to invite him.

Sinatra learned the Humphreys were coming and arranged to take Humphrey and Mrs. Humphrey to dinner the night before the astronaut event. A plain clothes cop (there were no more Secret Service) traveling with us and I would go along.

When we got to Los Angeles, I called an old high school buddy who had contributed to the 1968 campaign. He said his wife had never met Humphrey and wondered if they could come by just to say hello. I said sure. They talked to Humphrey for about 10 minutes in the lobby as he was on the way to another meeting. I then took them up to the Humphrey suite so we could reminisce more. Mrs. Humphrey had been taking a nap, but got up, came out, and sat and talked with my guests. They were transported. First, one Humphrey, and then the other.

I had told them that they would have to leave at about seven since someone was taking us to dinner. I did not tell them who it was. As the appointed hour approached, there was a knock on the door. I opened it, said, "Hello, Frank." My friends were wide-eyed and open-mouthed. As if they would not recognize him, I introduced them formally, "Meet Frank Sinatra," It was a one, two, three punch of recognition, and they floated out the door.

Soon, our little traveling party joined Sinatra in his limousine and we headed off for Beverly Hills. As we came around the corner to the restaurant, employees were in the street, arms up, stopping traffic. At the door, the owner bowed a bit and opened it, like a lackey greeting a king.

We met a couple of other Hollywood celebrities on the way to our table where, once again, there were folks falling all over themselves to serve the King. When we were seated, I said, "Frank." He responded with a chilly "Yes." I said, "This is the way they treat me in Minneapolis." Laughter was neither loud nor long.

A while earlier, the *Wall Street Journal* had done an article on Sinatra and his political fundraising. They called me for comments on his involvement with Humphrey and what he might have done for us. I was very careful and played down their pleasant relationship. Sinatra, I should have known, was used to adoration, not distance, restraint and understatement. He was not happy.

Humphrey's defeat was not a burden for Frank. Within weeks, he had established a new friendship with Spiro Agnew, short-term vice president under an ultimately shortened-term president. I don't know what Frank did when they were gone.

• • • • •

When I went to Kenya in 1967, I was excited since I might see Jomo Kenyatta and possibly meet him. He was the guerilla leader who had fought the British and driven them out, and was now head of the government. He was a hero of mine, not only from my left-wing days, but even as I had moved a bit to the center.

On my advance I saw him outside his office, just standing alone and looking around the grounds. That was sufficient, but since there would be a state lunch, I looked forward to actually meeting him there. The glorious day came. The attendance was limited and included no press. Our party of traveling journalists was small, and unanimously irate when they discovered they were not permitted to cover the lunch and speeches. Their logic was simple, but compelling. They had traveled a long way; they belonged where Humphrey was in order to report and, thus, merit their travel and their papers' expense. Beyond that, there was no reason to keep them out. They were invited in not to eat but to listen for a bit in every other country.

I carried that message to the Kenyan I had been working with, and he said he would raise the matter with Kenyatta. He was in the inner sanctum only briefly and came out to tell me the answer was no. No press. That response, of course, did not sit well with my companions. One, from the *Washington Post*, explained to me privately that he had just arrived in Nairobi and would be the *Post*'s resident correspondent in East Africa and really needed to be inside. It would help him establish his credentials and make contacts. He had talked to the other press traveling with us and they agreed that he should be the "pool" reporter, if no more of them could be admitted. A pool reporter goes in as a representative of the entire group and comes out to describe all that happened.

I went back to my contact and shared my new information. He went once again to see Kenyatta. When he came back, he had a solution. If I gave up my seat, the *Post* reporter, Anthony Astrachan, could sit in my place. Setting my awe aside, I reluctantly agreed: job before a free lunch.

When everyone was seated and Humphrey had been welcomed, a waiter carrying a large salad bowl tripped as he approached the head table, depositing a few vegetables on the leader. Kenyatta leapt to his feet, grabbed the substantial walking stick he used, and beat the waiter to the ground in front of an appalled Humphrey. Soon, other waiters carried the prostrate man out and the lunch went on as though nothing untoward had happened. (I'm glad Astrachan took my seat.)

As the lunch ended, Astrachan felt a hand on his arm. It was my Kenyan who said firmly, "If a word of this leaks out, you will be declared *persona non grata* and be out of the country in 24 hours." That produced a problem: fulfill his professional obligation as the pool reporter, reporting to the excluded journalists all that happened and then call the *Post* to tell them he was coming home after about a week in country.

He chose silence and staying put over tattling and going home. When we flew on to the next country, one of our group, Dr. Edgar Berman, a doctor who had latched on to Humphrey through his friendship with Humphrey's sometime difficult sister, Frances, whispered the story to a reporter for *Jet* magazine, a publication aimed primarily for a black American audience.

Edgar was puffed up, a little banty rooster, who was not on the staff, had little real influence, but felt, nonetheless, that he had a special, vital, unequalled relationship with Humphrey. Edgar was retired from a successful career as a surgeon, but felt he was a policy whiz on all subjects, and an arbiter on all disagreements. He was once described as a "horse breeder, world traveler, art collector, and bon vivant," and all that was true, if irrelevant.

He also told *Jet* that the waiter had been taken out and shot. I did not know that for certain, but it could well have been true. If it were, there was no need to share the information. When the other reporters, having been told the story by the *Jet* reporter, asked me for confirmation, I told them I would not check and would have no further words, except, I thought, with Edgar.

Edgar later wrote a book called, *Hubert*, describing in print his indispensable role, displaying his infinite knowledge, and his constant valuable advice to the man others of us, even most of his long-time friends, called Mr. Vice President. Like a lamprey, Edgar lived off his association with Humphrey. He was bright and pleasant, but much of the book about "Hubert" is an exercise in self-importance and self-promotion, a danger others have faced.

Thurgood Marshall, recently appointed to the Supreme Court, was with us in Africa. He was difficult from time to time, but more often pleasant and without pretention. At one stop, a State Department officer, probably at his first post, kept bugging the Justice for the title of his speech to be given the following day. Marshall, not a man who needed a prepared text, indeed did not have one, and thus no title for the program. But the young man persisted, insisted and made a general nuisance of himself. Finally, Justice Marshall, letting his words fall slowly from his lips, said, "The title of my speech is, 'Where is we now at?'"

The young man looked astonished, his jaw dropped open in disbelief, his pin stripes shivered, and Marshall, with a straight face and yet deeper drawl, said, "Son, everywhere I go in the United States, my people come up and ask, 'Thurgood, where is we now at?'"

• • • • •

I also got to know socially two senators from beyond Minnesota. While I was in Vietnam with Humphrey I was approached by a guy with a bowtie and big horned rim glasses who told me he had owned weekly newspapers in Illinois and wondered if he, a journalist of small towns and tiny audiences, could join our traveling national press. He seemed ready for rejection, but I welcomed him to join us, and we remained friends until his death in 2003.

Paul Simon was the son of Lutheran missionaries and seemed to have inherited a passion from them for making a better society. When he came to the House of Representatives in 1975, we renewed our previous brief friendship. After 10 years, he ran for the Senate and won with slightly more than 50 percent of the vote. Six years later he was re-elected with 65 percent. He was a committed and tough-minded liberal, but often found ways to co-sponsor legislation or work in some ways with Republicans.

His effort to get the presidential nomination in 1988 was a failure, and probably ill-advised. He drew a scant number of votes, was never close to the top, and gave it up quickly. The high point was, undoubtedly, appearing on "Saturday Night Live," a comedy show, with Paul Simon, the singer.

Gaylord Nelson, who had previously been governor of Wisconsin, was the other one. We had a mutual friend, John Hoving, and when Nelson had been drinking too much he would stop at John's house to sober up before going home to his wife's anger. One night, his cigarette kept slipping from between his fingers, and I would reach over, pick it up, and slip it back. A bit later, he looked up at me and said, "Sherman, you are so goddamned egocentric that you drop your own name."

In 1960, during the presidential primaries, Humphrey and his traveling party stayed at the governor's mansion. In the morning, Humphrey's chief aide came down the stairs with brief case in hand. Nelson's wife, Carrie Lee, had been an army nurse and was known for her outspoken and impolitic ways. She asked where Herb was going, and he said they had a breakfast meeting. She said persuasively, "I have prepared breakfast for nine people and you better eat here or I'm going to shove the eggs up your ass." They stayed and delayed their now second breakfast.

Nelson and Simon were, like Humphrey, consistent liberals and eminently decent men. They loved the Senate for what they could accomplish there.

One day in 1965, Humphrey buzzed me into his office. When I entered I saw Willy Brandt of Germany with him. Brandt, I learned later, considered Humphrey his best friend in the United States. Some months earlier, two of Brandt's assistants had come to the U.S. and called on Humphrey at Brandt's direction. Humphrey sent them to me to talk about American political campaigns and techniques. I don't remember now what we specifically discussed, but Brandt asked if I would come to Germany to talk to, and maybe train, some of his party people. Humphrey was pleased and I was honored that my wisdom had been internationally recognized and might soon send me across the Atlantic.

But, Humphrey, being careful, sent a question to the State Department asking whether that was okay. The word came back that it was, so long as I also offered the same information to the opposition party, a ridiculous request in the guise of diplomatic nicety. I would not agree to that and, thus, my career as an international adviser ended before it started.

Humphrey interceded at the White House when it appeared that President Johnson would not see Brandt because of two anti-Vietnam speeches he had made. Humphrey was successful and Brandt had a chilly half hour meeting with Johnson to which no photographers were allowed. Brandt was elected chancellor of Germany in 1969 without Johnson's help.

• • • • •

When Humphrey was a freshman senator, he visited Israel and stayed at the King David hotel. Needing a haircut he went to the basement barbershop. The barber asked him, as he must have every American visitor, "What do you do?" Humphrey told him he was a United States senator. The haircut was not free, but the barber felt honored.

After that, when a visitor said he was from the United States, the barber responded, "When you get home, write my friend, Hubert Humphrey." Within months and going on for years, Humphrey would get letters carrying greetings from the barber.

After the 1968 election, I went with Humphrey to Israel where Abba Eban, diplomat, graduate of Cambridge University, a bit stiff and formal, but a friend, hosted a lunch. When we entered the lobby of the King David, Eban was standing by the door of the room set for the lunch, and behind him a crowd had gathered to see Humphrey, an ardent friend of Israel from its beginning.

Suddenly, Humphrey threw his arms wide and began to move quickly toward where Eban stood. Eban's eyes grew wide, his body grew taut, as he anticipated an unwelcomed embrace. He should not have worried. Humphrey went right past him and hugged the barber who stood among the multitude. Eban looked relieved. The barber and the rest of those standing by looked delighted. Letters from shorn Americans increased.

* * * * *

When renowned cellist and composer Pablo Casals celebrated his 90th birthday on December 29, 1966, in San Juan, Puerto Rico, Isaac Stern, an illustrious violinist and friend of both men, asked Humphrey to speak at the ceremony. Stern and Eugene Istomin, another friend, told me that they were going to play a composition Casals had written, but vowed would not be played while dictator Francisco Franco was alive and still controlling Spain.

Stern had told me what the form of the music was. I, being a musical illiterate, went back to him and asked, "Isaac, did you say a sonata or a concerto?" He rolled his eyes, muttered, and then spelled, "Sonata: S-O-N-A-T-A." I said, "You son-of-a-bitch, I can spell, I just can't remember." It was in fact, Casals' "Violin and Piano Concerto."

The public part of the event was held in the courtyard of the governor's mansion, and Casals, barely five feet tall, and his wife, Marta, (soon to be a widow who later married Istomin) sat in the front row. The trio was not two bars into the composition when Casals recognized what it was. He rose almost magically just a few inches from his chair and then slowly sat down in obvious pleasure.

Later, about 10 of us had dinner, and Humphrey and Casals got talking about American TV westerns. Casals loved "Gunsmoke." It seemed an odd thing for a musical genius from far away. He soon explained that he had, as a very young virtuoso, traveled through the American West, often playing for applauding cowboys in boots, jeans, and Stetson hats. They made as much an impression on him as he must have on them.

• • • • •

DeWitt Wallace, the founder and owner of the *Reader's Digest*, had Minnesota roots and was very rich. His father had been the president of Macalester College in St. Paul. Humphrey had so charmed the current DeWitt when they had met earlier that Wallace seemed to feel that they had been lifelong friends though miles apart politically and ideologically.

One day Wallace invited Humphrey to come to the *Digest* offices in Pleasantville, New York, to visit with him and his senior editors. Huge numbers of people subscribed, read, and believed what appeared in the magazine, and Humphrey couldn't resist the possibility of capturing their attention, if only for a little while. (He ended up doing an article at Wallace's request.)

Humphrey took me along, and we ultimately sat with Wallace, who was quite old and a bit doddering, and eight of his editors and staff who were younger and doddering. They were as stiff and bristly as the old man was embracing. They asked questions and Humphrey was at his very best in responding. It was a great performance for a conservative audience who seemed quite hostile, or at least suspicious of HHH, before the dialogue.

As the meeting ended, Humphrey whispered to me, "Get the cufflinks." I said to a Secret Service agent, "Get the cufflinks." He brought back a manila franked mailing envelope filled with cufflinks that cost very little and were in their little plastic bags with a staple holding them shut. Humphrey then passed them out, and Wallace took his out of the bag and said, "You're are going to be our next president and a great one. I am so proud to have you here today. I would wear one of these on this shoulder and one on this." He crossed his arms displaying the links on his shoulders as he stood there beaming. I said, "Mr. Wallace, I have a third one here for your navel." There was a moment of awkward silence, and then Wallace laughed a little laugh. Then we all did.

When we got to the car and started off for the airport, Humphrey looked at me, shook his head, and said. "You dummy, if he hadn't laughed, I would have fired you on the spot." After a few days, he would call me into his office regularly and instruct me to tell the story to whoever was visiting.

One of the few black journalists in Washington during the 1960s was Carl Rowan. I met him first in Minneapolis when I was a janitor and he was a columnist for the *Minneapolis Tribune*. I got to know him better in the days that followed and then even more when we were both in Washington. He lived in an up-scale neighborhood and was mowing his lawn one day when a car stopped and the woman driving beckoned him over and asked, "How much do you charge for mowing a lawn?" He said the mowing was free, but he got to sleep with the lady of the house. The driver hit the gas pedal and was out-of-sight before another blade of grass disappeared. I can't vouch for this really happening, but Carl swore it had.

• • • • •

I learned fairly early that not everyone was Jewish. But it took a while to understand who all the others were. The population of Norway, Sweden, and Denmark was seriously depleted in the 19th and 20th centuries by emigration to the United States. Many of them found their way to Minnesota. A mixed marriage was a Swedish Lutheran and a Norwegian Lutheran. Wendy Anderson, governor, senator, employer, and friend, once told me that he was going to the Holy Land, and I asked why he was going to Israel. He said, almost incredulously, "Not Israel. Sweden."

The mayor of Minneapolis in the fifties was Eric Hoyer, who spoke with a Swedish accent. He said one day, "It took me a long time to learn to say "job," not "yob." And then they started calling them "proyeks."

I had a friend named Paul Skjervold whose last name was

pronounced like mine as though it were Sharevold. I met his brother one day and introduced myself and spelled my last name for him. "I am Norman Sherman, S, K, Yeh, E, R, M, A, N. He called Paul the next day and asked if I really spelled my name that way. In a moment, I stopped being Swedish. He took my S K Yeh away.

• • • • •

During the final week of the 1968 campaign, a couple of stars were recruited to be in our motorcade through Los Angeles. We were told that Sonny and Cher would bring their own car and that seemed okay to us until we saw it. It was a Rolls-Royce, high-profile, a bit elegant for where we were going, and made Humphrey's car look like a Model T. We thought it looked too rich and might offend folks along the sidewalks. There was fortunately nothing to be done. They got more cheers than Humphrey. People jumped up and down, cheered them, tried to break through to touch the car, and waved hello and goodbye as we passed. Not to Humphrey, but to Sonny and Cher.

• • • • •

Gregory Peck, movie star extraordinaire, handsome, tall, and surrounded by a few staff, came to see Humphrey. I led them over to the waiting room outside the Senate floor, near an office the vice president had just behind it. As he often was, Humphrey was running late, and Peck finally became visibly disturbed. I said, "Let me go see what is holding the vice president up."

I went past the Secret Service agent guarding the door and

told Humphrey that Peck was getting twitchy and maybe a bit angry. He told me to keep Gregory occupied for a few more minutes. As I approached the group, Peck and his entourage turned toward me. I looked up at our tall and distinguished visitor and said, "A funny thing just happened to me. The Secret Service agent mistook me for you." He didn't laugh much, but he relaxed a lot and soon Humphrey made him forget the delay.

• • • • • •

I wrote an article for the *Washingtonian* magazine in 1974. It said, "An old JFK lawyer and political operator tells of walking down K Street with two of his clients and stopping to talk briefly with Ben Bradlee, who was dressed in a flashy glen plaid suit. As Bradlee walked away, one of the clients asked, 'Who the hell was that?' 'He's the editor of the *Post*,' the lawyer replied. 'Jesus, I thought he was your bookie.'"

It was, indeed, the editor of the *Washington Post*, but that doesn't really describe his talent, power, and importance in Washington and to the country. Without him, the scandal of the Nixon abuse of power and the whole Watergate story might never have been exposed. The *Post* was probably the best paper in the country because of him and the people he gathered and directed.

He was an unlikely journalist, both loved and hated by his co-workers. Genius and despot, he was an intimate and long-time friend of John Kennedy and spent many evenings at dinner in the White House. He descended from two families already rich and powerful when the Kennedys arrived in the 1840s. He married into another leading Massachusetts family, the Saltonstalls. He went to Harvard, spoke fluent French and a bit of Yiddish. He also responded once to a compliant from a Senator, "You are picking fly shit from the pepper with boxing gloves."

I called him to say that I had been asked to write an article on him. He was nasty, crude, and dismissive. I responded in kind:

Dear Ben;

You made two points yesterday in our brief conversation that pissed me off.

1. You implied with a heaviness that invites, if not insists on, an interest in your unmade beds.

2. You said, 'I don't want to beat you out of any money,' as though my interest in doing an article on you was primarily for the money.

I am not interested in skewering you with your own phallus. You may be a superb cocksman, a man of great sexual prowess. Who cares? However good you are, you are a better editor which, of course, is our interest. Jack's interest and mine is in what you did with the *Newsweek* bureau and with the *Washington Post*. Neither you nor the *Post*, however, is so sacrosanct or pure that the *Washingtonian* ought only to sing your praises.

I squelched the impulse yesterday to tell you that I would give my fee, and it isn't much, you know, to the marriage counselor of your choice. If you think I am preying on you, I would be glad to do the article free or give the fee to some journalism scholarship fund. I don't see that this is relevant or important, but if you do, I'll do what makes you happy.

You are a public person who ought to be described as fully as, say, Senator Scott of Virginia for Washington readers.

The cover of *L'Express* is fine, but the *Washingtonian* is really a more logical place for such a story.

I thought, as a wanderer through the Washington scene who is not a journalist, that I might do an interesting piece. If you don't think so, fuck it, man. I'll write it without your assistance. Dealing with me, at least, you have a chance to check the story, if not to edit my copy.

Norman

I did not expect to hear from him, but a couple of weeks later, I did. He wrote:

Norman, baby:

As you recall our conversation, you should be pissed off. Agreed.

Let me just say that I have no concern about you and your commitment to do right with a piece about me. Over the years you have struck me as a man with a meritorious mixture of smarts and humor.

But since even paranoids have enemies, you will forgive me if I am not so sure about someone there in that magazine. For the record, let me point out the latest in this month's book:

1) Daniel learned about Quinn joining us from Quinn— the evening of the afternoon we hired her.

2) Bachrach did not threaten to quit, nor was she assured of juicy story assignments.

3) Bradlee is not finishing his book on Kennedy; he hasn't started it. And no one of the four principals was contacted by anyone from the magazine.

It does make a fellow wonder.

So, that's all for the birds as far as you're concerned. If you are still on, let's give it a fling;. I would like to check any quotes, since my language if often cruder that my love for words.

Yours in truth, Ben

• • • • •

Nasty and crazy mail was a steady diet in the Humphrey office with hardly a day not bringing some lunacy in writing. One letter came from Ohio with a simple message. The writer was going to come to Washington to kill Humphrey. That was against the law, and the Secret Service went to his home. When his wife answered the door, they asked to speak to the writer. She said he was on his way to Washington, having taken the family car. She seemed more put out by that than by his mission.

The agents got the auto license number and found him on the freeway. When the state trooper pulled him over, he was soon asked two questions: was he the writer of the letter and could they search his car. He consented without pause. The agents found no weapon and asked him how he intended to carry out his "mission." He raised his hands in front of his chest a bit apart and said, "With these."

• • • • •

When I had first come to Washington just before the 1963 legislative session, I met Congressman Morris Udall. He sent an aide to find me and tell me that Udall wanted to see me. Less than a day in Washington and I was already being sought out. What a "wow" moment.

Udall, I discovered soon, was a most decent and committed liberal, and a raconteur. He had a request: Don Fraser, as a new congressman, must ask to serve on the District of Columbia committee. It was a minor committee that few liberals chose and had been dominated for years by Southern bigots. Udall was at work to make it more responsive to the huge black population in the District. Fraser served with him there for many terms. Later, Udall, still a liberal power to be reckoned with, became seriously ill.

When he was in the hospital and approaching death, his friend and colleague in the House, Father Robert Drinan of Massachusetts, came to visit him. When Drinan entered the room, Udall had rolled in his bed toward the wall with his back to the door. Hearing someone, he asked without moving, "Is that you, Bob?"

Drinan said, "Yes, it is. How are you doing?"

Mo then rolled back toward Drinan, ignored the question, and said, "When I die, I want to be buried in Chicago."

Drinan, bewildered, responded, "Mo, you have no connection to Chicago, no family anywhere in the area. Why would you want to be buried there?"

Udall said, "I want to stay active in politics."

People in Illinois were known to have voted for years after their demise and Udall felt worthy of the tradition.

Udall often told the story of being grand marshal of a parade at a civic celebration in a small town in southeastern Arizona. He rode at the head of the parade on a borrowed horse. After the parade was over, he got off the horse and approached the folks in charge who had invited him. He said, "Thanks for the invitation and the wonderful stallion."

They smirked a bit and said, "Mo, you know that was a

mare." Udall responded, "It was a stallion. All along the route, people shouted, 'Look at that big prick on that horse.'"

• • • • •

Shortly after Hubert Humphrey died, I was asked to interview Joe Biden for the Humphrey archives at the Minnesota Historical Society. After his election in 1972, his wife and a child had died in an automobile accident. In his grief and beginning recovery, he decided he would not go to D.C. and the Senate.

Humphrey knew that Biden had been for Gene McCarthy for president in 1968 and not him, but he called Biden and urged him to come to Washington despite his tragedy. I found that out in my interview after Biden had referred to Humphrey as "the Boss" about a half-dozen times. I said, "Senator, do you call everyone older than you 'the Boss?'" He wrinkled up his face and said, "No, why do you ask that?" When I told him, he just shook his head, not even aware of what he had said again and again.

He then explained why he must have done it automatically. Humphrey had told him that it was no easier to mourn where he was than it would be in the Senate. Humphrey said he would be ready to counsel Biden at any time he needed it, to introduce him to the Senate ways, to help him over his difficult moments. Without Humphrey, the Biden national career might have ended before it began.

• • • • •

A couple of years after my mother died, brother Fred bought my dad a boat trip to Israel. Aboard the vessel, he met a lady of Italian descent, about half a foot taller, twice his weight, and not Jewish. We learned some of that from a picture we saw only later. Shortly after he left, we received a cable asking our permission to marry his companion of a few days at sea. Fred and Rose were furious, but I sent him a reply that said he should marry if he wanted. My siblings were slower. Before they could express their views, a second cable arrived: "About that matter I wrote you about, forget it."

Ginny came on the scene too late to savor many of his bits of whimsy or fancy, but she shared one notable event. My dad, with some help, retired to Florida, a haven for older Jews from around the country. Miami Beach had more Jews per square foot than Tel Aviv, and he lived up Collins Avenue among the downscale hotels. He wrote that he wanted to move to a more elegant residence. We all reluctantly agreed, and sent the additional monthly money.

After a few weeks, my dad wrote that the bathtub in his new quarters was too small. Put off by what I thought was a silly complaint I wrote him that a bathtub was a bathtub and he should stop complaining. I didn't say that at 5'1" he could fit in a sink.

During the 1972 presidential primary campaign, Humphrey made a brief effort to get the nomination, and I went to Florida along with Ginny and infant Lucy to help. When we walked into my dad's apartment and glanced into the bathroom, we saw a tub that was too small even for my diminutive dad. The bathroom had been built in a renovated and expanded closet.

* * * * *

Ghosts are used to anonymity, but even recognition can

be odd. On one occasion, Robert Strauss, a Texan, then head of the Democratic National Committee, asked a few of us to draft jokes for him to tell at the annual White House Correspondents Dinner. The press bathed and dressed up for the dinner, and Bob was a hit. He invited his covey of ghosts, Art Buchwald, an outstanding humor columnist, Frank Mankiewicz, Mark Shields, later a serious columnist and TV commentator of distinction, and me to lunch to hear our own words. We thought he was a ghost speaker, but laughed at our own jokes and congratulated him for his success. There was no question whose ego was swaddled by our gathering.

When I worked in the Department of the Interior for Bob Herbst, he stopped me one day in the hall and began telling me jokes I had written for him. They may have been unforgettable lines, but he seemed to have forgotten where they came from.

• • • • •

There was an occasional Secret Service moment that was less serious than safeguarding a president or vice president or finding a counterfeiter. Soon after Humphrey was elected, he was at the Navy Yard in Washington about to board a boat with a few guests for an evening on the Potomac. We were milling around since the Sequoia, a large boat that traditionally was used by presidents and vice presidents, was not there. A much smaller one, hardly large enough for all our guests, was at the dock. Someone at the White House had apparently ordered the demeaning change without telling Humphrey or our office. There was no plausible explanation offered. One could only assume it was part of the president's petty and mean campaign.

As we stood around, an old truck pulled up at a distance with two men in it. An agent was dispatched to see who they were and why they were there. Before the agent got into law enforcement, he had worked in the family junk business. When the driver and passenger explained they were there to pick up junk accumulated from the Yard's work, and they just wanted to see Humphrey whom they admired, the agent asked them questions about the price of some metals, whether they had gone up or down recently. The driver, amazed at the questions and knowledge, said "Jeez, you guys have to know everything."

* * * * *

A less famous person was a periodic part of my early DFL life. Miles Lord came off the Iron Range sharing the liberal genes of many there. We met at my first state DFL convention. I was walking down a hall in the hotel and a door opened. A guy I didn't know leaned out. He asked with an odd intensity, "Do you type?" When I said I did, he pulled me in and explained that he needed a speech typed to use when he sought endorsement for attorney general in an hour.

He was a gutsy, if freewheeling, attorney general who took on powerful business forces used to doing things their way while acquiescent conservative office holders looked on. Miles later was U.S. district attorney and then a federal judge, a bit of a wild ass through it all, but a flinty, consistent liberal. Miles became a close friend of Humphrey, providing easy companionship as well as comic relief for a busy senator.

One day, the two of them had been fishing with the Humphrey boys. They were looking scruffy when they came upon a bus stalled on the side of the road. Miles told Humphrey he would go check on why it was there. When he found that it was only a mechanical problem with help on the way, he told the passengers that there was a guy in the area who looked a lot like Senator Humphrey and often pretended that he was. "Just jolly him" were his final words as he waved and left the bus.

He went back to the car and urged Humphrey to go aboard and welcome the passengers, who were from California. Humphrey bounded in and announced that he was Senator Hubert Humphrey. A voice at the back yelled, "And I'm Governor Pat Brown." Humphrey loved to tell the story almost as much as Miles did.

In 1966, when there was a vacancy on the federal bench based in Minnesota, I learned that Gene McCarthy was going to urge President Johnson to appoint Miles, and I assumed Humphrey would second the motion. I spoke up to say I didn't think Miles had a judicial temperament and might become an embarrassment to both Johnson and Humphrey. I should have kept my opinion to myself.

Humphrey said firmly that I was wrong. He said, "Miles understands justice and he will be a people's judge and that's good enough for me." Miles proved him right and me woefully wrong. He made significant decisions on women's right, on the environment, on business practices, serving from 1966 to 1985, with almost four years as the chief judge.

● ● ● ● ●

One other guy almost met me, but I turned down his invitation. In 1981, to celebrate the posthumous award of the Congressional Gold Medal to Humphrey, President Reagan held a ceremony at the White House. I got a telegram inviting me to attend. I was too busy to respond.

•••••

Finally, I want to drop a name of someone who was not famous, not heralded as an expert in any field, and not a political leader. He was, without question, Hubert Humphrey's best friend for about 25 years beginning in 1945. While others might claim the role, only Freddie Gates deserved the description and was undisputedly it.

He was a high-school dropout, the son of Lebanese immigrants, an unpolished man whose sentences were, early on, sprinkled with "dese" and "dat." He ran a penny arcade on Hennepin Avenue in Minneapolis. You dropped a coin in a machine and bought yourself a few minutes of a pinball game with whistles and bells and no substance. It was not exactly a profession, of course, and some people disdained it and Freddie.

Indeed, in 1954, several DFL candidates for office or active in running the party came to Humphrey, in a formal way, and urged him to dump Freddie on the basis that he "was bad for our image." Humphrey spent no time defending Freddie; he just quickly said no and made it possible for his guests to leave without further talk. Mission unaccomplished.

According to Humphrey, when he was elected mayor, Freddie, a stranger, visited him, taking advantage of the easy-access policy. They chatted and Freddie asked if Humphrey was really going to clean up the prostitution and gambling in the city, the police corruption, and other underworld operations. He did not ask about high public policy, but about what he thought important and crucial for the city to become a better place for all of its people. Humphrey assured him that was a prime goal. They bonded.

Freddie almost immediately filled an important role beyond the skill or experience of more professional experts around Humphrey. He watched over whose money was welcomed into campaigns or projects. In a city where corruption was as present as lakes and snow, Freddie knew clean money from tainted. No contribution was likely to embarrass Humphrey with Freddie's ability to distinguish and authority to act.

Freddie soon assumed, or was given, an additional role. He watched over expenditures as well. Spending excessively was a sin, not just an abuse. He continued in both roles for the rest of his life even when a couple hundred dollars moved up to thousands.

Freddie's relationship with Humphrey was not of supplicant and patron, but of a special kind almost beyond description. There was a symmetry of spirit. The glue of decency bound them together, as different as they were. They may have never discussed the substance of legislation or program. Freddie was not an expert on arms control, or civil rights, or health care, or war and peace.

But they talked politics and people and Humphrey knew his own doubts, musings, attitudes were between the two of them and no one else. In a world where "Hubert said to me" gave status and represented real or assumed intimacy, Freddie repeated nothing and never quoted Humphrey in self-aggrandizement.

Unlike many more polished people who would knock their mothers over to be seen up close to Humphrey, Freddie never pushed to be in the picture, never bragged about his importance, never used his association with Humphrey to pad his pocket or inflate his reputation or ego or try to see some self-serving law passed. (Humphrey did get him appointed to a U.S. Post Office oversight board.) Governors and senators and supplicants look alike after a while. Freddie was one of a kind, helped Humphrey by being a good listener, an excellent judge of people and tactic, and helped protect Humphrey from the phonies who crept around.

And he advised me as well. When I worked editing Humphrey's autobiography alone in the woods, I decided that my isolation did not require a smoothly shaven face so I grew a rather handsome bushy beard. One day when I was in Minneapolis, Freddie looked at me and said, "If Hubert runs for the Senate again, you'll have to shave the beard." When I moved back to town, the first time I saw Freddie, he didn't say hello; he said, "Shave" and moved on. He knew when no one else did. Except me.

Humphrey, in his autobiography, noted that when Freddie died, there were four federal court judges at his funeral, two United States senators, the incumbent Minnesota governor and a former one. His image in their minds seemed to have changed even as he remained the same.

15. The State of the Nation

It has been a pretty good trip, certainly beyond any dream of early years. I have gone places I could never have anticipated seeing, and I have been involved in activity affecting my community and my country in constructive ways. I have called people who will have a place in history "friend."

Yet, I still find myself too often in despair. A large part of that feeling comes from the continued, even worsening, inequality in the distribution of wealth and opportunity in our country. That the rich get richer and the poor get poorer seems to be the goal of many who have more than they need. And many of those in the middle show vast indifference to the increasing disparity between rich and poor, even if they, themselves, are also victims.

Democrats—I among them—have believed that government should be an instrument for good to mitigate the excesses of our economic system, while Republicans would let the market determine winners and losers. This may be the defining difference between the two parties. Hubert Humphrey, in the tradition of FDR, believed that promoting the general welfare was the work of government. As he so often said, "We have had as the measure of our success that those who already have too much shall get some more, rather than that those who have too little shall get enough."

The numbers are shocking. In 1965, the top executives of large corporations generally made 20 times what a common worker in their companies made. By 2013 that ratio had changed—296 to one. The 400 richest Americans have a total net worth equal to about 150 million people. That means one rich creature for every 375,000 of the rest of us. One family, the Waltons of Wal-Mart, according to *The New York Times*, "have as much wealth as the bottom 42 percent of the country's people combined." (It is true that Wal-Mart, as I write this, is slightly raising its minimum wage for its workers.) The recently retired CEO of McDonald's who battles a livable minimum wage for its employees, earns $9.5 million a year. That disparity has consequences.

Public education, one of the major ways we distinguish ourselves from much of the world, is under constant attack, belittled, squeezed, and throttled. That comes in myriad ways: lower budgets, vouchers to private and religious schools, destruction of teacher unions, rage over curriculum and testing, and charter schools. A new batch of governors slashes university budgets while mouthing pious rationalizations and offering tax cuts to the well off. All of these efforts suck the energy and spirit out of a system from which much of our competence and genius comes. It is at our common core.

Another way in which Democrats like me would "promote the general welfare" is to assure that everyone entitled to vote has an opportunity to do so. Under the guise of "preventing fraud" (despite little evidence that it ever occurs today) Republicans and some Democrats of the old South work to keep those on the fringes of society from exercising this fundamental right. They are chipping away at the Voting Rights

Act of 1965 with help from conservative courts.

Healthcare has been out of the reach of many who work as hard as the rest of us. When Obama made healthcare a goal, it became the pejorative "Obamacare," a kind of social Ebola, a rallying cry beginning with many conservative members of Congress, then parroted in the hinterland, even as the Affordable Care Act has added millions of uninsured to the rolls of the insured. Healthy people produce more and are less of a drain on our economic life.

If we don't educate people, don't help them gain employable skills, don't provide access to healthcare, and discourage their voting, the results are predictable and should not be surprising. Young people with no training are left behind when they could be leading lives of benefit to both themselves and our country. Inevitably they, and many older folks as well become more than a burden, but a corrosive force.

A humane and decent society does not thrive on such disparity. It withers. Maybe we need a maximum wage on the rich and certainly we need tax policies that grow out of fairness and not greed. That would make my periodic worries about where we are going as an inspiring nation disappear.

Since 1980, Reagan has been a guiding light for middle-of-the-road, country-club Republicans as well as the more extreme right-wing who embrace his bromide that government is the problem in campaign after campaign, and then in office. It doesn't have to be that way. I am not alone in this.

An historian of Republican policy, Heather Cox Richardson, a professor at Bowdoin College, has recently written, "Eisenhower's policies were enormously popular, but they inspired the wrath of businessmen who claimed that taxes funding public programs were an unconstitutional redistribution of wealth. They demonized minorities, young people, women and Democrats, and with help of social conservatives, tied the Republican Party once more to big business.

"The consequences were predictable: after Reagan's 1980 election, economic stability turned into the Great Divergence, in which wealth moved steadily upward. In 2008, the economy crashed.

"Twice in its history, the Republican Party regained its direction and popularity after similar disasters by returning to its original defense of widespread economic success. The same rebranding is possible today, if Republicans demote Reagan from hero to history and rally to a leader like Lincoln, (Teddy) Roosevelt, or Eisenhower— someone who believes that the government should promote economic opportunity rather than protect the rich."

What the professor writes seems to be beyond the understanding of people we must depend on for an adequate today and a better tomorrow. For many congressmen, and more than a few senators, the public good is defined in a distorted way: lower taxes for the rich, fewer and weaker programs to help those in need and those in the middle, shut down government to achieve their ends despite its impact on families and our national economic health and safety.

The Republican speaker of the house talks fatuously of there being no need for more laws. Others talk of privatizing Social Security, repealing the Affordable Care Act, restricting food stamp and education funding. They say food stamps for the hungry or education or health insurance for us all need to be cut to balance the budget. A state senator here in Arizona shamelessly says food stamps should be used only for bulk foods and suggests even that be limited to beans and rice, a little Latino slur.

Where few will vote for a minimum wage of even $10 an

hour, when annual take-home pay for millions of Americans is about $20,000, complaints are now heard from some of our elected representatives that their $174,000-a-year congressional salary is too little.

They are driven by vaginal concerns: against abortion, frightened of contraception as a universally available option, riveted by same-sex marriage, in part because of their "concern about the children of those marriages." They ignore the fact that virtually 100 percent of gays and lesbians in our country are the products of heterosexual households as the conservatives beat their breasts (if I can use that word in public) in hostility and ignorance. They oppose love unless they define it. They decry a woman's right to chose an abortion if she wishes, but care little for offspring after they are born.

I would hope that conservative leaders would want to prove that they are not lackeys of wealth and power and ignorance, but instead would seek the greater good for all the people. Respect, hard work, and decency that existed during my years in politics, seem to have fled. Where Congress used to work long hours and full weeks, we now have three-day weeks. Republicans rail against "free-loading" public employees who do not work hard enough. They provide a better example of public waste. Where congressmen once had a few paid trips home each session, they now have dozens.

Where almost all members once brought their families to Washington to live as normal a life as possible, now family life is neither here nor there. Indeed, Newt Gingrich when he was elected Speaker of the House explicitly counseled freshman Republicans to sleep in their offices and leave their families at home. Connection, communication, and friendship among elected officials and their families, across party lines, were common occurrences in earlier days. All of that is now gone.

Manners that made legislating possible barely exist. Civility, dealing with opponents with respect, is gone. Compromise is a four-letter word. Middle ground is the road to hell. That is most apparent among the "patriots" who have stolen the Boston Tea Party and desecrated a precious moment of our history, disguising their bigotry, ignorance, and civic sadism into a sullen pseudo-patriotism and self-righteousness.

During my entire life there has been a consistent portion of stunted citizens for whom hate built on conspiracy theories and racial profiling is their fixation. They were there before World War II in the America First folks led by Henry Ford and Charles Lindbergh, both anti-Semites and against the social legislation of the New Deal. They were there when the John Birch Society was founded in 1960 and Fred Koch, father of today's trillionaire Koch brothers, was a leader. Daddy Fred said, "The colored man looms large in the Communist plan to take over America." Sour apples do not fall far from the tree. Those words may have changed over time, but an amended version of the delusion remains and the vitriol grows, bankrolled by heirs to a fortune and hate.

The wild men of the far right were there at the 1964 Republican national convention when they hooted and screamed and raged to stop Nelson Rockefeller from speaking. He was not conservative enough for them. Neither was Dwight Eisenhower for whom Rockefeller had worked. The nation, according to them, is filled with leeches who live off federal programs instead of working. Uppity blacks must somehow be subdued.

Their ugly belittling of Barack Obama is thinly disguised bigotry. He has the audacity to serve as president while black. The viral emails I get talk of a Muslim prayer room in the White House. As a Jew, I worry that the far-right spirit could easily descend into a new overt anti-Semitism. There will be new whispers: there is a Torah hidden in the Oval Office by Jews; circumcisions are being done by the Secret Service on federal property in the West Wing.

As the 2016 presidential race gets started, Republican candidates for president cater to evangelicals and the self-righteous from Iowa precincts to Liberty University in Virginia and any primary state in between. In their religious fervor, they have, I believe, lost the true and valuable meaning of their own religion. A deeply religious man I knew, Hubert Humphrey, often said, "Religion is more than a Sunday experience. It demands love, compassion, caring."

In days not long gone, most liberal and conservative media made a serious attempt at balance even as they saw things differently and expressed their own point of view. We depended on them. The most respected and influential reporters worked for newspapers and news magazines. With the decline of the print press has come the rise of rightwing talk radio and Fox News, stirring up their listeners with a bias masquerading as "fair and balanced." (MSNBC struggles to offset the right's distortions, but can't keep up with the deluge.) It is difficult to maintain a democracy when so many citizens are fed a kind of paranoid pap. As a result, they don't engage in discussion of the issues or listen to differing points of view. We can't even agree on the facts. And too often even the "objective" news media present two sides of an issue as though there were no gray areas in between.

I don't know the solution. I have only the hope that schools and churches and community leaders can stand up for reasonable dialogue in our complicated world. They have before, and we need them to do so now.

To make democracy work, Congress could begin again

to negotiate and compromise in good faith to find common ground. I would hope that they would heed John Adams, who said in 1809, "If I had refused to institute a negotiation, or had not persevered in it, I should have been degraded in my own estimation as a man of honor." If responsible conservatives would listen to Adams, it would help make democracy work for all of us. It could make the American dream once again universal and possible.

Until that happens, we will have a Congress that is dysfunctional, an irony since the idea of "congress" means coming together. Humphrey told Mondale as Fritz began his senatorial career, "Treat your rival as a friend." That idea seems to have disappeared, replaced by distemper and distrust, a spirit of "them" and "us," leading to stalemate enhanced by a new media.

It has been about 66 years since I cast my first vote, near 60 since I first worked in a political campaign. Through it all, good times and bad, I have remained hopeful and cheerful and confident that tomorrow would bring a better day for others as well as for me. I hope I have not been a fool.

16. Summing Up

We Shermans were not a closely-knit Jewish family. Geography, interests, personality kept us apart. We didn't talk to each other often, and we didn't visit for years at a time. Despite all that, I feel the need to conclude with what we all did and how we ended. Not all of it is pretty and might better be left unsaid, but my story is incomplete without it all.

My mother, as I have noted, died of cancer relatively young. She should have lived longer. Had she done so, our family, I think, might have remained one of some love and with more frequent and better communication than it has.

My father, for all his periodic simple behavior, was a decent person. He was not much of a father figure, but he was caring and sentimental about kids and grandkids, and generous with what little he had. He died in his eighties in a nursing home, distinguished only by a fight he had with another resident, canes whacking at each other after an anti-Semitic slur.

Sister Rose was a warm and good-hearted woman, mother of two successful children I still see and like. She had a sense of family that the rest of us lacked. She died of a heart attack in 1976. When she died, I tried to inform brother Fred of her death. Since he had always refused to have a telephone, I couldn't call him. Instead, I called the Henrico County police in Virginia. He had retired in Richmond, possibly to recapture some of the few good years he may have had as child and teenager. I asked them to deliver a message about Rose's death. A policeman went to his apartment and asked, "Do you have a brother Norman?" Fred said, "No," assuming accurately that it could only be bad news.

Marvin is approaching a hundred years, lives alone as a widower after a wandering life and career that took him back to Minnesota after World War II, and then to Arkansas, New Zealand, Colorado, Wisconsin, and finally to Arizona. He still talks of going back to New Zealand. He trained to be a refrigeration mechanic, but built houses, manufactured ice cubes in a small town in Arizona, and lived off the land in Arkansas where he retired for the first time at age 35. He had no savings, no steady income, a wife, a dog, an old car and a trailer, but he had said for years he intended to retire at that age. Reality did not intrude.

When there was talk of the federal government taking over land that they couldn't annex within incorporated towns, he organized his nearby neighbors, incorporated as Pruitt, Arkansas, and was elected mayor with all 18 votes cast. It is unknown if he served with distinction, but he kept the feds away for a time and his scruffy neighbors thought he was wonderful.

When he first got to Arkansas, he dug the basement for a house, put in some walls, a kitchen, and a bathroom, and got no further, living there with his wife, Marie, until they left their garden spot when he came out of his early retirement.

Fred deserves a book, most of it not cheerful or heart warming. He was a difficult man always, judgmental and interfering with siblings and outsiders, attentive to my mother, disdaining of my dad. And he was less than a blessing for me, no matter that he sometimes tried.

When I first married Jane, who was a fallen-away Unitarian (a short drop), he would not come to our home or acknowledge her existence. He was not very Jewish and she wasn't very Christian, but that didn't seem to matter. I finally prevailed on him and my dad to spend Thanksgiving with us. Fred was unable to speak to Jane directly. If she asked a question, he turned to answer me. The next year when he came again, he tried to respond to her directly, but couldn't get her one-syllable name out of his mouth with ease. He tried, tried, and finally gasped, Jaaane. It seemed close to a last breath.

A couple of years later, I drove out to his drug store in a Minneapolis suburb to share some sad news with him. Distraught and close to tears, I said when we were alone, "Jane wants a divorce." Without a pause, he responded, "You little shit, what did you do to that girl?" Oddly, I could only smile at his newfound allegiance. A couple of years later, he decided that he had had enough of the drug store and, taking time only to put on his jacket and empty the cash register, he locked the door and left. He didn't bother to sell the business. He just called the wholesale drug company to come get their goods, left the fixtures, paid the rent, and took off.

Many years later, his death was a sad excursion to suicide. He had continued to have no telephone for many years despite my urging him to do so. His logic was simple: he had no friends, so nuisance calls would be all he would get. As he got older, I said that he could fall, need help and a way to call out. He rejected my argument then as before. One day, when Ginny and I were visiting her parents in southern Minnesota, our daughter Emily called from our Maryland home. With excitement she said that Uncle Fred had called from his apartment in Hopkins, Minnesota, and had left a phone number.

I returned his call immediately, and he soon asked if I

remembered some conversations we had had about end-of-life. I thought a moment and remembered he had once talked about suicide if he were to become ill. I said, "Fred, for Christ's sake, you are not talking about suicide?" He said he didn't want to discuss it, but could I come to his apartment two days later? (He had moved back to Minneapolis after his time in Richmond.) He said he would leave a key to his apartment with the office.

I drove to Minneapolis early, checked in to a motel, and then sat wondering if I should interfere and go over immediately. It was a painful evening of confusion. I finally decided it was his decision, not mine. Intruding then would only delay whatever he had in mind. It was a long, sleepless night.

The next morning I went to the office as directed and was greeted cheerfully with "Fred said you were coming. Here is the key." I went down the hall to his apartment, already distraught at what I would find, and the chain holding the slightly open door from the inside was in place. I thought with some anger, "To the end, you make things difficult," and reached in to try to jiggle the chain loose. As I jiggled, his voice came clearly out, "Norman, is that you?"

He had saved deadly pills from his pharmacist days, taken them with a significant amount of whiskey, and wakened hung over with a headache. The pills were so old they didn't work. We went shopping for groceries since he had eaten all he had. A couple of weeks later he succeeded, although without pills and without me. In typical fashion, he left a note. In firm handwriting. He wrote, "Large Quantity Bubble Plastic wrap in my basement locker #94. These are keys."

Now to a happier litany.

Almost none of what I have described in earlier chapters since 1970 would have been possible without a fortuitous and fulfilling marriage, after my two failed ones. Certainly the last almost 45 years have been different from the first 40 because of a single person, Ginny Chambers.

Family weekend at Camp Hoover in Virginia, 1980: Lucy, me, Susan, Emily, and Ginny

By the time we got to Washington, I was approaching 45 years of age, and my older kids were in their late teens. I felt cheated of sharing their growing up and vowed to savor every childhood minute with however many children we had. Ultimately we had three girls, Lucy, Susan, and Emily. They were an attractive, smart, and pleasant lot (and still are), but I would have insisted on close involvement even had they not been.

I read them their bedtime stories, made them their school lunches, and we trained them to come to my side of the bed when a nightmare woke them up or if they needed help going to the bathroom. I even became an assistant coach for a soccer team.

They have brought me continuous joy, more than one could expect, and certainly more than I hoped for. Now, as adults, they find the bathroom alone, but some other things remain the same. Distinct and different, but with a shared sense of decency and concern for others, they permit me to feel that I have been a good model, teacher, and father. And now I am a grandfather to three of their children, Olivia Barker, Caroline Barker, James McDermott, and one now waiting to be born.

Ginny also salvaged my earlier empty years during which I had only periodic contact with Jane's and my older kids,

With children David and Anne, 1959

Anne and David, who were far away. When they were young, I tried every month to send them a book. I hoped that their reading what I had carefully chosen would bind us even at a distance. I thought that was real child support.

Once after Jane had gone to California to study more and teach, I saw them no more than briefly twice a year. On one visit, I was on the verge of tears as they got off the plane, came down the ramp, and approached me. David, about five, wore a little red cap, short pants, and a grin. He said proudly, "I didn't throw up on the airplane. Are you my daddy?" His sense of priority moved me.

Later, they both joined us in Washington. Ginny embraced them, welcomed them into our family as her own. They were never stepchildren in her eyes, but our children always. She took as much pleasure in them as I did. Both lived with us for a time, bonding with our girls who adored them.

Anne loved British literature and was the only person I have ever known who remembered the dates of the reign of every king and queen in its history. She worked on Capitol

Hill for Senator Birch Bayh before moving to England where she has been for over 30 years. Her daughter, our granddaughter, Helen has graduated from Kent University with honors.

David was a chess whiz, hanging out at Dupont Circle, a gathering place for chess nuts, earning a bit of money as he beat his challengers. He now works nights at the Government Printing Office proofreading the Congressional Record, among other federal documents. He is a chess Master and teaches it in schools in the D.C. area. Ginny has helped me stay closer to both of them than I might have alone.

In the years that followed our marriage, while I bounced around from job to job or free-lanced my writing, Ginny provided stability and unfailing encouragement, not only raising our kids beautifully, but going back to work when we needed money and health insurance. (Once asked how many jobs I had had during our marriage, she ingenuously asked, with a straight face, "How many 18-month intervals have there been?")

I have described here my roller coaster life with some self-satisfaction, but the ups and downs would have been a challenge beyond bearing to a lesser person than Ginny. Her love and tolerance made a good trip better, invariably satisfying or exciting, always fulfilling. She was both stabilizing and emancipating. I was very lucky to find an assisted-living arrangement while still relatively young and healthy.

Our retirement in Arizona where we could watch birds as we had for years, absorb the sun, avoid the snow and cold, and grow gracefully older has been wonderful. We have traveled to new places, discovered new things.

It has been a long way from my childhood in north Minneapolis and those smoke-belching tar blocks. I have burned coal for most of the years since. And I have followed my father's advice: "Norman, go somewheres."

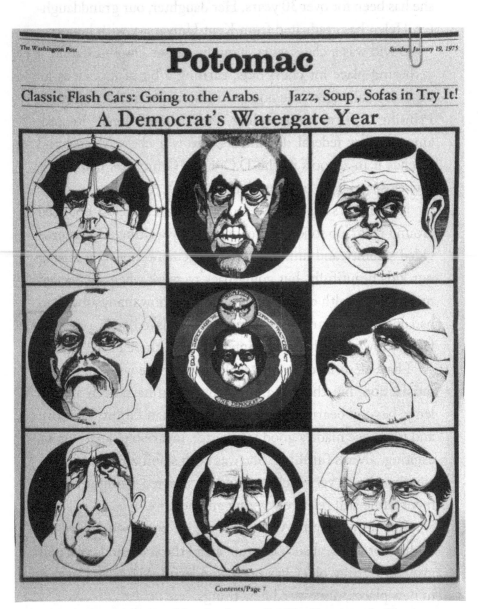

Cover of Washington Post Potomac Magazine, January 19, 1975, with me in stocks, Nixon's eyes overhead, and surrounded by Nixon Watergate cronies Jeb Magruder, Bob Haldeman, Chuck Colson, John Erlichman, John Dean, Gordon Liddy, John Mitchell, and Richard Kleindienst.

Special Section 1.
My Watergate Year

The cover of the Washington Post Sunday magazine on January 19, 1975 featured me. Surrounded by the faces of eight of Richard Nixon's closest advisers, I was a tiny little head in stocks, hands alongside my ears, a caricature of Nixon above my head. My bondage was encircled by "Equal Justice under the Corrupt Practices Act: The Democrat." Here's what I wrote.

A Democrat's Watergate Year

Though you have probably never heard of me, I am part of the Watergate gang. I recently pled guilty to a misdemeanor violation of the Federal Corrupt Practices Act and paid a $500 fine.

That ended a full year of public embarrassment for me and my family, expensive legal fees, and an endless drain of time and energy since I first received the subpoena from the Special Prosecutor's Office and the Ervin Committee.

As a result, among the few public words of Richard Nixon with which I agreed was his piety, "One year of Watergate is enough." My Watergate year was a surreal one in which my corrupt practices seemed like a mouse belch in the midst of a nuclear explosion. But if I have any lingering doubts about its reality, I need only recall that I shall forever be memorialized in the Watergate Special Prosecution Force Chronological List of Court Actions—LaRue, Magruder, Segretti, Krogh, Dean, Chapin, Porter, Jacobsen, Kalmbach, Colson, Haldeman, Erlichman, Mitchell, Strachan, Parkinson, Mardian, Barker, Martinez, De Diego, Liddy, Reinecke, Kliendienst, Connally, 14 leaders of corporate America, my partner, Jack Valentine, and me, Norman Sherman.

Next to my name is stated, "An information was filed on July 30, 1974, charging a one-count violation of Title 18, USC, Sections 2 and 610, aiding and abetting an illegal campaign contribution. A guilty plea was entered on August 12 . . ."

Before sentencing us, the judge said nice things about Valentine and me: it appeared we had not intended to violate the law, our former attorney had assured us that what we did was legal, we had provided all the information we had, everything we had said about our intent and actions had been corroborated.

It all sounded so good, I wondered what the hell I was doing there. If Maurice Stans had been in the courtroom, he might have thought the judge had given back our good names.

Alas, the judge's sympathetic words couldn't overtake the already published front-page stories in virtually every major newspaper in the country. Nor even that night's network evening news with an artist's rendition of my mug shot.

Yet the year, for all its misery, was not without its fascinating and even humorous moments.

My crime was diminutive compared to the more famous villainies of this period, but it launched me on a psychological journey where my sense of innocence, my self-justifications and rationalizations, buffeted by press coverage, and the shifting fears born of extended legal entanglements, wizened into uneasy acceptance of guilt, and an uncommonly clear vision of political morality.

Samuel Johnson once wrote, "When a man knows he is going to be hanged, it concentrates his mind wonderfully." That's the kind of year it was.

A Casual Start

In 1969, I quite casually started a business with my friend, Jack Valentine. Neither of us had had any prior business experience. I had been in and out of politics for most of the previous two decades and he had been working as a teaching assistant seeking a Ph.D. in American immigrant history. Nothing in either of our personalities or backgrounds suggested success in the corporate world.

But Valentine had a good idea and that seemed enough. In the mass-media-dominated campaigns of the 1960s, volunteers rarely had sufficient work to do. Valentine's idea was to have a computer match voter registration lists with telephone directory listings, making it easier for the volunteers to interview the appropriate people by phone.

In turn, the data the volunteer gathered, once stored in the computer, could be used for voter registration and fundraising drives, and for persuasive direct mail. Its ultimate value, of course, was in selective get-out-the-vote drives. Valentine's idea coupled the old politics of precinct workers with the new technology of computers. When well done, it produced superlative results.

Our first customer was Hubert Humphrey during his 1970 Senate campaign. I had been his press secretary while he was vice president, and it was that association, I believe, which inevitably attracted and, in the Watergate climate, possibly even required, the attention of the prosecutor and the press. When we got into trouble, every press account led with "former Humphrey aide" and I doubt seriously that we would have been prosecuted at all had I never worked for him. I became, I think, the most readily available token Democrat needed to offset the otherwise totally Republican lineup. Valentine, like a Siamese twin, necessarily became a target by association.

After our initial success in Minnesota in 1970, Valentine, Sherman & Associates rapidly grew to a million-dollar-a-year business, beneficiaries, in part, of the faddism that affects campaign management. All too quickly, however, we lost our reputation for competence and virtually went bankrupt.

Before that happened we made what we believed was a reasonable, legal and profitable business proposal to the Associated Milk Producers who were distributing campaign money to scores of politicians, lawyers, and public relations people in both political parties.

AMPI (that "I" stands for "Incorporated," a fact we somehow never considered) is a strange creature. It is a super cooperative which gets its money for politics through a check-off system, the take being determined by the number of gallons of milk delivered by members to the dairy. AMPI's political income has amounted to several millions of dollars in the past few years.

The First Mistake

Our pitch to them was simple. "Look," we said, "we work on political campaigns, but what we do is expensive. There is a lot of interest, but it is difficult to get the money as early as it is needed. If you will pay for part of the cost, the campaign committees can absorb the rest. Your money won't be squandered, but used in a sensible and productive effort.

Further, we will be developing millions of farm and rural names which you can use in your own organizing and propaganda efforts, and we will provide you an equivalent value of those names for any money you put into politics."

They talked immediately of two possible nonpolitical uses of our lists: selling insurance by mail, a staple and lucrative activity of other farm groups, and the sale of products through the mail.

Our first mistake was to believe them since they ultimately testified that they really had little interest in doing either of those things.

Our second and more serious mistake was in focusing on them as a political entity and not on them as a corporation, which they, indeed, were.

We knew that corporations as well as labor unions, by law, could not spend corporate or "treasury" money on political campaigns. In political jargon, it is "soft money" as opposed to "hard money."

Of course, it is easier to tap dollars already in the corporate treasury than it is to solicit voluntary contributions. A second advantage of this approach is that the money usually, if not always, can be deducted as a business expense.

The corporate officials who were convicted of giving illegal dollars to Nixon's reelection campaign had taken "soft" or corporate money and laundered it through some subterfuge: paying extra for a printing job so that a candidate might have his brochures or bumper stickers printed free, or paying unearned "legal fees" so that the attorney might channel the cash to a favorite candidate.

Had Valentine or I solicited corporate dollars from the Milk Producers, our guilt would have been obvious to us. It may be ingenuous almost to the point of disbelief, but we never considered the possibility that we would be paid with anything other than "hard" political dollars when AMPI committed over $100,000 for our voter data-gathering.

Months after the various projects were under way, weeks after we had complained to AMPI about not being paid, the first check arrived. It was a corporate check. It is unclear to us even now why they did not send political, clean money since they ended up with over a million of those dollars. In retrospect, we posited only two possible answers: one, that AMPI was saving all of it for the Nixon reelection coffers; two, that they wanted to hide their Democratic contributions as best they could in order not to offend those White House Republicans with whom they were negotiating for higher milk price support levels.

Retrospective wisdom suggests that we should have returned the corporate check and insisted on "political" dollars, but we didn't. We were afraid to cash the check for fear it was illegal, but we feared equally that returning it would, at worst, offend them enough to cancel their financing, or, at minimum, further delay their payment, a disastrous possibility since we were substantially overdrawn at the bank.

We went to our attorney. He had known our business from the beginning, he had been active as a campaign manager, and though we did not know it then, he had been retained earlier by the Milk Producers.

We asked him if it was legal to cash the corporate check and he said it was since we were supplying rural names for other uses to AMPI. (He later invoked the Fifth Amendment rather than testify under oath what he had advised us.) Elated, we cashed the check. The general manager of the Milk Producers afterwards testified under oath before the Ervin Committee that, " . . . we asked (their attorney) to prepare the deal."

Though we rarely had bothered to negotiate formal contracts with our clients, since most campaign committees automatically go out of business after the election and are, therefore, hard to sue, our attorney had belatedly drafted a contract covering our agreement with AMPI. We signed it and sent it on with a note saying they should contact our attorney if there were any questions.

We heard nothing and went blithely on, secure in the advice of our attorney. Our security died a cataclysmic death one October day in 1973, over two years after that first check, when a United States Marshall delivered a subpoena from the Ervin Committee to our office in Minneapolis.

My partner, a sensitive straight arrow accustomed to the life of academe, accepted the subpoena and proceeded directly to the men's room to throw up—an involuntary but periodic response he suffered throughout the ensuing wretched year.

Running Scared

It was a year during which we were to rethink our assumption that the advice of a competent attorney can always be trusted, an assumption without which business life, at least for amateurs, is infinitely more tentative, difficult and frightening. Our first instinct was to go voluntarily before the Ervin Committee and the Special Prosecutor's office without a lawyer, laying out the facts as we knew them. More experienced, and probably more sensible heads, urged that we get an attorney.

It was clear we couldn't use the last one, but, I said, "Goddamit, we're not going to retain some high-priced Washington attorney like we have something to hide. We aren't guilty of anything so let's not act scared."

But we were scared. The Milk Producers had developed the image in the press of political "Bonnie and Clydes," notorious public enemies. We knew that anyone working with them might be embarrassed, but in our most paranoid moments, we never considered the possibility of becoming defendants in any court proceeding.

The next shock was the advice that we get a criminal attorney. Since Minnesota doesn't have that much white-collar crime, criminal attorneys usually deal with dramatic acts of murder, assault, burglary, prostitution, and occasional kidnapping. And now, the two of us. Seeking a criminal attorney seemed an implicit admission of guilt.

Valentine and I made a basic decision which became the most important instruction to our new attorney, "We will cooperate fully by providing all records and recollections. The one thing, above all else, that we will not be guilty of is perjury in order to protect ourselves or anyone else."

Essentially, we made it easy for the prosecutor's office. Since no one else so peripherally involved had been indicted, one wonders, moral considerations aside, whether cooperation was indeed the wisest approach.

The night before our grand jury appearance, Valentine and our criminal attorney arrived in Washington and we spent the after-dinner hours in a hotel room going over our files and our recollections. And over. And over. Neither I nor Valentine has the recall of a John Dean and it was a struggle to remember who talked to whom and at what time about each detail.

The evening was a mess. We smoked too much, we spurred each other's tension, we both thought the attorney was not paying enough attention. We were like gauche teen-agers anticipating a blind date with someone's fat sister. We hoped it would be over quickly and that no one else would see us.

At one point, I went to the bathroom and noticed that our attorney traveled with a hair-blower. Somehow it undermined my confidence in him. Endlessly, we recited all we knew and when the lawyer's patience had been pushed to the limit, we went to Valentine's room and recited our monologues yet again. We began to bore each other, but could not stop talking.

I have been around Washington and politics long enough to be somewhat callous, but Valentine is, by nature, a Boy Scout filled with inordinate pride and concern for personal honor. The mere facts of the subpoena and an impending grand jury appearance had crushed his spirit. He was so depressed that he looked more and more like a man who had, indeed, violated whatever law he could. His bloodshot eyes sank deeper and deeper into dark, dark circles.

By morning when I returned, he was a basket case. He had managed about two hours' sleep, smoked two packs of cigarettes. I had slept more and smoked less, but had needed to wipe my hands to hold tightly to the steering wheel driving over. I heard my own voice, half an octave higher than normal, wondering aloud, "If we're innocent, what in Christ's name does a guy who is guilty feel." No one answered.

No Smiles

We arrived at the prosecutors office at 14th and K. Bigger enchiladas than we must have gone to Jaworski's office and found impressive surroundings. Our arena of truth bore the unmistakable stamp of a temporary government agency. A uniformed guard sat at the one working desk in the middle of an odd-shaped room that had not been repainted when the previous tenant moved out. When we mumbled why we were there, the guard shoved toward us a pad of forms. We filled in name., address, identification; he silently handed us red, laminated, numbered lapel passes.

He pointed us to two standard metal and leather chairs in

the corner. Since there were three of us, one stood awkwardly while two sat. My head told me to go to the bathroom. When I got there, my bladder told me it was already on empty.

While we waited, young assistant special prosecutors and their secretaries moved in and out displaying their passes in the casual way of regulars. No one smiled much and conversation was subdued, but intense. They are people on a mission, you think, and our minds moved for the first time that morning from ourselves to what they are doing and you are glad. But only for a moment. You come back quickly to yourself, fearful of people on a mission.

The atmosphere corrodes another level of innocence. If the ambiance is not precisely hostile, it is, at least, strongly adversative. And that mood heightens with the sudden appearance of your escort. "We will interview you separately. You can have your attorney with you."

In the small, cluttered office of "your" assistant special prosecutor, you try to explain that the invoices are on letterhead because you never got around to printing invoice forms. You try to explain away confusion because you never had a bookkeeper and your secretary had been a dropout from stewardess school.

You wish you had been more orderly and your memos less ambiguous. You begin to sound absurd and defensive. You blurt out what must be a cliché: "If I had intended to violate the law, I would have concealed it more artfully. I would have disguised things."

The young man questioning you raises his eyes from the yellow legal pad on which he has been scribbling and smiles a humorless smile, allowing he has heard that one before. Now, in addition to everything else, you feel stupid.

Your attorney helps you answer a question, explains an

invoice, and you both resent and appreciate him. When you leave after an hour, you are damp with perspiration and concern. Doubts which began with a subpoena and multiplied with the need to retain a criminal attorney, now run amok in your mind. "Jesus, am I guilty? What are the consequences going to be?"

The humorless smile is contagious and you smile one at Valentine as he thumps past you. For the next hour you sit alone in one of those two chairs out front, focusing on the inevitable office coffee pot with instructions taped to it, a cup of coins next to it. You try the men's room again, then skulk back to the chair.

Enter the Jury

When the preliminary interview is over, the five of us—two prosecutors, our attorney, Valentine and I—pile into a cab to the Federal Court House where the grand jury sits. You avoid the obvious topic, but it is difficult to remain silent, so you half-whisper, mumbling something about a recent sports event.

At the courthouse, you slide from the cab hoping to look inconspicuous. One of the prosecutors pays the driver and you start for the door. You involuntarily slow down when you notice a photographer friend, Nikons hanging around his neck, intended for more notorious witnesses, you hope. He clasps his hand to the side of his head and proclaims, "Oh, no, Norman, not you, too," I respond with a feeble smile and feel not only guilty, but convicted.

There was further evidence that this was not an auspicious day. The grand jury had taken off for lunch and we were asked to come back in half an hour. The prosecutors vanished and we descended to the dreary basement cafeteria for lunch. None of us ate much and while we sat there, several other newsmen I knew stopped by to say hello. Mercifully, no one asked what I was doing there.

Lunch over, I led the way to the elevators, moving like a wooden Pinocchio.

We got off the elevator at the sixth floor, turned left and left again down a dingy corridor past a free-standing wooden sign which said, "Grand Jury Members Only."

After a brief wait, you enter the grand jury room alone when you are beckoned. The room itself is small and plain. You sit at a table with a microphone, a court stenotypist at your right hand; at your left the forelady of the grand jury who swears you in, and opposite you at another table with its microphone for the two members of the Special Prosecutor's staff.

Behind the forelady loom the other 22 grand jurors, terraced in four or five rows. Several chew gum, one knits, and most are middle-aged and black. You rise to be sworn in and you promise to tell the truth. You give your name and they ask you to spell it. S-H-E-R-M-A-N, you hear your own voice say. It is not grand enough to be Kafkaesque, but there is a definite schizophrenia, a depersonalization at a very personal moment.

The man across from you says that you may be a potential defendant and that anything you say may be used against you. You begin to perspire, not in gleaming Nixonian splendor, but just quietly under the arms.

As the questions begin, you think, "I didn't set out to violate the law. I'm not even sure I did. I didn't buy anyone and I didn't sell anyone. I didn't abuse any public trust." You've answered all the questions that morning, but they are repeated for the grand jurors and for the record under oath.

You wonder, "Should I turn to the jurors when I answer the questions or should I speak to the attorneys who are asking them?" With a sudden jerk, you glance at the jurors. There are no smiles. Of course, there is nothing to smile about. But if you've learned life can be bittersweet, and maybe even absurd, you want to smile, to say, "Isn't all of this ridiculous, my being here."

Paid in Full

My appearance is brief. Maybe 10 minutes, maybe 20, I lost all track of time. When the prosecutors have on record what they want, they turn to the jurors who may now ask questions, but in my case they don't. I take that as a good sign. Then a voice says, "Thank you, Mr. Sherman," and I am out. Once again there is that awkward wait while Valentine has his turn.

Then we are told to go downstairs and fill out forms so that we can be paid for one day in court. The witness fee is $20 plus travel, in my case 11 cents a mile for driving the six miles from Chevy Chase. Finally, it is over.

You are no longer a virgin. You've been had and you feel corrupt, a view reinforced through the ensuing months by more hours interrogation from the Ervin Committee counsel and auditors, by press queries and news stories, by explanations to friends, to the children and other family, and by the time you waste just thinking about your status and reputation.

In addition, endless events conspire to cut deeper into confidence. Valentine's wife was chairman of the Ethics in Government section of her League of Women Voters chapter. She was so humiliated by all the press coverage that she tried to resign, but her colleagues graciously refused. It didn't help much.

Valentine's mother, a week out of the hospital after major surgery, saw her son on the network news and phoned hysterically, crying, "My son a crook. I should have died on the operating table."

My son came home one day to say he had just overheard two little kids down the block talking. One said, "My daddy says Mr. Sherman is a bad man."

One day, as I drove through the Minnesota countryside with my 12-year old nephew, he said, "Hey, Uncle Norm, about that bribe you took . . ." I interrupted him and tried, unsuccessfully I'm sure, to explain it wasn't a bribe.

Recently when an old friend used my name for a reference, her prospective employer, the editor of a prestigious journal and a literate Washingtonian, asked, "Isn't he in jail?"

"Shut the Door"

One event more than any other typified for me the lunacy of the year, my own roller-coaster moods, and how Washington rumors are fed. Late one morning, a colleague called me into his office and said in a conspiratorial half-whisper, "Shut the door." He said he had just talked to David Shoumacher of ABC, who was supposedly about to call me. Leon Jaworski had told Shoumacher I was soon to be indicted. I froze, fought off a wave of nausea, and accepted it as fact.

With buckling knees, I walked back to my office, shut the door and sat for 20 minutes. Then I called my wife. Had the story been about anyone else, I would have spent the time on the phone tattling the tale a dozen times.

Once in reasonable control, I called Valentine, whose only response was a shocked, strained gasp, "I can't breathe, I can't breathe." When he recovered, I said I would call the prosecutor's office and then call him back.

At first, "my" prosecutor, an assistant to Jaworski, would not talk to me, asking through his secretary whether I didn't have an attorney. My mood fell even more. I persisted and said, "Yes, I do, but if the rumor I've heard is true, I'm going to fire him and get another."

The prosecutor spoke to me and told me what I wanted to hear. "The rumor," he said, "is not true." He explained further that because his law firm had earlier represented John Connolly on other matters, Jaworski had recused himself from the milk case and, therefore, had none of the facts before him.

My mood rebounded instantly. As I interpreted our conversation, it seemed that they had little interest in Valentine and me. The attorney had concluded our conversation by saying, in a pleasant way I thought, "If we take any action, you will hear it directly from me and not from a reporter."

I was relieved and manic. Almost gleefully, I called Shoumacher to squelch the rumor and to find out how it had started. Its origin was classic. While my friend had been on the phone with Schoumacher, he said, "I'll call you back. Leon Jaworski is on the other line." In the call back to my friend, Shoumacher asked about Valentine and me and the possibility of our being indicted. It was only a probing question, but my friend thought it was a tip-off. As it turned out, Jaworski had called just to answer an invitation to the upcoming TV Correspondents' Dinner.

On Trial

Weeks passed, the rumors flowed and ebbed, and finally the rumor turned into fact. Whether I had read the phone conversation wrong or conditions changed, I do not know.

We heard officially from the Special Prosecutor's Office that they intended to file an "information," which is like an indictment but not moved through the grand jury, charging us with one misdemeanor count of aiding and abetting an illegal corporate contribution, if we were prepared to plead guilty. The impression was left that we could choose our court if we'd plead guilty.

In order to get the whole misery over with, I could stomach a guilty plea, but Valentine was angry and disagreed adamantly. He felt we had been patsies while others, including our original attorney, had been untouched by the prosecutors. Our new attorney believed a not-guilty plea would probably result in a felony indictment.

Subsequently, when several of the Milk Producers were indicted, I was able to persuade Valentine that, however innocent our motives had been, we were guilty, and that the time had come to end our personal year of Watergate. He reluctantly agreed, something he would not have done had he sufficient money to keep fighting.

We asked to be tried in Minnesota and we were. Our reason was simple: the sentencing mood in Washington then seemed capricious and, therefore, dangerous; and St. Paul's chief judge, a former Republican congressman, had a reputation for consistency.

Shortly before, he had fined the chairman of 3M $500 for laundering corporate money through a Lebanese bank.

We entered the St. Paul courtroom for the first time in mid-August, 1974. It is impressive, with high ceilings and a rich, grey carpet befitting the monochromatic majesty of the room—the walls, the jury box, and the bench are all dark walnut. Before court convened I thought with some irony, "Finally, I'm in the big leagues. No more grey metal chairs."

I went to sit with Valentine in the defendants' chairs until, at the appointed hour of 9 a.m., a door opened at the rear of the room. Watching intently for the judge, I heard the bailiff intone, "The Court all rise. Hear ye. Hear ye. The United States District Court of Minnesota is now in session. Be seated please."

The judge, robed in traditional black, glided to his seat

above us all. In front of his high bench sat a court reporter and a clerk. A few feet away, opposite the judge were the prosecutor's table, a lectern with a microphone and the defendants' table to which we were called. The rest of the court was empty except for a couple of reporters, several U.S. Marshals, and a few friends conspicuous in the dark pews.

Strangely, I found myself only half listening as my own thoughts struggled to intrude. I once had received a traffic ticket for running a stop sign, but that had been 20 years before. I had mailed in my fine. I had always thought of myself as honest and law-abiding. I'd been around politics all my adult life and had never taken anything or sold anything. Once, I think, I was offered a bribe, but I wasn't really sure.

Yet here I was: guilty, embarrassed, and humiliated. In the Watergate mood, I stood as one alleged betrayer of the public trust among many—Haldeman, Ehrlichman, Mitchell, and Sherman. It seemed unreal to me once again—out of all proportion. I hoped it would all be over soon.

The prosecutor read the charge; the judge asked us if we had legal counsel and were satisfied with it. He asked whether we understood the charge, and finally he asked, "How do you plead?"

"Guilty." By that time, my mind was concentrated wonderfully. I was fixed on the judge and when asked for a statement, I moved five feet from where I stood to the lectern to deliver my statement of contrition. I spoke softly and directly to the judge, my voice breaking as I read hurriedly. It was part real emotion, part show biz and we waited then for the sentence. (The maximum could have been a year in jail and a $1,000 fine,)

None came. Instead the judge asked for a pre-sentence investigation, released us on a $1,000 personal recognizance bond, banged his gavel, and was gone. Valentine and I were left hanging, twisting slowly, slowly in the wind.

The Ultimate Shame

It was now 9:20 a.m. We stood in a stupor outside the courtroom until a U.S. Marshall moved up and, in classic law enforcement fashion, whipped out his I.D. and asked us to come down to his office as quickly as we found it convenient.

We weren't clear why and he didn't explain, but we went. Once again, we were taken in turn to an inner room, this time to be fingerprinted and have mug shots taken. While the humiliation was private, it was possibly the ultimate shame.

For the fingerprinting, the marshal took off his coat, exposing the holster and gun riding on his hip. All of my pent-up hostility unloaded on him, though I didn't verbalize it. I thought, "If you were a little bigger and a lot smarter, you'd be a professional football player." While I glowered, he gripped my wrist and hand and warned, "Don't try to help. It just smears the print and we'll have to do it all over again." I made my hand go limp, afraid I might be charged with entering and smearing.

After washing off the black ink, I waited silently while he diddled with his camera. He took two shots, peering at his portrait work as he peeled off the Polaroid backing. I hated him as I had not hated anyone else in the entire process. The system makes you a supplicant to higher authorities—the young attorney who interviews you, the grand jurors who sit lumpenly, the judge—and when you find a peasant like yourself, you psychologically turn on him.

When I returned to the outer office to switch places with Valentine, I noticed something I had missed when we first came in. In a corner through a standard doorframe was another room. With the door closed, I would have thought it a closet or another office. With it open, I saw a cell for prisoners in transport, complete with an open toilet and forbidding grey metal bars. Slouched on a bench was a woman dressed in prison blue work clothes.

Valentine's eyes followed mine, he seized my arm in a frenzy and asked, "Are we going to jail?" There was no time to answer as he followed the marshal out of sight to be fingerprinted and photographed.

Later when we reviewed the incompleteness of the morning, we convinced ourselves that a pre-sentence investigation could only help. Though Valentine's fear of jail seemed, even to him, excessive, it never disappeared from either of us during the two-month long investigation.

A Target of Rage

In a relatively private, but gently ugly way, that investigation was more intimately distressing than most of what had gone before. We were assigned to a probation officer, a kindly and decent civil servant, who told us that he only did "special cases" now that he was the chief probation officer for the federal courts in Minnesota. His concern for us was almost painfully paternal, genuine and helpful.

Like a high school sophomore buttering up a teacher, I tried during our two-hour interview to get him to like me. Nice guy that he was, he could not prevent the process from being demeaning.

In an elaborate, eight-page document, I answered all sorts of standard fare: education, jobs held, financial status.

Then the questions got psycho-social: family history, including when you left home (almost 30 years ago), why you left (my mother died), what your religion is (Jewish), how frequently you attend church (occasionally), the name and address of church and pastor.

You've left those last two blank and skip sections on skills, interests, and ambitions. You wish you had been married only once and that you had moved less frequently. You cravenly want to apologize for a life style you have enjoyed and would not change. You obsequiously try to show that, underneath it all, you uphold those values the probation officer and the judge admire.

As that first interview ended, I was also reminded that I must solicit three character references. Like the finger-printing, this became a target of rage. I thought, "Here I am approaching 50. shuffling about asking people to attest to what a good boy am I." There comes a moment when you want to scream, "Let's stop this crap. Just give me the year in jail and leave me alone." But, of course, you don't. You just keep smiling. You keep answering.

The Sentence

Finally, the sentencing is set. All of the papers are in order. You stand once again in the courtroom and the story is played out.

You expect that, by now, your emotions are in control, but they are not. As the judge delivers his peroration, you think, "My god, he is going to let us off." You are giddy. Then he says, "$500. One week to pay." The giddiness and hope are replaced with a virtual cacophony of emotions: relief, anger, and the chronic emotion of the year—a sense of disproportion that you were selected for this honor.

And then the bittersweet sense of irony surges forth. It is unlikely that the judge noticed a faint smile flicker across my face when he pronounced sentence, but I could not suppress something I had thought of often during the previous weeks. The judge had been elected to Congress in 1946 and had run again in 1948 when he had lost to Eugene McCarthy. In that time of pre-Watergate morality, campaigns of Republican candidates were largely financed in that district by a small group of very rich industrialists. It is unlikely that someone in those campaign committees over 25 years before, just when I was first active in politics, did not violate the same law for which I was now being sentenced. I wondered if that possibility had crossed the judge's mind.

The morning after and in the days that followed, friends stopped to offer me their congratulations. I thanked them for the gesture and the concern. Was it a victory of some sort? I had been convicted of a federal crime and paid a fine. Did I get away with something?

I think not. I look back with fatigue on a draining experience of family hurt, money wasted, time lost, reputation sullied. My crime wasn't much, but I realize, as one measure, that if I wanted to work for a politician or office holder again, I probably couldn't. Who would want to hire a Watergate miscreant?

Aftermath

While the unctuous bleating of Maurice Stans and the deeds and lies of others make it difficult, I even look back with some begrudging sympathy for men I detest—Nixon and his sycophants—and understand their garrison mentality, under siege by the special prosecutor and the courts and particularly by the press.

Though many of my friends are journalists, my overriding emotion of the year was dislike for journalists, whether they were doing their job, as it affected me, well or poorly. I was almost as unhappy with good reporters legitimately trying to explain what was gong on as I was with the opportunists betting on me to give them their minute on the evening news.

Good reporters and bad plugged into every story the fact that the maximum, penalty for my crime was one year in jail and a $1,000 fine. That was true, but no one had ever received the maximum, no one had ever gone to jail. Its repetition made it seem a real possibility. It upset family and friends needlessly. Most devastatingly, it left the impression—with people who never understood or particularly cared about what I had done—that I was lucky not to be in jail.

The year simply was an obscenity. Perhaps, however, it had redeeming social value. If the corrupting influence of special interest money has been destroyed permanently, if the abuse of democratic political institutions can be avoided forever, I suppose my discomfiture was worth it.

● ● ● ● ●

That is what I thought then. Here is what I think now.

My 1974 crime was really no real crime and, significantly, the statute has vanished, no longer on the books. Even if it was sufficient for a prosecutor to pursue, it pales compared to today's legal abuse of our political system. The money question has not been resolved. Corporate money is everywhere and getting worse by decision of the Supreme Court. Karl Rove and the Koch brothers and their ilk are powerful beyond reason. They do not want to improve government, as best I can tell, so much as just buy it, hiding a villainous and greedy heart of indifference behind shibboleths about lower taxes and smaller government no matter what the consequences. My hope is that good people, of both parties, will not accept the desecration of democracy.

When my Watergate year was over, I assumed it would be a lasting personal burden. At least for a peripheral creature like me, and I assume for most others more centrally involved, except for Nixon, it has had none of the effects I anticipated. No jobs denied, no isolation, no exclusion from politics or government and, in fact, my personal anguish is simply long gone, if not quite forgotten.

Special Section 2.
HHH Memo to LBJ on Vietnam

On February 15, 1965, just short of a month after he was inaugurated, Humphrey sent a memo to the president expressing his opposition to further involvement in Vietnam. I had nothing to do with it, but the war dominated the spirit of our country and its politics for much of the decade, so I reproduce it here.

The war Johnson inherited from President Kennedy had 19,000 advisers in Vietnam and about 400 American military had died. By then, Kennedy had already begun to say that the United States was overcommitted in Southeast Asia. If the new president had remembered Kennedy's concern or listened to Humphrey, we would have been spared a lot: 50,000 dead Americans, 150,000 wounded, billions of dollars spent, and a troubled, divided country. The lives of well over two million civilians in Southeast Asia would not have been lost. I had known for a long time what a military death does to a family and hated to see it happening to others.

Though he had sometime earlier supported the war while Senator, he now spoke strongly against it. As the new vice president, Humphrey wrote:

I have been in Georgia over the weekend, and for the first time since Inauguration, have had time to read and think about fateful decisions which you have just been required to make, and will continue to be making, on Vietnam. I have been reading the Vietnam cables and intelligence estimates of the last two weeks. Because these may be the most fateful decisions of your Administration, I wanted to give you my personal views. You know that I have nothing but sympathy for you and complete understanding of the burden and anguish that surrounds such decisions. There is obviously no quick or easy solution, and no clear course of right or wrong. Whatever you decide, we will be taking big historic gambles, and we won't know for sure whether they were right or wrong until months or perhaps years afterwards. The moral dilemmas are inescapable.

I want to put my comments in the most useful framework. In asking me to be your Vice President, you made it clear that you expected my loyalty, help, and support. I am determined to give it. I don't intend to second-guess your decisions, or kibitz after the fact. You do not need me to analyze or interpret information from Vietnam. You have a whole intelligence community for that purpose. You do not need me for foreign policy advice. You have a Secretary of State and whole staffs and departments to do that. I am not a military expert. Plenty of others are.

But because I have been privileged to share with you many years of politics in the Senate, because we have recently come through a successful national campaign together, because I think your respect for me and my value to you significantly consists of my ability to relate politics and policies, and because I believe strongly that the sustainability of the

Vietnam policies now being decided are likely to profoundly affect the success of your Administration, I want to summarize my views on what I call the politics of Vietnam.

1. In the recent campaign, Goldwater and Nixon stressed the Vietnam issue, advocated escalation, and stood for a military "solution." The country was frightened by the trigger-happy bomber image which came through from the Goldwater campaign. By contrast we stressed steadiness, staying the course, not enlarging the war, taking on the longer and more difficult task of finding political-military solutions in the South where the war will be won or lost. Already, because of recent decisions on retaliatory bombing, both Goldwater and the Kremlin are now alleging that we have bought the Goldwater position of "going North."

2. In the public mind the Republicans have traditionally been associated with extreme accusations against Democratic administrations, either for "losing China," or for failing to win the Korean War, or for failing to invade Cuba during the missile crisis. By contrast we have had to live with responsibility. Some things are beyond our power to prevent. Always we have sought the best possible settlements short of World War III, combinations of firmness and restraint, leaving opponents some options for credit and face-saving, as in Cuba. We have never stood for military solutions alone, or victory through air power. We have always stressed the political, economic and social dimensions.

3. This Administration has a heavy investment in policies which can be jeopardized by escalation in Vietnam: the President's image and the American image, the development of the Sino-Soviet rift, progress on détente and arms control, summit meetings with Kosygin, reordered relations with our European allies, progress at the United Nations, stabilizing

defense expenditures, drafting reservists.

4. American wars have to be politically understandable by the American public. There has to be a cogent, convincing case if we are to enjoy sustained public support. In World Wars I and II we had this. In Korea we were moving under United Nations auspices to defend South Korea against dramatic across the border, conventional aggression. Yet even with those advantages, we could not sustain American political support for fighting the Chinese in Korea in 1952.

Today in Vietnam we lack the very advantages we had in Korea. The public is worried and confused. Our rationale for action has shifted away now even from the notion that we are there as advisers on request of a free government to the simple and politically barren argument of our "national interest." We have not succeeded in making this national interest interesting enough at home or abroad to generate support. The arguments in fact are probably too complicated (or too weak) to be politically useful or effective.

5. If we go north, people will find it increasingly hard to understand why we risk World War III by enlarging a war under terms we found unacceptable 12 years ago in Korea. Politically people think of North Vietnam and North Korea as similar. They recall all the "lessons" of 1950-53: the limitations of air power, the Chinese intervention, the "Never Again Club" against GI's fighting a land war against Asians in Asia, the frank recognition of all these factors in the Eisenhower administration's compromise of 1953.

If a war with China was ruled out by the Truman and Eisenhower Administrations alike in 1952-53, at a time when we alone had nuclear weapons, people will find it hard to contemplate such a war with China now. No one really believes that the Soviet Union would allow us to destroy Communist

China with nuclear weapons.

6. People can't understand why we would run grave risks to support a country which is totally unable to put its own house in order. The chronic instability in Saigon directly undermines American political support for our policy.

7. It is hard to justify dramatic 150 plane U.S. air bombardments across a border as a response to camouflaged, often non-sensational, elusive, small scale terror which has been going on for ten years in what looks largely like a Civil War in the South.

8. Politically in Washington, beneath the surface, the opposition is more Democratic than Republican. This may be even more true at the grassroots across the country.

9. It is always hard to cut losses. But the Johnson administration is in a stronger position to do so now than any administration in this century. 1965 is the year of minimum risk for the Johnson Administration. Indeed it is the first year when we can face the Vietnam problem without being preoccupied with the political repercussions from the Republican right. As indicated earlier, our political problems are likely to come from new and different sources (Democratic liberals, independents, labor) if we pursue an enlarged military policy very long.

10. We now risk creating the impression that we are the prisoner of events in Vietnam. This blurs the Administration's leadership role and has spillover effects across the board. It also helps erode confidence and credibility in our policies.

11. President Johnson is personally identified with, and greatly admired for political ingenuity. He will be expected to put all his great political sense to work now for international political solutions. People will be counting on him to use on

the world scene his unrivaled talents as a politician. They will be watching to see how he makes this transition from domestic to the world stage.

The best possible outcome a year from now would be a Vietnam settlement which turns out to be better than was in the cards because LBJ's political talents for the first time came to grips with a fateful world crisis and did so successfully. It goes without saying that the subsequent domestic political benefits of such an outcome, and such a new dimension for the President, would be enormous.

12. If, on the other hand, if we find ourselves leading from frustration to escalation and end up short of war with China but embroiled deeper in fighting in Vietnam over the next few months, political opposition will steadily mount. It will underwrite all the negativism and disillusion which we already have about foreign involvement generally—with serious and direct effects for all the internationalist programs to which the Johnson Administration remains committed: AID, United Nations, arms control, and socially humane and constructive policies generally.

For all these reasons, the decisions now being made on Vietnam will affect the future of this Administration fundamentally. I intend to support the Administration whatever the President's decisions. But these are my views.

Acknowledgments

Without Ginny, good wife, good mother, good editor, (and her late cousin, John Schamber,) this book would never have been started or finished. Having listened to my stories over and over again for many years, Ginny thought putting them to paper and sending them to John as he had asked, might provide the basis for beginning this memoir. With both of them encouraging me, I began and continued. Ginny has also cleaned up my language and checked my syntax while trying to make sense of my narrative. She also remembers events I have forgotten.

John Stewart has worked for many years to educate me, first on the legislative process, afterwards on the substance of what we had been doing. He has recalled with precision events we shared working for Hubert Humphrey. He is the best example of a public servant I have known—wise, self-less, persistent in the pursuit of a better society for us all, but concerned especially with the least fortunate, those who suffer discrimination, those who barely survive in poverty. He has done so through government, within his church, in every aspect of his life.

Others have read a preliminary version and made suggestions for additions, deletions, or clarification or have provided information. First among them is Mary Margaret Overbey. When she was fresh out of the University of North Carolina with a master's degree in English, she showed up in the Humphrey office carrying a letter signed by Humphrey in response to one she had written. I interviewed her and, impressed by her academic record, her demeanor, her promise, I hired her for $400 a month. She remains in Washington, proving I was right and wise.

William Dickinson was a fellow visiting professor at Louisiana State University after a long career as a journalist and editor of the Washington Post Writers Group. Bill read an early version and encouraged me to continue.

Clarke Chambers, my long-ago professor of American history and a benefactor in several ways over many years also read a beginning draft and cheered me on. His approval was important for he more than any other teacher or friend sharpened my academic interest in American government and traditions. He focused me on knowing the past to better understand the present and to grasp what good government could do in a democracy like ours.

As we prepared for publication, my friend Sandy Lerner and my son David gave the manuscript a final edit, assuring me that there were no remaining typos, misspellings, or unclear statements. At least that is what I think they said.

Others around the globe have listened to my stories and a few have urged, "You ought to put that on paper." They prefer to remain anonymous, but I thank them for their persistent encouragement.